# Pharaoh's Magicians

# Pharaoh's Magicians
*Evolution, the Bible,
and Modern Gnosticism*

Gregory C. Benoit

WIPF & STOCK · Eugene, Oregon

PHARAOH'S MAGICIANS
*Evolution, the Bible, and Modern Gnosticism*

Copyright © 2011 by Gregory C. Benoit

All rights reserved. Except for brief quotations in critical publications or reviews, no part of this book may be reproduced in any manner without prior written permission from the publisher. Write: Permissions, Wipf and Stock Publishers, 199 W. 8th Ave., Suite 3, Eugene, OR 97401.

Wipf and Stock Publishers
199 W. 8th Ave., Suite 3
Eugene, OR 97401

Unless otherwise specified, all Scripture quotations taken from the New King James Version, Copyright © 1979, 1980, 1982 by Thomas Nelson, Inc. Used by permission. All rights reserved.

Scripture quotations marked as NIV taken from the HOLY BIBLE, NEW INTERNATIONAL VERSION. Copyright © 1973, 1978, 1984 International Bible Society. Used by permission of Zondervan Bible Publishers.

Scripture quotations marked as ESV taken from The Holy Bible, English Standard Version® (ESV®), copyright © 2001 by Crossway Bibles, a publishing ministry of Good News Publishers. Used by permission. All rights reserved.

ISBN 978-1-61097-416-5

Manufactured in the USA.

# Contents

Foreword .................................................................... 1

— Section 1: Reading the Bible —

1: Evolution, Gnosticism, and the Bible ............................... 5

2: Genesis 1 ............................................................. 13

3: Genesis 2 ............................................................. 41

4: Genesis 3 ............................................................. 64

5: Selected New Testament Passages ................................. 89

6: First Adam and Last Adam ........................................ 103

— Section 2: Rewriting the Bible —

7: Rewriting Genesis 1 ............................................... 121

8: Rewriting Genesis 2 ............................................... 144

9: Genesis 3 and Adam ............................................... 154

— Section 3: Heretics in Our Midst —

10: What is Gnosticism? ............................................. 165

11: Pharaoh's Magicians ............................................. 179

— Appendix 1: Alleged "Sources" —

The So-Called "Sources" of Genesis ................................ 197

Bibliography ............................................................ 221

# Heresy

Hairesis (αἵρεσις) denotes (a) a choosing, choice (from *haireomai*, to choose); then, that which is chosen, and hence, an opinion, especially a self-willed opinion, which is substituted for submission to the power of truth, and leads to division and the formation of sects, Gal. 5:20. . . such erroneous opinions are frequently the outcome of personal preference or the prospect of advantage.

—W. E. Vine, *Vine's Expository Dictionary of New Testament Words*

# Foreword

People today tend to think of Gnosticism—when they think of it at all—as an outdated heresy which flourished in the first two centuries AD. But this notion is grossly inaccurate on two levels: first, the heresy is far more ancient than the first century; it was actually invented by the serpent in the Garden of Eden at the very beginning of time. Second, Gnosticism is far from outdated or old-fashioned; it is alive and thriving in the world today, and its false teachings have polluted the theology of the church. The one thing that Christians today do understand correctly about Gnosticism is that it is a heresy. What is less understood is that it is a heresy which is being embraced and taught by the leading Bible scholars and teachers of our day, and as such it needs to be purged out.

This book began when I was preparing a series of sermons on the book of Genesis. In all innocence, I purchased copies of the most influential commentaries on Genesis: Gordon Wenham's *Word Biblical Commentary on Genesis* (Thomas Nelson), and Victor P. Hamilton's *New International Commentary on the Old Testament: The Book of Genesis* (Eerdmans). I was taken aback to discover that both of these commentaries attempt to rewrite the first three chapters of Genesis in order to accommodate the religion of evolution—so I purchased other commentaries from other series by other authors—only to discover that they, too, had adulterated God's Word in an attempt to force evolution into the text.

It is important to understand that evolution is a religion. It is a faith-based teaching on the origins of the human race, one that cannot ever be proven any more than one can hope to conclusively prove that Genesis 1 is a literal record of the truth. One believes in evolution by placing one's faith in the teachings and claims of modern science, despite the widely held notion that science is proven fact which requires no act of faith.

It is a religion in the sense that whoever or whatever created mankind is mankind's God. One's creator has the final authority over one's life and destiny. If God created man as described in Genesis 1, then He is the final authority over mankind's destiny. If mankind evolved, then that final authority belongs to Death, as death is the driving force behind the myth of evolution.

This book addresses both evolution and Gnosticism, as evolution is a modern permutation of that ancient heresy—but it does *not* address any scientific claims or pseudo-evidence. This book is concerned only with what the Bible teaches on the subject of man's origins, and therefore it will address only what the Bible says. The premise of this approach is simple: one's beliefs concerning the origins of the human race are based upon faith; no empirical evidence can ever be produced to conclusively prove one view over another. One is free to place one's faith in the teachings of men, which we commonly refer to as "science;" one is free to place one's faith in the teachings of the Bible as the final Word of God; but one is *not* free to claim that the Bible endorses the false religions of the world.

This book will demonstrate that last statement, that the Bible does not and cannot be made to endorse the Gnostic teachings of evolution.

# Section 1:
# Reading the Bible

# 1

# EVOLUTION, GNOSTICISM, AND THE BIBLE

Modern science is wrong. I cannot prove this assertion using modern scientific tests and theories and studies; I say it on faith. And when I speak of "modern science," I am speaking explicitly of modern theories concerning the origins of the universe in general and of mankind in particular. I say that I cannot prove that science is wrong using scientific methods because I am not a scientist. I have never studied physics or astronomy or paleontology or chemistry or any other esoteric branch of modern science.

I believe that there is a God, but I cannot prove this assertion, either. On the other hand, modern science cannot prove that God does *not* exist, yet much of modern science is founded upon the belief that there is no God. Scientists exercise faith just as much as Christians do—perhaps even more so. I suspect that many of their theories concerning the origins of the universe are built upon their own exercises of faith, built upon the presupposition that there is no God who created the heavens and the earth out of nothing.

It is not my purpose, however, to debate with scientists on any level. If you are looking for a book that presents scientific evidences for the truth of creation, you will be disappointed in this one. I am not qualified to hold scientists accountable for whether or not their tests are reliable, whether or not their data are accurate, whether or not their interpretations of data are sound, whether or not they are even telling the truth when they *present* their data.

Yet it is important to point out that most people do exercise faith when they believe what modern science tells them. The average person, like me, is not qualified to examine the methods of carbon dating, for example, to see whether they are reliable, to discern what presuppositions they are built upon. Most of us cannot hope to hold science accountable to be telling us the truth, and we exercise faith in the veracity of scientists when we accept what they tell us as fact.

I have chosen to take a different step of faith. I have chosen to believe that the Bible is telling me the truth concerning the origins of the cosmos in general and of mankind in particular. The Bible, however, tells me something that is radically different from what modern science tells me, and a straightforward reading of Genesis demonstrates that the two beliefs are absolutely incompatible. This means that I must be willing to look foolish in the eyes of my contemporaries when I say with conviction, "there is no such thing as evolution."

There are, unfortunately, many Christians today who are unwilling to pay that price, unwilling to look foolish to the world around them by placing their faith in the Bible as the Word of God. This would be somewhat understandable (though not excusable) if these people were just ordinary Christians like you and me. But that is not the case; these people are leaders in the Christian faith, great teachers who are praised and exalted in seminaries and churches throughout the western world. They are the great theologians who have written thick, multi-volume commentaries on the book of Genesis, theologians who are viewed as the great scholars whose opinions carry great weight, teachers whose voices boom with doctrinal authority. And they are corrupting the church with their false doctrines.

These theologians tell us, almost universally, that the Bible actually teaches the doctrines of evolution. I say "doctrines of evolution" deliberately, because I believe that evolution is a pagan religious system, and as such is incompatible with the teachings of Scripture. Yet our great teachers are telling us that the two—Scripture and evolution—are perfectly (or sometimes imperfectly) compatible, and some go so far as to claim that Genesis *insists* that we read evolution into it. This is a false teaching, bordering (at best) upon heresy, and it must be resoundingly rejected and purged from the church's pulpits and seminaries.

This book is built upon the assumption that the Bible is the word of God, that it is divinely inspired and contains truth—truth which is consistent with itself from Genesis to Revelation. I intend to examine the Bible to see whether it can be made compatible with the teachings of evolution, focusing primarily upon the first three chapters of Genesis. If we discover that the Bible will *not* countenance this teaching, then those theologians who are teaching a false gospel will be called to an account. It is my belief that most modern commentaries on Genesis are filled with error, and many are preaching outright heresy.

So the reader is cautioned not to look for scientific evidences in this book, nor to expect it to address "intelligent design" or any other evolutionary debate. This book is a Bible study primarily, and a debunking of the so-called "higher critics" secondarily. Belief in any system of "origins" is an act of faith, whether one believes in evolution or creation or some adulterous amalgamation of the two, and those who build their faith upon the Bible as the Word of God will be well rewarded by studying it to find answers to this debate. This book hopes to help in that direction, as we go carefully through Genesis and other passages to see what God has to say. It is my intention to let the Word of God speak for itself, stripping away the false premises of modern theology.

## Darwinism is a Religion

Evolution is not a new idea. It is actually a modern version of ancient pagan mythologies which taught that the world was brought into existence over a long period of time through the forces of "the gods" as they struggled against one another or against the forces of "chaos." The modern permutation of this ancient religion replaces "the gods" with the forces of death and survival, but the end results and underlying assumptions of the two mythologies are the same.

Darwinism is a form of naturalism, an ancient pagan teaching which assumes that there is no other plane of existence outside of the universe which we inhabit. This assumption leads to the conclusion that there is no God; or, if there *is* a god, he or she or it is part of the cosmos which we inhabit. In the case of Darwinism, that god is the force of death, the greatest power that exists which drives all species to struggle against it. Death, in the evolutionist's scheme, is the one force which is unchanging in our world—death is immutable, and it is all-powerful (or omnipotent) in that there is no other entity within our cosmos which can defeat it.

Christianity, on the other hand, is a form of supernaturalism, which believes that there are planes of existence outside of our own—Heaven, for example. Christianity, obviously, teaches that there is a God who exists outside of space and time, a God who is eternal, who created all that exists, a God who is greater than death itself. Christians believe that God alone is immutable and omnipotent, and the New Testament makes it clear that Jesus Christ defeated death once and for all.

So right off the bat we have a serious problem when we try to intermingle these two religious systems, religions that are based upon mutually exclusive premises. One cannot be a naturalist *and* believe that there is a God who exists outside of creation, because the naturalist rejects the idea that any other planes exist—there is no Heaven, there is only the earth and the universe surrounding it. The Christian, on the other hand, cannot accept the notion that God exists only within our universe, because then He would be a part of it, not its creator—He becomes "one of us," not "other," not God.

Yet many Christians like to call themselves "theistic evolutionists," claiming that God actually used evolution to create our universe. Others try to shun the "evolution" part while still embracing the false doctrines of that religion. These theologians invent many names for themselves, including "progressive creationists" and "framework theologians." But one cannot take bits and pieces of many religions and amalgamate them into one new religion. This is what the so-called New-Agers have attempted in our culture, and it is what the Gnostics have attempted for millennia. This is called a syncretistic religious system, which attempts to select the nicer parts of many religions and mix them together into a theological stew. Theistic evolutionists and progressive creationists and day/age theologians and framework theologians and many other false teachers are attempting to take the parts of Darwinism that they like and mix them together with the parts of Scripture that they like. Each of these theologians does what is right in his own eyes, and the result is that we have as many ludicrous theories as we have modern theologians. Which is to say, far too many.

Part of this confusion grows out of one's basic assumptions concerning modern science in general and Darwinism in particular. Modern westerners tend to view evolution as science, as provable (and already proven) fact, like simple mathematics. But evolution is actually not science, it is faith. It makes extensive use of the "natural sciences" simply because it is a naturalistic religion. Natural science is to naturalism what prayer and occultism are to supernaturalism: the "tools of the trade."

Science is merely the learning of man, the theories of man, the hypotheses of man. As such, science is flawed and subject to error. Science, like mankind, is fallible; yet modern Christians tend to operate on the assumption that it is infallible, that once a "scientist" makes a pronouncement there is no further room for discussion. But a theory that is based upon a false premise will ultimately be proven false. Evolution is naturalistic; it is based upon the premise that there is no God, that nothing exists outside of our known cosmos. Its foundation is false, therefore its conclusions will also be false.

Christians delude themselves when they think that they can take pieces of this false religion and intermingle them with Christianity. They think that they can embrace science's claims that the earth is billions of years old, while also embracing the Genesis account of creation. But these Christians must come to grips with the reality that those scientific claims are based upon a false premise—therefore, *all* scientific claims concerning the origins of the universe *must* be treated as false. This is a simple rule of logic.

The flow of logic is like a chain, each link in the chain depending upon the integrity of the preceding link. If one link is found faulty, then the entire chain is broken, and all subsequent links fall off. If modern science's claims that the earth is a billion years old are founded upon the presupposition that there is no plane of existence beyond our known cosmos, then that claim of the earth's age must be rejected as false because the preceding links of logic have been proven false.

I say "proven" guardedly here, because the fact is that all these assumptions are actually acts of faith. One exercises faith concerning the origins of the earth and the existence of God simply because these things cannot be proven or disproven in any laboratory. Yet we all exercise that faith, naturalist and supernaturalist, Christian and pagan alike. The Christian and the pagan choose to place their faiths in different directions, but each of them has made a conscious choice to act out his beliefs in faith that the source of those beliefs is reliable and trustworthy.

## Mankind's Creator is Mankind's God

Modern Christians tend to view the whole evolution controversy as of secondary importance, at best. After all, what difference does it really make whether man evolved or was created in six days? We can't hope to prove the truth one way or the other, so let's all just get along and have some cookies. What we tend to forget, however, is that whoever or whatever created mankind is mankind's god, by default. We are answerable to our creator, just as a machine is answerable to the man who designed it. If the machine isn't working right, the designer steps in and fixes it. The machine has no say in the matter.

Man's creator makes the rules, and mankind is subject to his laws. Man has no say in the matter. If we evolved from the lower species, we did so in order to survive. We had no choice in the matter, if that premise is true. It was evolve or die, plain and simple. Death was the motivating force which drove mankind up from the ooze, and we are, therefore, subject to the "laws of evolution."

Darwinists even use that phrase, "laws of evolution." What they don't seem to recognize, however, is that one must have a law-giver if one is to have a law. Who wrote the laws of evolution, the law of "survival of the fittest?" Death wrote that law, according to Darwin. Death, therefore, is the god to whom all mankind is subject, the one whose laws mankind must obey, according to evolution.

Paradoxically, if mankind evolved he also is subject to his *own* laws. If there was no creative agent beyond death that produced us, then we also have ourselves to thank for our high level of evolution. Once mankind has submitted himself to the laws of death, he is free to go about worshipping himself.

We see both aspects of this false religion in the west today. We see the culture of death rising paramount in America, with abortion rights, euthanasia, death with dignity, assisted suicide, and so forth. We also have become a culture of self-love and self-esteem, the liturgy of the church of self.

Darwinism is the religion of death, and modern science, anthropology, philosophy, and so forth are its high priests. Darwinists see death as the one fixed constant in the universe, the one thing that has not changed over the course of millions of years. Death itself is outside of evolution, because it is the pre-existent force which *defines* evolution. Death is evolution's god, immutable and omnipotent. It is heretical, therefore, to attempt to intermingle this false religion—even *parts* of this false religion—into the Scriptures.

## Modern Gnosticism

Gnosticism is an ancient heresy which Paul condemns.[1] It is a syncretistic religious system, which means that it borrows bits and pieces from other world religions and melds them together into some sort of homemade theology. As I mentioned above, the modern New Age movement is an example of this approach. Another important element of Gnosticism, however, is its view that one cannot hope to know God without some secret knowledge, some mystical "higher knowledge" which is not available to the common man.

This element of Gnosticism is profoundly apparent in modern science. The common man cannot hope to fully understand the scientist's theories of the age of the universe or the origins of life on earth, because they are clothed in esoteric jargon and premised upon highly technical hypotheses which the unlearned cannot hope to fathom. This is not a surprise if one keeps in mind that evolution is a religion, and it does not present any grave problems to the Christian other than sometimes appearing foolish in the eyes of the world.

The problem, as I have stated above, is that the church's leading theologians today have devised their own syncretistic theologies, attempting

---

1 See, for example, Colossians 2. "Beware lest anyone cheat you through philosophy and empty deceit, according to the tradition of men, according to the basic principles of the world, and not according to Christ" (Col. 2:8). See Section 3 for a more complete treatment of Gnosticism.

to mix into Scripture bits and pieces of the Gnosticism of Darwin—each theologian selecting which bits and pieces he likes best, so that there is no universal consensus amongst them as to *how* these incompatible schemes fit together.[2] The one point of agreement among our "higher critics," however, is that the Bible needs to be reinterpreted and effectively rewritten in order to accommodate their own flavor of gnosticism.[3] The tricks that they play in accomplishing this theological adultery are clothed in high-flown jargon and invented terminology, and are based upon unspoken assumptions that the common man is not aware of.

The most basic assumption of most of these "higher critics" is that the Bible is not the inspired Word of God. These theologians are the modern descendants of a group of German philosophers who were influential during the mid-1800s. Those Germans rejected the idea that the Bible was a special book, and began to look for proofs that it was merely the work of men without any intervention from the Holy Spirit. Our modern commentators, of course, do not openly confess this tenet of their faith, yet it is the foundation upon which they have built their entire reading of the Bible.

This poison of gnosticism has sickened the church of Jesus Christ in the 21st Century, and it threatens to rob us of our sacred text, the book upon which we build our understanding of the person and work of Jesus Christ. To counteract this poison, we will begin in the following chapters by studying selected passages from our sacred text—the Bible—to see whether it endorses the tenets of Darwinism. We will attempt, as best we can, to read it from an honest layman's point of view, trying to leave behind our own agendas as we do so. In Section 2, we will look more closely at the false teachings which these theologians espouse, and we will try to see through the many sleights of hand which these magicians of Pharaoh play with the text. In Section 3, we will examine Gnosticism itself, and look at its modern manifestations—including the ways that modern gnosticism has crept into the teachings of the church today.

---

2 This, incidentally, is true of the ancient Gnostics, as well, whose writings lack a unified consensus on their theological schemes. But all Gnostics, ancient and modern, agree that the Bible cannot be understood by the common man without some form of mystical "higher knowledge," available only from its highly educated priests.

3 Throughout this book, I use the word "Gnostic" in two ways. I capitalize it when referring to the heretics of the first and second centuries AD, and I use lower-case "gnostic" when referring to their modern descendants. This is done simply for clarity.

## The Basis of Our Beliefs

As we investigate the claims of modern theologians that the Bible endorses elements of evolution (such as the "day/age theory" and the "framework hypothesis," which claim that God took a million years to create the earth), we will discover that our views of creation affect the very core of our beliefs concerning the person and work of Jesus Christ. As I said above, this is not a mere matter of opinion, not a peripheral issue over which Christians can "agree to disagree." Our understanding of creation and of the origins of mankind will determine whether or not we can trust what the New Testament tells us about the death and resurrection of Christ. If God used evolution in any form while creating mankind, then Jesus did not rise from the dead.[4]

Modern science disagrees with the teachings of the Bible concerning the origins of mankind, and Christians must face the fact that the two belief systems are irreconcilable. This book is a call to God's people to come out of the world, to reject the false teachings of modern science on these matters and to embrace the Scriptures as our sacred text, our only way of reliably coming to understand who God is and what He expects from His people. Attempts to integrate the false teachings of evolution into that sacred text only succeed at depriving God's people of God's revelation of Himself—it does not satisfy the unbelievers around us who embrace the teachings of evolution.

"Choose for yourselves this day whom you will serve, whether the gods which your fathers served... or the gods of the Amorites, in whose land you dwell" (Josh. 24:15).

---

[4] I recognize that this is a bold statement, but I will demonstrate in the coming chapters that it is not hyperbole but actual, logical fact, the inescapable conclusion which we are forced to confess if we allow evolution and gnosticism into our reading of Genesis 1.

# 2
# GENESIS 1

Let us begin at the beginning by investigating what God's Word has to say about the origins of mankind. We will address many of these verses again later to find out what modern gnostics say about them, but we must first let the Scriptures speak for themselves.

## In the Beginning: Day One

***1. In the beginning.*** Moses[1] opens his history with a phrase which suggests that he is about to tell us a story—a sequential story. Modern readers who picked up a story opening with "once upon a time" would immediately expect a fairy tale. In a similar way, readers can expect that the author of Genesis is preparing to follow a logical sequence of events in the story that he's telling. The story might include some "flashbacks" along the way, perhaps some interjections and elucidations, but for the most part the reader immediately expects that the story will move forward chronologically from the "beginning" to the end. It may seem an odd way to begin our discussion of Genesis to emphasize this point, but by the time we get to reading what the modern "higher critics" have to say on Genesis 1 (such as suggesting that the six days of creation are not described in chronological order), we will see how important it is to begin properly.

***God created.*** Here is the central theme of this chapter—indeed, of the entire book.

Moses begins with the creation of the universe, then moves on toward God's creation of His covenant people. In fact, the theme moves forward throughout the entire Bible, leading us to God's restoration of His creation, and culminating in His creation of the New Jerusalem which John describes in Revelation. Certainly other themes are treated along the way, but the inexorable thrust of the entire Bible is concerned with God's creative and redemptive work among mankind. It is no coincidence, therefore, that the Bible opens with these words which define its central theme.

---

[1] It is not my purpose in this book to prove whether or not Moses is the author of Genesis. I do, however, wholeheartedly reject the modern fairy tale that Genesis was written by a group of editors and "redactors." For the sake of simplicity, therefore, I will refer to the author as Moses, since that is the belief which has held sway for several thousand years.

This is merely the first glimpse that we have of divine inspiration of this sacred book, and we will examine many more as we go along. It is important, however, to begin by recognizing that Moses himself probably had no idea that one day his writings and many others' writings would be gathered together into a sacred text and studied as a unified whole called the Bible; nor did he stop and think to himself, "How should I introduce a main theme of God's word?" Modern critics will be telling us that the "authors" of Genesis took their ideas from pagan myths, in effect denying the book's divine inspiration. As we proceed, therefore, I will point out a few of the countless bits of evidence which indicate that God Himself inspired Moses to write the words which we now know as Genesis.

**God created the heavens and the earth.** There is abundant speculation concerning exactly when "God created the heavens and the earth"—and, for that matter, what exactly is referred to by "the heavens." The traditional understanding is that He created earth and its surrounding environment—what we refer to today as "outer space"—on day one, prior to calling forth light (v. 3).

Some modern commentators argue that this view is contradictory to verses 14 and following, where God creates the sun and stars; they prefer to assume that earth, outer space, stars, planets, etc. all existed already prior to "day one" when God called forth light. Others argue that the earth and heavens pre-existed before God began to form them, and may have been there for billions of years, may even have taken billions of years to form via evolution. The old-fashioned "gap theory" posited that God actually created the earth *twice*, destroying the first version and creating it anew.[2] Still others argue that God's first act was to create heaven and earth, while verse 2 and following describe "subsequent phases in God's creative activity."[3]

Moses does not specifically state that God spoke the earth and heavens into being, yet it is more faithful to the text as a whole to assume so than to assume otherwise. Bear in mind that whatever theory one posits here is mere assumption, mere theory. One's theories, however, need to accord with our

---

[2] There are numerous versions of the gap theory, each suggesting a different reason and timeframe for the reconstruction of the earth. The most popular version was promoted by C. I. Scofield in his study Bible. Very few still hold to this theory, but those who do generally quote 1 Peter 3:5-7 where Peter mentions that "the world that then existed perished, being flooded with water." Peter is speaking, however, of the flood in this passage (Genesis 6—9), not of any re-creation of our planet.

[3] Gordon Wenham, *Word Biblical Commentary: Genesis 1—15*, 11.

known facts, and we know for a fact that God speaks and it becomes so in Genesis 1.

One possible theory might be that God began by creating what we call outer space, with earth in the midst of it, prior to beginning the six-day creation cycle—perhaps at the time that He created what Christians refer to as Heaven, the "dwelling place" of God and His angels (as distinct from "the heavens" or "outer space"). Presumably, by this theory, He spoke and brought into existence outer space, empty except for the "formless and void" globe that would become earth. This, however, mars the important seven-day process by appending time to the beginning. On this basis alone we can probably rule out this theory.

The simplest explanation is the traditional view, and it is also the most straightforward reading of the chapter: that God began His creative work by calling the earth and outer space into existence, then continuing to call forth light, and so on—all on the first day of creation. Thus, it seems most likely and most true to our text to understand that God is calling earth and space into existence at the very beginning of day one of the creation week.

What is absolutely sure, and no theory or assumption, is that we do not know conclusively. We do not know because we are not told explicitly. God did create man in His image, complete with curiosity and a passion to know the truth, so it is good for man to speculate and inquire. But man must also be humble enough to remember that there *are* "things past finding out" (Job 9:10), and what went on before man was created is surely one of those things. Our speculations, otherwise, can lead us well into false doctrines and heresy. It is best, then, to accept Genesis 1 at face value, not trying desperately to make modern science's theories fit in between verses and behind words and under some "sub-text" and above the heads of common men.

**2. *without form and void*.** Most modern Bible commentators tell us that the Hebrew phrase here actually means "chaos." We will address this sleight-of-hand trick later, but for now it is important to understand that there is no sense of chaos in Genesis 1. The Oxford English Dictionary defines "void" as "not occupied or frequented by living creatures; deserted, empty."[4] The NIV translates this phrase as "formless and empty," emphasizing the emptiness

---

4 All definitions given, unless stated otherwise, are from *The New Shorter Oxford English Dictionary*, Lesley Brown, ed. Oxford: Clarendon Press, 1993. The word "void" can also be used "of speech, action, etc.: ineffective, useless, leading to no result"—a sense that will become pertinent when we consider modern misreadings of Genesis.

of the initial stage of the world at the very beginning of creation. Something that is empty cannot contain chaos, since chaos is the struggle of two or more entities; an empty object contains no entities that can struggle.

Something which is "without form" is an unshaped mass, such as a lump of clay or a piece of unsculpted marble. The word "void" or "blank" can even refer to a piece of metal, awaiting the imprint from the hammer of a metal smith. The sense of this phrase is that the earth and the heavens were unformed and unshaped, masses of material awaiting the creative imprint of God Himself, like a huge lump of clay ready for the gentle, shaping hands of the Potter. This sense of gentleness, in fact, is latent throughout the first three chapters of Genesis, as we shall see as we go along.

There is no sense of struggle in this creation account, no sense of vying forces working against one another—in short, no sense whatsoever of "chaos." On the contrary, we shall discover a multitude of evidences that God's hand is gentle, tender, and loving throughout the six days of creation—and beyond, even after Adam falls into sin.

**darkness.** Darkness is not an entity, it is the *absence* of an entity, the simple absence of light. Darkness is the natural state of the universe, while Light is the effect of God's presence. Many forms of ancient paganism, however, teach that the universe came into being through the conflict of vying forces. This concept is described, for example, in the *yin/yang* symbol. The pagan teaching is that two forces—darkness and light, order and chaos—struggled together at the beginning of creation, producing through their conflict the elements of our world. This concept, of course, defies logic, since struggling and fighting brings only destruction, not creation; but logic is not the issue here. What matters is that we recognize what the Bible teaches, and the Scriptures make it abundantly clear that the universe was brought about, not by struggle, not by multiple forces or beings working either in concert or in conflict, but solely by the loving hand of God. As we shall see, God does not share His glory as Creator with any other being, not even the angels.

**deep . . . waters.** Evidently the earth was originally engulfed by water with no dry land showing.

**Spirit of God.** We have already been told that it is God who is the Creator, so it is no surprise to discover that His Spirit is "hovering" over the face of the waters. But who or what exactly *is* this "Spirit of God"? If we are beginning to read the Bible at the beginning, we have not yet met the Holy Spirit of the New Testament, and this becomes a valid question to ask. Is this Spirit the one who is creating? Is it He who speaks in verse 3? We are not given these details, so we must allow the text to speak for itself if we are to find any answers. The chief rule which we must bear in mind as we study Genesis—or any other book, for that matter—is that "context is king."[5] Whatever understanding we come to on such questions must be supported and endorsed by the context of Genesis (and, eventually, of the Bible as a whole).

The Hebrew word translated as "Spirit" or "spirit" in all modern versions of the Bible is the same word which means "breath" or "wind." The same is true of Greek and Latin, and this etymology is also evident in modern English. I will discuss this in more detail in Section 2, but for now it is enough just to point out this linguistic relationship of "spirit" and "breath." The question does arise at this point, however, of whether Moses is suggesting that God has some form of "duality," whether he is saying that God is both Creator and Spirit.

The wording "*and* the Spirit of God was hovering over the face of the waters" [emphasis added] suggests that the Spirit was not alone in the work of Creation; that the "God" referred to in verse 1 is somehow a separate entity of sorts from the Spirit of verse 2. The New Testament, of course, explains this duality by teaching us of the triune nature of the Godhead: Father, Son, and Holy Spirit. But we have not gotten to the New Testament yet, nor has Moses himself. Is it fair, therefore, to expect that Moses understood Trinitarian theology? I do think that the ancient Jews understood at least the duality of the Godhead, as we read of the Spirit of God throughout the Old Testament. But the larger point here is that Moses was not required to understand God's triune nature—*if* we believe that he is writing what God inspired him to write. He did not need to know about the "fossil record" that would become so important to mankind's thinking in the distant future when he wrote about the six days of creation; he was responsible only to record what God told him to record.

**hovering.** Henry Morris suggests that God is turning on the energy of the planet at this point, producing electromagnetic and gravitational forces which will enervate the earth.[6] This may well be the case—certainly the introduction of light in the next verse seems to support the idea—yet it is not all that Moses is telling us. The "hovering" of the Spirit speaks of a gentle caressing, literally "moving gently" as *The Interlinear Bible* transliterates the

---

5 I am indebted to my friend Dr. Dave Reid for this pithy phrase.
6 Henry Morris, *The New Defender's Study Bible*, 8.

Hebrew.[7] It paints a picture of a mother hen gently fluttering above her nest, of an eagle hovering patiently and protectively above her eyrie. There is a sense of tenderness commingled with power in this chapter. The Omnipotent God is tenderly caressing His creation, even as He speaks it into being.

Again, this is the antithesis of ancient pagan teachings, which claim that the earth came into being as the result of raging conflict amongst powerful, superior beings. It most assuredly is also the antithesis to the doctrines of evolution, which require that death be the motivating force which produces change or evolution. For that matter, there is thus far nothing *living*, so how could death even be a motivating force for change? The planet itself is, at present, not a living entity, let alone a sentient being, and it therefore cannot be expected to "evolve" itself into some different state of being. The only way that change can take place on the planet is for some outside force to intervene, to separate the waters from dry land, for example. This is the very doctrine which Scripture teaches and which evolution denies, and as such the two theologies are mutually incompatible—it is only the Christian Darwinists who attempt to intermarry them.

It is also worth noting that, at this point in creation, the Spirit of God evidently has covered His light in some fashion. We learn from the Gospel of John, if we permit ourselves to skip ahead to the New Testament briefly, that God is Light (we will consider this and other passages at greater length in another chapter), yet here we are told that the waters are covered in darkness, even though God's Spirit was hovering directly above them. The picture is that of the Creator, the Master Potter, pausing briefly above His great lump of clay just prior to getting to work on creation—and the first step, as we see in the next verse, was to turn on the light.

**3. And God said.** God begins His creative work by speaking, not by acting. This comes as a bit of a surprise, given the powerful forces which Moses has pictured above, poised and ready for action. Yet this also implies that God's creative power is contained in His Word alone. This is a mystery, one which will become somewhat clearer when we look at the first chapter of John, yet a deep mystery nonetheless. It could perhaps mean that God is laying down some deep principles and laws of His creation, laws which will then carry on His creative work in their own power. This, of course, is the exact idea which is espoused by Christian Darwinists, as they suggest that God ordained the laws of evolution at the very beginning of creation,

---

7 *The Interlinear Hebrew-Aramaic Old Testament*, Jay P. Green, Sr., ed., 1.

then sat back and allowed those laws to bring all things into being—with only occasional divine interventions. Yet it also could mean that God's words contain power; that His word alone causes creation to occur. We will need to depend upon the context to bring a better understanding as we go along.[8]

God's speaking also implies a careful deliberation on His part, an intricate and detailed planning that went on prior to His speaking the first word of creation. Evolution, on the other hand, is a theology of randomness, denying the external creative intelligence of God. Christian Darwinists, as I have already pointed out, attempt to squish God into evolutionary theology, claiming that evolution is God's tool, the creative force which He used to carry out His design. Yet this scheme is unfaithful to both theologies, to the theology of Moses as well as the theology of Darwin. Darwinism rejects the concept of a divine planner, an "intelligent designer;" it is a theology designed to explain creation *without* the inconvenience of a Creator. We shall see as we go along that even an atheistic evolutionist is more faithful to the tenets of his belief system than a Christian Darwinist, who attempts to rewrite not one but two religious theologies to suit his own desire for compromise.

***Let there be. . . and there was.*** At this point, one might argue that God's words, "Let there be," indicate that He is setting down some law of creation, as in "let there become." This might well be the line of thinking behind the Christian Darwinist: that God is establishing certain evolutionary laws, forces which will then continue His work of creation in their own right. It might also be taken to mean that He is stating His long-term purpose for some element of creation, and that He then sets about creating that element—regardless of how long it might take for that element to actually appear, even if it takes a million years for "light" to evolve. God's saying "let there become" merely means, in this scheme of thought, that He intends to evolve light, not that He made it appear instantaneously.

But the following words, "and there was," contradict this idea. The implication of this formula is that the created element—in this case, light—appears instantly. This is the traditional understanding of the passage, and it is, more importantly, the sense which the text demands.

Let's say that a man stands in his kitchen and decides that he needs a new table. It is conceivable that he might exclaim, "Let there be a table!" It is more likely that he would say, "We need a new table," but we will not force

---

[8] We know, of course, that the Word is Christ Himself, and that He is the agency of creation which is alluded to here. We will discuss this in more detail, however, in chapter 4.

our modern ways of speaking onto Moses and his generation. Nevertheless, a person retelling the new-table story would not say, "George said, 'Let there be a table,' and there was!" He would say, "George said, 'Let us have a new table,' and he went out to his workshop immediately and got busy building it." Tables need to be built, after all; it would be a miracle if a man spoke and a table appeared instantly.

But this is exactly what the text of Genesis is telling us: that God said, "Let there be..." and instantly "there was." There is no room in the text for the suggestion that God spoke a desire for light, then set about for millions of years to create that light from scratch. He spoke, and it was—instantaneously. How many times have you heard someone say, "Let there be light!"—at the same time flipping on the light switch? It is an old joke, and it demonstrates that we understand instinctively the meaning demanded of this wording: that "let there be... and there was" implies an instantaneous fulfillment of the command.

The Hebrew itself makes this even more clear. "Let there be light" is two Hebrew words which might be transliterated, "Be light!" It is in the imperative voice—a command—implying instant fulfillment rather than gradual accomplishment. So now we find George standing in his kitchen, staring at an empty space, suddenly commanding in an imperious voice: "Be table!" In this telling of the story, we expect to see a table suddenly materialize in George's empty kitchen, accompanied by a cloud of magical smoke.

The Hebrew verb "to be" can also be translated "become" or "became." This is the way that the same word is used in Gen. 3:20: "And Adam called his wife's name Eve, because she was [became] the mother of all living." Context, once again, determines how we understand this important little verb, both in Hebrew and in English. The context of 3:20 demands that we understand Eve to have become the mother of the human race—not an instantaneous transformation, but one which has unfolded over the course of time. Once again, context is king; and the context of "let there be... and there was" demands that we recognize the instantaneous appearance of the thing being created, not its gradual appearance over millions of years.

It is also worth noting here that the verb "to be" is related to God's name: "I AM." In creating the universe, God is expressing part of His ineffable nature, imparting Himself into His creation. "As I AM, so shalt thou be!"

This passage raises another question: to whom is God speaking? In later verses, He will apparently be addressing some aspect of creation, such as the earth: "Let the earth bring forth. . . ." (11). Here, however, His audience is not specified. Is God addressing Himself when He commands, "Let there be light"? He does this later in this chapter, as we shall see, but in that instance He says, "Let us create. . . ." It is conceivable, however, that God is in fact addressing Himself with this command to bring forth light, that He is telling the Spirit to unveil His light. The traditional view is that God is simply commanding that light be brought into being out of nothing—*ex nihilo*, as the Latin Vulgate phrases it. There is much mystery surrounding God's creation, much that we do not know and cannot fully understand; as always, we must be sure that the context of Genesis supports any theories that we put forward.

Finally, science tells us that the universe began with a big bang. Moses, on the other hand, seems to be telling us that it began with a soft voice. We shall see in Genesis 3 that God speaks to man in a soft voice, like the "still small voice" which Elijah would hear many years later. This passage emphasizes, as I've already said, the gentleness and loving caress with which God created our universe, and it is fitting to think that His voice did not boom with thunderous authority but rather spoke gently with the calm assurance of fulfillment.

**Light.** Note that the text does not say "a light," but "light." We are accustomed to having light in our world which shines from a specific source, whether from the sun or from light bulbs or some other identifiable source. Here, however, we encounter light which has no source—for the sun and stars have not been created yet. Perhaps the space surrounding the unformed earth was suffused with brilliant light at this point in creation. God is light, after all, and He is omnipresent, so it is conceivable that all space was glowing with brilliance. It could mean that God instituted the *principle* of light, that He created the energy forces which we call light.

Yet the immediate fulfillment—"and there was light"—suggests that visible light suddenly appeared in the space surrounding the unformed globe. I tend to think that God revealed Himself to His creation right at the beginning, that He unveiled some aspect of His glory, His quality of being The Light. It might even be, as I've suggested above, that the Spirit of God unveiled His light as He hovered above the watery globe. This sense, incidentally, can help us to understand the "evening" and "morning" of this chapter, as we shall see in a moment.

**4. It was good.** God will repeat Himself often during the course of His creation, frequently taking time to step back from His work, examine it, and declare that it is good. Moses lets us know that God declared His work good from the very first element of creation, when He introduced light. He usually will do this at the end of the day, once a particular aspect of creation is completed; but here He declares light itself good, before He has finished His work for the day. This suggests that light is complete in itself; it does not require separation from darkness or separation of night and day or even the naming of the elements to become complete: it is complete and entire of itself. This is a mystery, and I cannot pretend to comprehend its full significance. It is, perhaps, enough to say that God is Light, complete and perfect in Himself; He has no need of creation to be fulfilled or perfected. He is.

Christian Darwinists, alas, will claim that God used evolution to move His creation to various points in the continuum which He deemed to be "good." This would require, from a logical perspective, that God allowed some element of evolution to occur until He felt that it had attained "goodness," then that He stopped that bit of evolution because it was complete. (When God declares that something is good, it is roughly equivalent to saying, "It is finished." This thought in itself could certainly be pursued further in relation to the work of Christ.) This, of course, creates a host of problems if one is trying to be faithful to the tenets of evolution, as we shall discover in future verses. For example, God declares fish and birds to be "good," or "finished," yet evolution claims that fish evolved into mammals, implying that evolution's work was *not* complete.

**God divided the light from the darkness.** Light is separated from darkness in our world by shadows, whether cast by objects in bright sunlight, or cast by the earth itself, which we know as "night." Shadows, however, require that light be focused from a single source, such as the sun. We would not have night-time if the entire universe were suffused with glowing light, for example. Thus, it is possible here that the Spirit of God has focused His light, shedding it forth from a specific point in space, perhaps where He was hovering over the waters. This would imply that the darkness is the shadow cast by the earth itself as God's Spirit hovered above.

This might also account for the "evening" and "morning" of the first few days, prior to the creation of the sun. Skeptics have made a fuss over the question, "how can there be evening and morning without the sun?" It is a silly question, but one which we should answer, nonetheless. First, the sun is not what determines night and day, it is the earth itself as it revolves upon its axis. Any light coming from any single source, shining down upon the globe, would create darkness on one side and light on the other. Thus, if the Spirit in fact has revealed His light from a specific point in space, then there was indeed a "night-time" on one side of the globe.

Second, notice that Moses says "evening" and "morning," not "night" and "day." This is a small distinction, admittedly, yet it is worth mentioning. If light is suffused throughout the universe, rather than shining forth from the Spirit at a specific point in space, then there would be no night-time; the entire globe would be surrounded by light at all times, even while it revolved upon its axis. In such a case, one might speak of it as "morning and evening" to denote the passage of time.

These are all mere speculations, but there is one thing that does come clear from this verse: the Bible, as I've said already, will not endorse the eastern concept of "yin/yang," of two conflicting forces at work in creation. Light and darkness, for example, are not separated until after creation has begun, and they are not presented as metaphors for some giant contest between heavenly forces. I emphasize this because the "yin/yang" concept of conflict between forces is central to the religion of evolution, which is built upon the premise that there is an eternal conflict between life and death. A species evolves, according to their tenets, because it must either change or die. The Bible, on the other hand, demonstrates right from the beginning that the earth and the universe came into existence *without* conflict—in harmony, not in chaos.

This verse also denotes God's first law of His creation: light must remain apart from darkness. God will establish numerous "separations" in this chapter, but in chapter 2 we will learn of a particularly important separation which God commanded: mankind was to remain separated from death. This is the one law that is violated, as mankind is the one creature in God's creation with the capacity to disobey. I mention it now because it is important to underscore this fact: the Bible teaches that mankind did not evolve from some lower order of creation, and it simply cannot be forced to accommodate that false belief. God separated mankind from death; it was man himself, as a sentient and accountable being, who brought death into the world.

But God's laws were not revoked when man sinned, and His law still stands separating light from darkness. As sons of the Last Adam, God's people are called upon to re-submit themselves to this commandment

(2 Cor. 6:14). Evolution, as I continually point out, is a religious system, a system of darkness, and we are in error when we attempt to commingle the two.

Finally, it should be pointed out that evolutionists have no explanation for the origins of light. Christian Darwinists tend to overlook this, and work out their own theories concerning Moses' words. The more honest among them say, "Well, scientists have not told us yet how light was evolved. When they do, we will figure out a way of working it into Genesis." The lowest of the breed, however—the ones who write commentaries—have the audacity to tell us that Moses is not speaking chronologically in Genesis 1, and with that dismissive absurdity they pretend that light is evolved on day 4 with the creation (excuse me, the evolution) of the sun. We shall hold these commentators accountable beginning in Section 2.

**5. *God called the light Day.*** A person who names someone or something is demonstrating authority over the person or creature being named. Bestowing a name is a sign of lordship, of headship, even of ownership, and it was not done lightly in the ancient world. We shall discuss this further in a moment, but for now it is worth noting that God Himself holds authority over the earth's diurnal cycles; this is not an element of His creation which He gave to Adam to superintend.

***The evening and the morning.*** As I pointed out in verse 4 above, skeptics constantly carp that there could be no day and night prior to the creation of the sun, a quibble that is silly at best. It is the earth's rotation, not the sun, which determines day and night, and any light source could produce the darkness which we know as "night-time" on one side of the revolving globe. Furthermore, note that God is naming *light* "day," not sunlight. Technically speaking, by this definition we do not even need to have a revolving globe for God to name His light "day." He named it, and it is thus by definition; it is called day simply by God's fiat, because He named it such.

I must reiterate here that we are examining Genesis by the rules of literary interpretation for the most part, not by scientific analysis. In other words, we are allowing Genesis to speak for itself, and at times comparing what it says with the Bible as a whole. Details in Genesis which seem to conflict with modern science must be dealt with in some other forum; we are no more concerned with what scientists have to say about Genesis than we are with what the ancient pagans had to say. We are certainly free to say that Genesis is "unscientific," and to thereby dismiss it as wrong. But we are *not* free to say that "science and Genesis do not agree, therefore Genesis must mean something other than what it seems to be saying."

I put forward in verse 4 above several possible explanations for the "morning and evening" here, but the real issue comes back to the *ex nihilo* concept which I mentioned earlier: God can create something out of nothing if He so chooses, and Moses is here claiming that the earth experienced "morning and evening" because God ordained it to be so. One does not even need to know that the earth rotates on its axis to understand this.

Modern critics love to stress what Moses knew and didn't know (as if they themselves have access to Moses' knowledge), and they would be quick to suggest that Moses couldn't be expected to know that the earth rotated on an axis while simultaneously revolving around the sun. (It is, in fact, very likely that the ancient Egyptians did understand these things, at least in a rudimentary way.) This brings us back, once again, to the issue of divine inspiration. What Moses knew or didn't know is not the point; the point is that he *did* write these things, and he wrote them under the inspiration and direction of God Himself. The entire debate becomes quite silly, suggesting that "morning and evening" prove that Genesis cannot mean what it seems to be saying—yet it is just such minutiae which modern Bible critics use to distract us from the important teachings of this book.

*The first day.* I pointed out at the beginning of this chapter that Moses is planning on taking us chronologically through the six days of creation, and here he underscores that fact once again. He is saying, in effect, "thus ends day one; now on to day two." He uses this formula throughout the early part of Genesis, often concluding a section with the phrase "this is the genealogy of" such and such a person. It marks the conclusion to one section and the introduction to the next section—in this case, the conclusion of day one and the beginning of day two. Not a terribly incisive bit of insight, pointing out that Moses is telling us that this is the conclusion of day one. It is self-evident; why belabor it? Why, indeed. We shall see in Section 2 that those things which are self-evident in Genesis are treated as "problems" and "mysteries" by our modern Bible scholars.

This formula in chapter 1 also underscores the fact that Moses is describing a literal period of 24 hours—a literal day, not a metaphorical "day." He informs us of this by saying, "there was a morning, followed by an evening—it was the first day." He repeats this same formula for each of the six days, and the smallest child would recognize that he is speaking of a 24-hour period of time. Christian Darwinists, however, have willfully blinded themselves to the painfully obvious, insisting that Moses doesn't really mean a 24-hour period of time—he really means millions of years. We shall discuss the various permutations of this misreading in Section 2. For now, it is enough to note that the text means exactly what it says; there is no hidden layer of mystical secrecy.

## Day Two: The Firmament

**6. *Be a firmament.*** Here, again, we have the Hebrew verb "to be," as God literally commands: "Be expanse!" This firmament, translated "sky" in the NIV, has been subjected to ample debate—as has nearly every word of this chapter. (Satan attacks most diligently at the core of Christianity. If this passage were of peripheral importance, as modern Christians seem to believe, it would not be the center of such heated controversy.)

Henry Morris suggests that the earth was originally surrounded by a thick canopy of water vapor which dissipated during the flood.[9] It is interesting that evolutionists themselves make a similar claim. Scientists claim that an original layer of helium and hydrogen was dissipated by a "solar wind" [see comments above concerning the Spirit of God hovering] and replaced by a dense canopy of carbon dioxide and water vapor. This book, however, is not concerned with what modern science has to say; it is concerned solely with what the Bible has to say. The fact is that we do not know exactly what the firmament constituted simply because Moses doesn't tell us.

***Divide the waters.*** Here again, we see God dividing and separating elements of His creation. At first glance, it seems surprising to find God being a "divider," a role usually assigned in Scripture to Satan. The Greek word for the devil, *diabalos*, means "divider." It literally means "to throw across," to throw a line of separation or demarcation across something which is unified, and this is what the evil one loves to do among God's people. (It is no coincidence, after all, that the whole evolution debate has divided the church in modern times.)

But in this passage, God is not separating good from evil, for evil has not yet entered the world. Later in Scripture, darkness will come to be equated with sin, but at the time of creation, *physical* darkness was a part of the unified goodness of God's plan. On day two, God separates the "waters from the

---

9 Henry Morris, *The Genesis Record*, 59–61.

waters," dividing the moisture in the atmosphere from the waters which, at that point, still covered the entire globe.

It is, therefore, good for God's people to discriminate between those things which God has separated—dark from light, wet from dry, up from down. It is also the reason that Satan works so hard to outlaw "discrimination," the ability to distinguish one thing from another. Even the word "discrimination" has been brought to mean its exact opposite: the separating of one group of people from another, where no separation should exist. Meanwhile, we are virtually forbidden to distinguish between those things which *are* different and which should be kept separate: male from female, right from wrong, up from down. The evil one has worked steadily since creation to remove the separations which God ordained. Conversely, the enemy also works constantly to separate those things which God ordained to be united: marriage, churches, brothers. (Compare Proverbs 6:16–19, which states unequivocally that God hates such dividers.)

**8. God called the firmament Heaven.** Once again, we find God naming part of His creation. As I've already stated, naming something demonstrates lordship, authority, ownership. God will later command Adam to name the animals, but here we notice that He has retained for Himself all authority over mankind's environment. He names day, night, heaven, earth, and sea (v. 10). In an age of perpetual political scare tactics concerning global warming, ozone holes, acid rain, and so forth, it is good to know that God Himself has control over the environment. This also should serve to warn mankind of his solemn role as steward of the environment; it doesn't belong to us, so we should be all the more careful in how we use it.

*second day.* Moses concludes the second day of creation, following the formula which we have already noted, demonstrating that this is a chronological account—but he diverges from the formula in an interesting way here: God does not call the firmament "good." This is the only day of creation which, evidently, God does not deem as fully good yet.

Some have suggested that God is not quite finished with the "watery" parts of creation, as He will separate sea from land on the next day. But this is unlikely, since each day He completes some aspect of His creation, and it is unlikely that on this one day God didn't finish what He had started in the morning. (Again, just to emphasize what I have said above, this also demonstrates that evolution is not part of God's plan, requiring as it does millions of years to reach some stage of completion. God does not leave His creative work unfinished at the end of the day.)

Another clue to the completeness of God's work on day two is that He separates that which needs to be separated—in this case, He divides the "waters above" from the "waters beneath." This is a vertical separation, whereas day three will bring a horizontal separation of the seas from the dry lands.

I would suggest that God intended, even before creation, to ultimately remove all barriers which exist between God and mankind. That would include the barriers which He Himself would create in making the world habitable by His creatures, which is symbolized by the firmament, the great barrier of sky and space which stand, at least figuratively, between earth and the "dwelling place" of God. The firmament surrounds earth much like a womb or cocoon, protecting our fragile environment from the uninhabitable regions of outer space. But none of God's creation is intended to remain indefinitely within the womb; God intended from the beginning that His creatures should grow to maturity, becoming productive participants in His on-going plans. For mankind, this maturing included Adam facing a test: would he choose to obey God, even in the face of direct opposition from the evil one—and even from his own wife? This is what Bible commentators refer to as the "probationary creation."

Of course, if the "canopy theory" described above is correct, then we know that God did remove it during the flood—although that was surely not the way that He would have removed it if Adam had not sinned. But on a larger level, I would suggest that God does not deem the firmament "good" for the reason that it is a boundary, a line of separation which is different from the other separations that He makes: it separates man from God. This is not something which He deems good, and it is only temporary. One day we know that He will, indeed, remove all barriers between Himself and us, and in that day all things will once again be "very good."

## Day Three: Dry Land, Seas, Plants

**11. Let the earth bring forth.** With the earth now habitable, God calls forth life. We see something new on the third day, as God commands part of His creation to produce something for the first time. He is still creating solely by the power of His Word, yet now He is *not* creating *ex nihilo*, out of nothing. He is, instead, choosing to use elements of what He has already created to produce some entirely new entity. It is important, however, to recognize that the dry land could not have produced anything if God had not commanded it to be so. Dirt does not spontaneously produce grass; grass seed must first be planted in the dirt.

Having said that, God did not plant grass seed on day three and then watch it grow. He commanded it into being, and it sprang up instantly, once again creating by *fiat*, by simple word of command. This solves that ancient riddle concerning the chicken and the egg: the chicken came first—or, in this case, the apple tree came before the apple seed. Plant life did not grow first from seeds, but solely from the Word of God.

It is possible that trees did not just suddenly appear full-grown with a cosmic *poof*; perhaps they grew up from the soil, passing through the various stages of maturity which trees still pass through today—seedlings, saplings, young trees, mature trees—doing so with extraordinary speed. Whether or not they appeared fully grown or sprouted through their normal stages, we do know this: In one day, plants and trees of every type and variety sprang up from the earth and grew into maturity, their branches probably laden with seed-bearing fruit before the evening arrived.

We should also note at this point that God is the one doing the creating here, even though the earth is participating in the process. It is similar to a potter who creates a bowl from a lump of clay: the clay is participating in the process in the role of providing the material for the bowl, but the creation is solely the work of the potter. We would not say that the potter and the clay cooperated together to co-create a bowl, and we cannot suggest here that the earth (or any other force) is participating with God as co-creator of life.

It is important for us to grasp the concept that the earth was extraordinarily fecund or fertile during the early days of creation. The ground brought forth at God's command, and life sprang into being and grew toward maturity with miraculous speed. God expects His creation to produce, to be fruitful—not merely to eat, sleep, and exist.

C. S. Lewis pictures this nicely in *The Magician's Nephew*, in which several characters arrive in Narnia just as Aslan is singing all things into existence. One of the people, an evil witch, throws a piece of iron at Aslan which she had violently torn off of a London streetlamp. The iron bar sticks into the fertile soil of Narnia, and promptly begins growing into a gas lamp (the same lamp that the Pevensie children discover in *The Lion, the Witch, and the Wardrobe*). Later, some coins fall out of the magician's pocket, and they, too, grow into gold and silver-bearing trees. The magician, an avaricious old soul, gets the idea that he could make himself quite wealthy on earth by growing gold and battleships and whatever else he plants in Narnia, but Aslan explains the truth to the others. " 'He thinks great folly, child,' said Aslan. 'This world is bursting with life for these few days because the song with which I called it into life still hangs in the air and rumbles in the ground. It will not be so for long. But I cannot tell that to this old sinner, and I cannot comfort him, either; he has made himself unable to hear my voice. If I spoke to him, he would hear only growlings and roarings. Oh Adam's sons, how cleverly you defend yourselves against all that might do you good!'"[10]

Lewis' warning is well-taken. Those modern commentators who insist that creation could not have occurred in six days manage only to deafen themselves to the clear messages of Genesis.

*According to its kind.* God ordains that each created entity should reproduce itself "according to its kind"—which is, after all, what "reproduce" means! Our modern Xerox machines reproduce documents "according to their kind," making exact copies of the original placed on the glass. A copier that changed the original would not be considered an "evolutionary marvel;" it would be considered broken.

Roses produce roses. There is certainly flexibility within God's scheme of creation for pink roses, yellow roses, white roses, and this is yet one more aspect of the delight which God takes in His creatures. He loves individuality and variety; consider snowflakes, such an insignificant part of creation, yet no two are the same. But roses, nonetheless, bring forth roses; a rose bush will never produce a cumquat (without man's meddling), no matter how many millions of years go by.

Evolutionists themselves speak of the "sudden appearance of plant life," recognizing that plants did not gradually materialize from lower orders. But they then go on to define "sudden" as meaning thousands of years! As though any sane man considers a thousand years to be "sudden." Tell a Darwinist that his tax refund will arrive "suddenly"—within the next thousand years—and see whether or not he really believes in his own definitions.

---

10 C. S. Lewis, *The Magician's Nephew*, 153.

## Day Four: Sun, Moon, Stars

**14. Lights in the firmament.** This is the first mention of any specific light source in all of creation. It emphasizes the fact that light depends solely upon God, not on the sun or any other created element.

Further, Genesis here teaches us that the heavenly bodies exist (at least in part) for the benefit of earth and earth's inhabitants. Modern man would scoff at such an idea, claiming that it is immensely egotistical for man to suggest that the sun exists for his benefit. (As though it *isn't* egotistical to suggest that mankind evolved himself out of the lower orders.)

Modern science has the attitude that mankind is of little value or significance. We do, in fact, seem quite insignificant when one views the vastness of the heavens, the distances and breadth of the galaxies. The world looks into outer space and says, "Man is nothing." The Christian looks at the same wonders and exclaims, "What is man, that God is mindful of him? How amazing that God sees us at all, let alone numbering the hairs upon our heads!" When one moves God out of creation—or even attempts to move Him one step backward behind the pagan myth of evolution—one loses respect for all aspects of that creation, and most notably of mankind himself. We can see this contempt at every turn of the globe today, with abortion, euthanasia, cloning, farming of human embryos in the name of "science," and countless other debasements that are becoming commonplace in our culture.

Science long ago determined that the earth is not the center of the universe, dating back to Copernicus and Galileo, to the discovery that the earth revolves around the sun. Yet God's perspective seems to be otherwise, according to Genesis 1; not that the earth does not rotate around the sun, but that the sun *exists* for earth's benefit. The purposes of the heavenly bodies, according to Genesis, are as follows:

**To divide the day from the night.** Once again, God commands His creation to carry out His will, part of which is to divide and separate those things which He has separated. Notice also that He does not command the sun and moon and stars to separate light from darkness; He has already accomplished this. The heavenly bodies are commanded to continue one aspect of this separation, dividing day from night.

**Signs.** God's people are forbidden to dabble in astrology and other forms of divination, yet here we learn that one purpose of the heavenly bodies *is* to provide mankind with signs and indications of God's involvement with His creation. One example would be the star or "heavenly light" which appeared around the time of Jesus' birth, announcing His incarnation to the magi and enabling them to find Him. Did this star or "light" serve any other purpose in creation? We are not even sure today what nature of heavenly body it was that appeared, but it is certainly clear that its appearance—if not its very existence—was primarily for the purpose of providing a sign to the men of earth. How very extravagant is God's creation!

*seasons . . . days and years.* God ordained, from the beginning of time itself, that mankind should pay attention to the passage of time. This purpose of the heavenly bodies, furthermore, is for the benefit of mankind alone. Animals and plants do not study the stars, nor do they count the passage of days and months and years.

**15. To give light on the earth.** Finally, Moses tells us outright that the heavenly bodies exist in part to bring light to earth. This does not mean that the sun does not shed light on the other planets in our solar system—although, if modern science should prove correct concerning the conditions on those other planets, that sunlight is of little or no value to any planet other than earth. God's perspective, at least as far as Genesis is concerned, is centered solely upon planet earth, and mostly upon mankind who is given stewardship of that planet. This does not necessarily mean that there is no other life in the universe; it does mean, however, that man should not be wasting his time looking for it. God is concerned with man's relationship with Himself, and that should be man's central concern, as well.

This business of the heavenly bodies has other implications for modern science besides whether the earth is at the center of the universe. Scientists tell us that the light from the stars takes millions and billions of years to reach earth, and from that postulation they conclude that the stars must be billions of years old, that the light which we see when we gaze up at night left the stars that long ago. Christian Darwinists also like to point out this postulation, arguing that science has proven how far away the stars are, and proven how long their light takes to reach earth, all of which has proven that the universe is a bazillion years old and therefore Genesis must either be wrong or mean something other than what it says.

The basic answer to this is: I don't know. I don't know how far away the stars are; I don't know how fast light travels in outer space; I don't know when the light rays which I see at night were emitted from any given star or planet. I do know, however, that Genesis states clearly that the stars were brought into being instantly at God's command; that they were created on the fourth day of creation, *after* plant life was created; that plants would not have survived a billion years without the sun; that Moses tells me clearly that the plants were created only *one day* prior to the sun; and that I must exercise faith no matter what I believe on these matters.

Henry Morris suggests that God created "light trails" at the time of creating the stars, so that the light emitted from them was instantly visible on earth.[11] This is possible, I suppose—but it is equally possible that *science is wrong*! We must remember that modern science is nothing more than the aggregate, accumulated knowledge of mankind, and man is frequently wrong. Our understanding of heavenly bodies is predicated entirely upon theories and suppositions, since no man has ever traveled outside of our own solar system. This does not mean that those theories and suppositions are wrong; but it certainly does *not* mean that they are accurate, either. There is every reason to anticipate another Galileo or Copernicus or Einstein who will one day shake up the accepted scientific theories with some new discovery or postulation. At that time, all the other theories which have been built upon the debunked theories will also be shattered. Who can say whether or not this will include the speed of light in outer space, or the distances of the stars?

As I said previously, these things are all matters of faith. We can choose to place our faith in the knowledge and theories of learned men, or we can choose to place it in the Bible. We cannot, however, choose to force the Bible to say what it does not say, solely to gratify our own caprices of belief.

**17. Set them in the firmament.** We tend to picture God flinging the stars into space, scattering them at random; but Moses tells us here that God *set* them in place, individually and deliberately. Psalm 147 further tells us that He knows the exact number of the stars—and that He calls each by name!

The Hebrew word for "set" has a generous, positive connotation. It is used of placing a ring on a person's hand (Gen. 41:42) or of setting a helmet on someone's head for protection (1 Sam. 17:38). Isaiah 42:1 uses the word to describe the coming Messiah's anointing of the Holy Spirit; it is used in Deut. 12:15 to speak of God's placing a blessing upon His people. David tells us in Psalm 8:1 that God has set His glory above the heavens.[12] Once again we see the gentle and loving hand which God uses in every aspect of His creation. There is no hint here, or anywhere else, of "chaos" during these six days.

---

11 Morris, *The Genesis Record*, 11.
12 *BDBG*, 678–81.

***To give light on the earth.*** Moses once again reiterates God's earth-centered perspective in creation.

## Day Five: Fish and Birds

**20–23.** The planet can now accommodate and feed other living creatures besides plants, so God brings forth sentient life—or "life that moves," as the King James words it. Plant life was a marvel, springing as it did from the earth on God's command, but here we have an even greater marvel: creatures that can swim and fly!

It is interesting that fish and birds are created on the same day. (The King James suggests that the waters brought forth both fish and birds, but most other modern translations do not make that connection.) Mammals will not appear until the next day, whereas evolution teaches us that mammals *and* birds both evolved from fish—millions of years later, of course. (This is the magic wand of the Darwinist: wave a few million years at it, and absolutely anything can be explained away.) Fish, according to their doctrines, also preceded plant life. Genesis most obviously does not agree with this timetable, yet many Christians persist in claiming that Genesis can be read to accord with evolutionary theology.

We shall see in Section 2 that modern Bible commentators try to get around this "difficulty," melding Darwinism into Genesis, by telling us that Genesis is not meant to be taken either literally or even chronologically. Yet, even if we were to allow this preposterous claim, and buy into the absurdity that Moses means a millennium every time he speaks of the "morning and evening" of a particular *day*—even then, we would still find fish and birds appearing during the same "epoch." Even if we permit the silly "dischronologicization" (I did not invent that word!) of the modern commentators, by which they explain away the fact that birds and fish are created *after* plant life and not before: even then, we find that Genesis stubbornly refuses to be commingled with the theologies of Darwin, because evolution preaches that fish and birds evolved millions of years apart, not during the same epoch. We simply cannot mix evolution into Genesis, no matter what tricks we play with the text.

**20. Abundantly.** The Hebrew here is literally "swarming swarmers." The sense is that God, once again, is amazingly prodigal in His creation. Here again we see an aspect of God's tender love and generosity, as He fills His seas with an abundance, with swarms upon swarms of living creatures. He fills "the open firmament of heaven" with all manner of fowl, and the phrase itself of "open firmament" implies a generous expanse of open space to accommodate them.

**22. God blessed them.** This is the first time that God has addressed His creation directly. And once again, Moses underscores the *lack* of hostility or chaos during creation, as God shows forth the tender love which He has for all levels of His handiwork. His first words of direct address are words of blessing and fruitfulness, not of cursing and death. Would it be a blessing to His creatures to be immediately placed under the dominion of death and suffering? Yet this is precisely what Christian Darwinists are suggesting, whether or not they realize it, by claiming that God used the forces of evolution to perfect His creation.

God also commands His creatures to be productive, to participate with Him in His creation work, like a potter exhorting a lump of clay to be malleable to his hand and not to fight against him. It is also noteworthy that He expects His creatures to be focusing on the next generation, not on themselves. (Sin, as we shall see in chapter 3, ruins this focus.) God does not seem to be worried about over-population; He has already created "swarms of swarms," and now He turns right around and urges those swarms to "be fruitful and multiply." The modern fixation on "over-population" is just one more facet of the Darwinist mindset, the cult of death.

## Day Six: Animals

**24. Let the earth bring forth.** Once again, God calls upon His creation to participate with Him in His further work, this time to produce land animals. God has taken care, furthermore, to populate each layer of His creation—land, sea, and air—leaving no plane empty of living beings.

It is hard to picture exactly what took place over the next few hours of day six, but presumably the ground began to heave up into mounds of dirt, and animals of every size and description broke free. Lewis, again, presents a compelling and entertaining picture of this possibility in *The Magician's Nephew*. We cannot be certain that this is what happened for the simple reason that we are not told, but by this point in the chapter we *can* know for certain that it happened immediately, powered solely by the Word of God; it did not take a million years; and it did not involve death.

Once again, God is not creating in a vacuum, not creating *ex nihilo* as He did during the initial stages of creation; rather, He is utilizing the materials which He has previously created to carry on His work to completion. God is still creating today, but He is not creating any new creatures or materials. He has chosen to use His existing creatures and materials to continue His perfect work, and now He expects His children to cooperate with Him in that work. Our Father expects His children to be fully involved in His redemptive work in the 21st century, just as much as—or more so than—the lower orders were involved during the first week of history.

*According to its kind.* Notice how frequently Moses reiterates this concept. Evidently the concept is important, and God has Moses underscore it at each stage of living creation. Modern evolutionists in general, and Christian Darwinists in particular demonstrate the willingness with which mankind chooses to believe that a worm can bring forth a canary. The emphasis also suggests the possibility that the ancient Israelites were confronted with the ancient pagan myth of evolution in their own day, and God wanted Moses to emphasize the truth for men of all cultures and times.

We will discuss this further in Section 2, but I will mention in passing that modern Biblical commentators love to claim that Genesis is merely a political tract designed to refute pagan myths. They cite various examples of what they feel to be proof of this, but oddly enough, none of those commentators ever points to this reiteration of creation bringing forth its "own kind" to suggest that Moses was trying to refute pagan evolutionary beliefs in Genesis 1. (The religion of evolution is not a new invention, remember; pagans in Moses' day had their own versions of it.) We shall see in more detail that the commentators dare not point to this phrase as proof of Genesis being a "polemic," because that would preclude them from intermingling the doctrines of evolution into Genesis—which they are loathe to forsake.

This phrase means just what it appears to mean: that like begets like. Cattle reproduce themselves as more cattle. Cattle do not bring forth "creeping things" or birds or fish. And nothing, as we shall see in a moment, begets man.

## Day Six: Mankind

**26. Let Us make.** Here, for the first time, we are privileged to witness God planning His next creative act. Previously, He has commanded the earth to bring forth, or simply has spoken something into being from nothing whatsoever, but now He makes us privy to His plans prior to creating. This is just one of the many ways that the text demonstrates how unique and special mankind is, the pinnacle of God's creation.

This deliberation reveals another significant difference from previous creations: God is going to create mankind Himself. Notice how He commands the sea to bring forth fish (20) and the earth to bring forth animals (24), but He does not make such a statement regarding mankind. The fish and birds and animals are all brought forth from the earth and waters at God's command, but His hand is not upon the earth and waters (as far as we are told); it is merely the power of His Word which brings them forth.

This time, however, we shall discover that God will bend down Himself and create man from the dust of the earth—with His own "hands." The fish and birds and animals are creatures of earth and sea. The cattle, one might say, are created *of* earth and *from* earth, motivated by God's Word. But mankind is created *of* earth *from* the hand of God. Man, therefore, is a creature of God and earth, the only part of His creation that can make that claim. Even the angels themselves are not so created.

***In Our image.*** Here we have another distinction between man and the lower orders of creation. Birds, fish, animals, even creeping things were all created "after their kind," but man is created after God's own likeness. The lower orders of creation are of the earth, earthy; man is of God *and* the earth, and therefore bears a dual nature; he is both earthy and heavenly. This is another element of our God-likeness, as God is shown here as a duality, as God and Spirit. When Christ comes of Mary, we shall discover that God Himself is both spirit and flesh, taking on Himself the very dual nature of mankind.

A creature's nature reflects its parents, springing as it does from its own kind. Cattle reflect the earth from which they literally sprang, but man reflects both earth and God. His earthly parts are his physical flesh and, alas, his mortality (which is *not* part of his original design; we shall discuss this more in a future chapter); while his Godly part is his immortal spirit.

But why does God say "us" in this verse? To whom is He speaking? Moses has already told us (v. 2) that the Spirit of God was hovering over the newly forming planet, so the most natural reading here would be to assume that God is speaking to Himself—or to His Spirit, if you prefer. (This, of course, becomes a "problem" for the gnostic Bible scholars of today, as we shall see in Section 2.)

Moses has made no mention whatsoever of any other heavenly entity besides God, so it seems unlikely that he would suddenly refer obliquely to the angels without naming them. Furthermore, there is only one creative entity here: God Himself. The mystery of God's dual nature has been touched upon in verses 1 and 2, where Moses speaks first of "God," then of the "Spirit of God" hovering over the waters. The Bible teaches clearly, not merely in this chapter, that man is created in God's image and in His image alone. So God cannot be suggesting to the angels or to anyone else, "Let's make man in our image(s)." Indeed, mankind alone bears the image of God; not even the angels are made in His image. Therefore, God would have needed to say, as I just worded it in the previous sentence, "in our images," not "in our image." Surely He would have worded it this way had He been speaking to cattle, for example, since cattle are made in the image of the earth from which they were taken. It is quite clear that God is addressing Himself here.

That probably seems self-evident to any honest reader of Scripture, but I am forced to belabor the point because of the reprehensible tricks of modern Bible scholars, which I will address further in Section 2. They will tell us that the "editors" of Genesis couldn't be expected to understand Trinitarian theology, and that the book itself is little more than a retelling of ancient pagan myths anyway, so therefore God could not be speaking to Himself here.

Now, Moses certainly did not have a complete understanding of God's triune nature, since the full revelation of that did not appear before the birth of Jesus Christ. Yet he clearly *does* have some understanding of the fact that God is both "God" and Spirit, since he introduces both aspects of the Divine nature in verses 1 and 2. And it only takes two to make an "us." But the bigger issue here is that of faith: if we are willing to accept by faith that Genesis is divinely inspired, that God Himself revealed to Moses in some way what He wanted Moses to write, then we will recognize that the human author—Moses—does not need to fully comprehend all the subtle nuances of what he was recording. His job was merely to record what was revealed to him, whether or not he fully understood it himself. This was probably true of Isaiah when he prophesied about the virgin birth; it was unquestionably true of John when he recorded the Revelation, as he tells us so himself.

This is one of the miraculous powers of Scripture, that its fullness and perfection unfolds more and more with each successive generation. Imagine the delight of the early Christians when they re-read Isaiah with a suddenly clearer understanding of those ancient prophecies. A future generation will re-read Revelation and will marvel at its perfect accuracy—while a future generation of Gnostic commentators will undoubtedly scoff and suggest that Revelation was actually written during the 20th century by a team of editors and redactors. This divine inspiration is the reason that we hold the Bible to be our sacred text, and it is high time that we silenced those in our midst who persistently deny it.

**27. Male and female.** God creates both Adam and Eve on the same day—a very busy day, as we shall see in chapter 2—and both are equally unique in all of creation. Both male and female bear the image of God; in fact, the two together are required to fully understand just what that "image" means. Nevertheless, the two are not interchangeable; each bears a unique role in creation, which will become more evident in chapter 2 when Moses goes into more detail on all that occurred during day 6.

**28. Be fruitful.** Once again, God is not afraid of "over-population." On the contrary, God's command to "fill the earth" (rendered "replenish the earth" in the KJV) appears to be needed if he is to also "subdue" the earth, fully exercising his "dominion" over creation. This is the opposite of the world's view. Those who adhere to Darwinist theology view every intrusion of mankind in a negative light, suggesting (without actually saying it aloud) that the world would be better off without man. There is no doubt that mankind has often exploited God's creation in a destructive and gluttonous manner; this is just one result of the fall of man, causing us to violate even those that we were created to protect. In fact, we shall see that Adam's first such violation is to desert his own wife the moment that his eyes are "opened."

Yet a love of God's creation is not really what motivates modern evolutionists on this matter. They do not hesitate to kill and destroy when it suits their own purposes, even to the point of sacrificing their own unborn children. Evolution is a cult of death, and as such is adamantly opposed to all elements of life. It is no surprise that God's command—"be fruitful and multiply"—should be such an offense to the adherents of death.

**Subdue.** It is possible that a Christian Darwinist might make noises about God's command to subdue the earth—although I have not encountered this argument as yet. But one might try to suggest that God was commanding mankind, before he even existed, to claw and climb his way out from among the lower orders, subduing and overcoming those weaker pitiful beings, and ultimately standing forth in his own supremacy—a demigod in his own right. (After all, is this not the gist of Darwinism?)

This idea of subduing, should it ever be posited, would hold a negative connotation. We shall see in chapter 2 that "dominion" refers to stewardship, not to tyranny. Adam is not commanded to lord it over the animals by brute force (or even by cunning; we shall see where *that* tactic leads in chapter 3), but rather to lead them: to be "leading over," not "lording over," if you will. Mankind is called to exercise a loving, tender care for God's creation, and this is one of the reasons that God's own loving tenderness is demonstrated so frequently during creation. God Himself models for man just how to properly care for His creation.

**31. Very good.** God concludes His creative work by standing back and examining it. Behold, He declares, it is beyond "good," it is *very* good! We shall discover, when we examine other books from the Bible, that God detests death. It is unthinkable, therefore, that He would declare His work "very good" when death was reigning over His creatures. And without death, evolution is impossible.

God has repeatedly declared that His work is "good," but by the end of day 6 it has become "very good." What has changed? It is finished, for one thing, and God is clearly in the business of finishing what He begins (Phil. 1:6). That which makes it complete, however, is the creation and establishment of mankind—both male and female. Even the creation of Adam alone was not enough, not "very good." It was not until God had created Eve and established her at her husband's side in Eden that God declared His creation complete and very good.

This concept of completion is directly contrary to the doctrines of evolution, which teach that mankind is still evolving. We have not yet become what we are "destined" to become (although a Darwinist would never openly speak of destiny, since it implies the existence of a God with a plan); we are still in the process of evolving into godhood. The Bible stands firmly opposed to this concept; mankind cannot evolve himself into godhood, nor can mankind evolve himself out from under the curse of death. Yet Christian Darwinists persistently ignore the fact that Genesis declares God's creation complete at the end of day 6, insisting instead that we can intermingle evolution into God's Word. This claim is a heresy.

# 3
# GENESIS 2

In Genesis 2, Moses zooms in for a close-up look at day 6 of the creation week. This chapter does not contradict chapter 1 in any way—but we will see later that modern theologians try to claim that it does.

## Finished

**2. God ended His work.** Creation is now complete, according to Genesis, and God is in His Sabbath rest—He is no longer creating anything new, *ex nihilo*, out of nothing. His creative work ever since has been focused on making Himself known to mankind, particularly (as we shall see in chapter 3) since mankind has been cut off from fellowship with Him virtually since the day after He finished. The remainder of the book of Genesis, and of the entire Bible, demonstrate that God is now busy working within the history of mankind.

As we have seen from chapter 1, Genesis claims that God finished making the earth, including mankind, in six literal 24-hour days. We are certainly free to disbelieve this claim, choosing rather to place our faith in the teachings of men, but we are not free to suggest that Genesis says otherwise.

**3. Blessed and sanctified.** God once again blesses His creation, but this time He is blessing a day of the week. This is different from His previous blessings, where He spoke to specific tangible entities which He had created, such as man, animals, etc. This time, He is blessing an intangible thing, an abstract concept in a sense, an element of the passage of time. This suggests that there is an inherent blessing built into the laws of creation, a blessing that is available to those who observe a particular day in a particular manner.

Moses will elucidate further on the Sabbath blessing in the book of Exodus, but the text here does contain a clue to this blessing, as God models the requisite behavior for His children. In other words, Moses tells us that "God rested" on the seventh day, and it is logical that His children, those created in His image, would find His blessing by imitating His actions.

It is also worth noting that this blessing is not necessarily limited to mankind, as the text does not specifically indicate that it was a blessing for Adam and Eve. Thus it is that the Lord commands His people (Lev. 25) to give a year of "Sabbath rest" to the land itself by allowing fields to lie fallow for a year. Even dirt needs rest, and will be blessed when it does, according to God's laws. Jesus will later inform His disciples that "the Sabbath was created for man, not man for the Sabbath," so we must recognize that man is chiefly responsible for understanding and recognizing the Sabbath. This is only logical, since man has been created specifically to oversee God's creation, and one aspect of that oversight must include the observance of the Sabbath. Remember also that God created the heavenly bodies specifically (in part) so that man might pay attention to the passage of time. The Sabbath is just that: a marking of time, to keep one day set apart for the Creator. This is a blessing, not a curse—the curse of the Law comes after the fall—and it is a blessing which the Creator has woven into the very fabric of His creation.

This is also the first time that God sanctifies some element of creation. It raises an interesting question: all of creation is perfect, sinless and deathless, so what does God mean when He "sanctifies" something, making it "holy?" The Hebrew word translated "sanctified" means "to set apart as sacred; consecrate; dedicate." The English word "consecrate" means "to set apart as sacred; dedicate solemnly to a sacred or religious purpose; make fit for religious use."[1] It is worth noting that both words have the sense of being "set apart." Evidently, when God sanctified the seventh day, it was not that He was purifying it of something unholy, but rather that He was setting that day apart from the other six days of the week.

This may help us to understand what God intended of the Sabbath, if we consider that men are called upon to set it apart from the rest of the week, to make the Sabbath "fit" for God's use. This clearly includes the need to rest from one's work, which tends to demand all our mental focus and physical efforts. This is, as the Lord teaches clearly in the New Testament, an area of Christian liberty as each believer must grapple with the most proper way of making the day fit for God's use. Nevertheless, setting apart a day for the Lord is a principle which God wove into His creation from the beginning, and the believer who ignores this commandment cannot hope to experience the special blessings which God set apart for those who obey.

Notice that Moses does not specify that there was morning and evening on the seventh day. This in itself implies that creation is complete, since the "morning/evening" formula was used on the preceding days to lead into the next day's work. God has completed His creation; He is no longer adding

---

[1] *Shorter OED*

new species to His repertoire. He created the animals and other forms of life which He intended, then created man as creation's supervisor or steward—the crown or pinnacle of His creation. There is nothing more to be added.

This obviously goes directly against the principles of evolution, which insist that new species are evolving in the present day. This also suggests, of course, that man himself is evolving into some higher entity; if we carry this thinking out logically, we will realize that evolution teaches that mankind can one day become God—or at the very least, "like God." If there is any doubt as to where *this* idea comes from, we shall address it directly in chapter 3.

God's Sabbath rest, furthermore, did not conclude at the end of the seventh day. This suggests that God still expects His creatures to observe the Sabbath, even in the frenetic 21st century.

## Transition

**4. *This is the history.*** This phrase introduces a formula or device which Moses will use frequently in Genesis, the "generation of" formula (which theologians refer to as "the *toledot* structure," *toledot* being the Hebrew word meaning "generations"). It serves as a transitional device, ending one section of Genesis and introducing the next section. Moses uses the "generation of" device to accomplish two purposes: to recapitulate the information which he has just given us (and add in some small new details), and to introduce the new topic which he is about to address.

Compare, for example, Gen. 5:1–5: "This is the book of the genealogy of Adam. In the day that God created man, He made him in the likeness of God. He created them male and female, and blessed them and called them Mankind in the day they were created. And Adam lived one hundred and thirty years, and begot a son in his own likeness, after his image, and named him Seth. After he begot Seth, the days of Adam were eight hundred years; and he had sons and daughters. So all the days that Adam lived were nine hundred and thirty years; and he died."

Moses opens chapter 5 by summarizing what he has been telling us in chapters 1 through 4. He then adds some new details which he had not told us before: how long Adam lived, that he had other sons and daughters, even that God "called them Mankind" on day 6—a new detail which Moses did not give us in Genesis 1 or 2. He adds entirely new information about Adam, carrying out his genealogy all the way to Noah—which introduces the reader to the person that he's going to talk about next: Noah. In this way, Moses has both concluded section 1 by reiterating key points on Adam, and introduced section 2, in which he will discuss Noah.

He is doing the same thing here in Genesis 2: he is summarizing what he has already told us in chapter 1, adding a new detail concerning mists watering the ground instead of rain as a sort of transition leading into his next topic—the creation of the man who would "till the ground." This seems straightforward enough when one is reading these verses, but few things in Genesis are ever straightforward to our modern Bible commentators, and we will be startled in Section 2 to learn what *they* see in this passage.

It is perhaps worth taking the time here to compare two contemporary translations of this passage, noting what a world of difference punctuation can make. Here is how verses 4 through 7a are rendered in the New King James Version:

> This is the history of the heavens and the earth when they were created, in the day that the LORD God made the earth and the heavens, before any plant of the field was in the earth and before any herb of the field had grown. For the LORD God had not caused it to rain on the earth, and there was no man to till the ground; but a mist went up from the earth and watered the whole face of the ground. And the LORD God formed man of the dust of the ground....

Here is the same passage in the English Standard Version:

> These are the generations of the heavens and the earth when they were created, in the day that the LORD God made the earth and the heavens.
>
> When no bush of the field was yet in the land and no plant of the field had yet sprung up—for the LORD God had not caused it to rain on the land, and there was no man to work the ground, and a mist was going up from the land and was watering the whole face of the ground—then the LORD God formed the man of the dust from the ground....

You will notice that the punctuation choices of the English Standard Version cause the verses to suggest that God created man "when no bush of the field was yet in the land and no plant of the field had yet sprung up"—which would suggest that God created man prior to day three. The New King James, however, punctuates the verses such that the clause "before any plant of the field was in the earth and before any herb of the field had grown" is connected to the previous clause, "in the day that the LORD God made the earth and the heavens". Thus, the NKJV suggests that verses 4 through 6 are a sort of short-hand review of Genesis 1, reiterating that God created the earth in the beginning, before any plant existed, and so forth.

As I have already pointed out, this is precisely the formula that Moses uses elsewhere in Genesis, and it is quite reasonable to assume that he is using it here: reiterating what has come before, leading into what is to follow. But with a few tiny bits of punctuation, the English Standard Version has changed the meaning of the passage significantly to imply that man was created on day two rather than day six.

It's important to know that the Hebrew contains no punctuation such as commas or dashes; these punctuation points are added in English translations to help clarify the passage's sense. This means that it will be up to the discretion of the team of translators who are producing any modern translation to gather the sense of the verses and render them as faithfully as possible into modern English. Once again, context must be king. That context must include what comes before and what comes after these verses; that, after all, is what is meant by "context." Adding a comma or a dash or any other punctuation can actually cause this passage to contradict (superficially, at least) what we have already been told in Genesis 1.

Moses tells us in chapter 1 that mankind was created on day six, while plants and herbs were created on day three. There is no compelling reason whatsoever to punctuate these verses to contradict that, particularly as there is no punctuation given in the Hebrew in the first place. It only makes sense, if one is called upon to add punctuation in English, to do so in a manner that accords with chapter 1; doing otherwise suggests that the translator has some agenda other than accuracy within context.

If one presupposes that Genesis is the work of mere men—and particularly, of numerous mere men who are writing, editing, and redacting at various wide-spread periods of history—then it is not problematic if chapter 2 presents a slightly different time-table of creation from chapter 1.

If, on the other hand, one presupposes that Genesis is the work of the Holy Spirit, "dictating" the words in some fashion to an individual author (also known as divine inspiration), then it *is* a problem if the two chapters conflict. One might argue, of course, that discrepancies cast doubt upon the divine inspiration itself, indicating that Genesis is merely the work of men rather than the words of God. But when these "discrepancies" are produced by a simple shifting of flexible punctuation—punctuation that is not even *present* in the original Hebrew—then one must reconsider how one punctuates rather than casting doubt upon the inspiration of the author. Unless, of course, it is the intention of the "scholar" to cast doubt upon divine inspiration.

**5. *God had not caused it to rain.*** Moses adds a little more detail here, as he generally does in his "generations of" transitions. (See Genesis 5, where we learn how old Adam lived to be, and what other children and grandchildren he bore.) We now learn that God had not used rain to water the earth during the early days, at least during creation week.[2] It is possible that He continued to water the ground with mist rather than rain well into human history, as well; Moses does not tell us. Henry Morris posits that it had never rained on the earth prior to Noah's flood. All that we can be certain of, however, is that it had not rained prior to the creation of man.

God used a gentle mist, rather than rain, to water His new plant life. Once again, we discover the gentleness of God's hand upon His creation, even to the point of providing the water needed for survival by the most gentle method imaginable. Mist is more gentle than rain falling from the sky, and it is also more pervasive—it gently infuses the entire plant, not merely the tops of its exposed leaves. This might suggest also that all of creation was still in complete accord with God's will prior to man's sin, such that even the earth itself waters its own plant life, as a mother nourishes her offspring at her own breast. This clearly changed at some point after the fall of mankind, when nourishment for the earth had to fall from above because creation itself had abandoned the plan of God.

---

2 A few modern translations, such as the NIV, use "springs" instead of "mist" (contrary to BDBG and other Hebrew dictionaries), but the discrepancy is immaterial. The end result of springs watering the ground would include watery mists, especially in a warm climate without rain. It is quite possible, indeed, that both springs and mists were present.

## Creation of Man

**7. *God formed man of the dust of the ground.*** Here, again, Moses offers us some new information which we hadn't known from chapter 1. We had known that God created man in His image, both male and female, but now we are told that God formed the man Himself using the dust of the ground as His physical material. Again, this is part of the "generations of" formula which Moses uses frequently, adding little extra details even as he summarizes what he has said previously. These new details do not in any way conflict with the details given in chapter 1, nor do they imply that this is a completely different account of man's creation, nor does this information suggest that two different people wrote chapters 1 and 2. Yet just such absurdities as these are suggested by modern Bible commentators.

## God's Garden

**8. *God planted a garden.*** God once again sets about modeling for man what he was created to do. Man, created in His image, is placed in the garden to care for it, but God begins by showing him how. This is repeatedly the case in these chapters, as God shows man what He wants him to do by doing it Himself first—from taking a rest on the Sabbath to caring for His creation, even to the point of being reconciled with those who harm him, as we shall see in chapter 3.

Notice that the text does not say that God planted any new *varieties* of trees. In fact, the verb "planted" is different from the formula which Moses uses in chapter 1, where we see God speaking and plants springing into being directly from the soil. Perhaps God planted seeds here, and trees and shrubs sprang up miraculously fast; perhaps He transplanted some trees from elsewhere and moved them to Eden; perhaps He spoke them into being as in chapter 1; or perhaps they sprang up on day 3 along with everything else. We just don't know, simply because we are not given the specific details.

Regardless of how He did it, there is no conflict between what we are told here and what we are told in chapter 1. On day 3, He created trees, shrubs, grains (grass), and so forth by *fiat*, by His word of command. On day 6, He "planted" a garden—whether using existing materials, speaking into being some new ones (perhaps He did so to create the trees of Knowledge and Life), or whatever method He chose—and this new information concerning day 6 in no way conflicts with what we were told in chapter 1. There is actually no reason to presume that He is even creating by *fiat*, as He might simply have chosen to "plant" by hand!

**9. Pleasant to the sight.** Here we see another aspect of God's generosity and prodigality. His creatures needed trees that were "good for food," to be sure, but there was no reason for them to be nice to look at. Providing for His creatures' survival would have been generous enough, but the Creator went far above and beyond all that His creatures could have hoped or imagined, making all aspects of survival also bring pleasure! Once again, this is the antithesis to the concept of chaos and struggle, the antithesis to all that is preached by the doctrines of evolution.

## Two Unique Trees

*The tree of life . . . the tree of the knowledge of good and evil.* These two trees are evidently unique in all of creation. (It is conceivable that others like them grew elsewhere outside of the garden, prior to the fall of man, yet the context seems to suggest their uniqueness.) God has placed them at the very center of the garden, and He has planted the garden for the express use of Adam—all of which suggests that these two trees are for the sole use of Adam. We don't know, of course, what would have happened if Adam had not sinned, but the presence of these trees at the center of the garden seems to indicate that God intends to use them for some important dealings with Adam.

We can only conjecture what that entire purpose was, since Adam was never permitted to eat from the Tree of Life. Perhaps God would have invited him to eat from the Tree of Life once he had demonstrated his voluntary obedience and loyalty to His commands, once he successfully endured temptation and was found faithful. We do know that this is exactly what happened once Christ, the Last Adam, proved Himself faithful, as His children will one day be invited to eat freely from the Tree of Life in the New Jerusalem (Rev. 2:7; 22:2, 14).

What exactly *is* the Tree of Life? Does it offer some sort of magical fruit which would bring eternal life when eaten? Once again, we do not know simply because we are not told. It is important to understand, however, that Adam at this point already possessed immortality. Paul tells us in Romans 5 that death entered the world because of Adam's sin (and this fact alone makes the Bible incompatible with the doctrines of evolution), so therefore we can be assured that Adam was not subject to death at this point.

Many modern commentators, however, claim that Adam was not immortal when he was created, believing that the fruit of the Tree of Life would somehow magically confer immortality upon him. This notion is not supported anywhere in the Bible, and the New Testament teaches just the opposite. The text before us, however, does not expressly answer the question one way or the other, so we will belay the debate for the time being.

The Tree of Life may have been strictly for the purpose of God's ceremonially making a covenant with Adam. This is, of course, purely speculative, and speculation is always very risky. But my point is that we have no reason to believe that the fruit itself was imbued with some magical properties of conferring eternal life—indeed, we have reason to believe otherwise, as I have just suggested above. It is quite possible that God intended to use the Tree of Life in some symbolic fashion to make an everlasting covenant with Adam, once he successfully resisted the temptation of eating from the Tree of Knowledge of Good and Evil. Alas, we shall never know for certain.

What exactly is the Tree of Knowledge of Good and Evil? Is this some magical fruit which conferred knowledge of good and evil upon Adam the moment that he bit into it? We shall see soon enough that Adam's eating brought sin and death into the entire world; was this a result of some magical quality within the fruit itself? This seems rather unlikely, and this time we can see what a stretch of common sense it is to imbue these two trees with magical fruit.

Modern Bible commentators generally treat this fruit as some mystical symbol, viewing Adam's eventual eating of the fruit as symbolic of some theoretical element of man's free will. Gordon Wenham tells us that the fruit is symbolic of "moral autonomy," representing man's desire to make decisions for himself apart from faith in God's sovereignty.[3] Bruce Waltke assures us that the fruit confers "ethical awareness."[4] There are as many other abstract theories as there are gnostic commentaries on the book of Genesis.

There is nothing in the text here to support any such abstractions. It is much more likely that both trees are merely fruit. We will see in Genesis 3 that even the Tree of Knowledge is good for food, for example. The Lord's command to Adam had to do with Adam's obedience, not with some magical quality contained within the forbidden fruit itself. It will be Adam's act of eating, not the fruit itself, which brings death and sin into the world.

---

3 Wenham, *Genesis*, 63–64.
4 Bruce K. Waltke, *Genesis: A Commentary*. Grand Rapids, MI: Zondervan, 2001, p. 86.

Nevertheless, the fruit itself is very real; it is not some picture of abstract principles, as modern commentators try to make it. Adam's eating the forbidden fruit is an act of simple disobedience, not some mystical statement of autonomy or attempt at humanistic ethics.

Thus we see what I referred to above concerning the Tree of Life: that the tree itself is not imbued with magical properties, but instead stands as a sort of covenant "marker" between God and man. God uses the Tree of Knowledge as the one small bit of food which Adam is not allowed to eat, permitting Adam to demonstrate his obedience by simply refraining from eating it. In a similar manner, He may have intended the Tree of Life to be a covenant "marker," inviting Adam to eat from it as a symbolic sealing of some eternal covenant between God and man.

And now that I've spent so much time addressing these questions, I must return to my overall conviction that these are *all* mere speculations, and are of little value as such. The text is what we must be concerned with, avoiding the temptations of wandering too far from what has been revealed to us.

## Eden's Environs

**11–12. Havilah, where there is gold.** Moses tells us that there was gold and other valuables in Havilah, someplace near Eden. Presumably, this land was known to the ancients of Moses' day, and by Moses' time people had evidently discovered the gold. Nevertheless, this also brings up a dangerous presupposition which modern readers make concerning Adam and his immediate family: that they were primitive and very unlearned. Even conservative Christians make comments about "man's discovery of fire" and "the invention of the wheel,"[5] implying that "early man" (another loaded term: Adam was the "early man," according to Genesis) was too dull-witted to know how to cook his supper.

Yet the opposite is far more likely true. Let us remember, first of all, that God created Adam directly, by hand. He was, therefore, the perfect man. He was highly intelligent, extremely clever and quick-witted, strong and agile and inventive. He had a hunger to learn about his new home, setting about immediately to understand the animals and to name them. Furthermore, he apparently walked in the garden daily with God Himself, speaking with the Creator face to face! He was probably inquisitive, and it is not far-fetched to

---

5 For example, see *NIV Archeological Study Bible*. Grand Rapids, MI: Zondervan, 2005, p. 10—where the Sumerians are credited with inventing the wheel.

picture him asking God all manner of questions concerning the brand new world.

It is not unreasonable, therefore, to assume that Adam may have known that gold and other useful ores were buried underground, and have been quick to recognize that those ores would be useful to him. The ores themselves could well have been "brought forth" during creation just as life was brought forth. We do not need to assume that it took ages for diamonds to be created, for example.

But many of our modern assumptions embrace the false doctrines of evolution, even when we sometimes don't realize it. Genesis tells us that God created plants and fish and animals as fully grown entities; He could just as easily have created gold and onyx and diamonds the same way. Genesis also tells us that He created Adam as a mature, intelligent man; but our tendency is to think of him as childish and naive—at best. It is a doctrine of evolution that man began as a brutish savage and gradually became civilized and cultured, and modern Christians automatically put Adam into that false picture.

We must be on guard against such false assumptions, as they are influenced and engendered by the evolutionary theology of our modern world. If we are to make any leaps of faith concerning Adam and Eve, it is far safer to think that they might have created tools themselves than to think that they were too stupid to invent the wheel or discover fire.

## Adam the Gardener

**15. *To tend and keep it.*** The Hebrew word for "tend" invokes the sense of serving another person, willingly or otherwise, in the act of tilling the ground. It is used elsewhere in the Old Testament to mean both forced labor to an overlord and voluntary service to the Lord. The same word is used in Exodus 3:12, for example, where it is translated "serve God." Mankind was created to serve the Lord and to work, not to wander aimlessly through Paradise.

The Hebrew word translated "keep" implies watching over something, guarding it, caring for and preserving and protecting. This immediately brings up the question of what there was to protect the garden *from* in a perfect world, but that question becomes moot in chapter 3 when we discover that evil has already infiltrated under the guise of the serpent.

These details are still pertinent to mankind today: man is still accountable to God for the protection and nurturing of His creation.

## God's First Command

**16. God commanded the man.** This is the first time that God has issued a command. Now, this is interesting because God has previously been issuing the command "let be" to His creation, commanding the earth to bring forth plant and animal life, and so forth. Yet Moses does not tell us that "God commanded the earth to bring forth . . . and it was so;" God merely *speaks* and His will comes to pass. This use of the word "command" here may underscore the fact that man has the option to disobey God's word, whereas there is no hint of that option at any other point in creation. The earth hears God's voice, and His word becomes reality—as though the earth does not even have the option of resisting His will.

This is underscored by God's following words in verse 17, in which He explains what will happen if man refuses to obey His command. Again, this is a very new thing that we are seeing on day 6 of the creation week: never before has God explained what would happen if His words were not obeyed. There is no hint prior to this that any part of creation was even capable of disobeying His word—it is not entertained even as a possibility. Apparently, mankind is unique in creation in this way, that he alone has the option of obeying God. (I'm speaking here of temporal creation, not including the angelic orders.) This, then, is one aspect of what God means when He tells us that man is created in His image.

It is worth noting here that God gives this commandment to Adam alone—not to Adam and Eve. It is my belief that the Tree of Knowledge was a test for Adam alone, providing him with the opportunity both to obey God and to begin his own role of headship over creation. What will Adam do when he is faced with temptation? What choice will this creature of free will make when faced with two options: obey God or disobey God? And further, how will he react when his lordship is threatened? What will he do when the woman, created to be his helper under his leadership, usurps that position and urges him to follow her lead? Will he stand firm and obey God's word, or will he crumble and capitulate his authority to someone else? Here in verse 16, God is placing before Adam the test that he will face, and He tells him up-front what the ground rules are and what the consequences will be for failure.

**17. You shall surely die.** Here we have God's first *negative* command—indeed, this is His first stern word in the whole week of creation. All His words thus far have been words of blessing, words of creation, words of approval, and this new commandment sends a jarring note into Paradise. This once again underscores the difference between what Genesis teaches us about creation versus what the evolutionist claims: in the Christian Darwinist's dogma, God begins to create, then issues the command, "Survive!" In Genesis, God produces a fully-mature creature in one day, then cries out, "Flourish!"

Here we also discover that Adam was created immortal. He was not subject to death; God's warning that he would die if he ate the fruit would make no sense if he were already destined to die. The Lord is not saying, "look out, that fruit is poisonous and eating it will drop you in your tracks." He is warning Adam that he will lose his immortality and become subject to death if he chooses to eat it.

Yet, even in this negative-sounding pronouncement, God is actually doing something very positive: He is giving His premier creature an opportunity to demonstrate that which sets him apart from the rest of creation, to act in his capacity as God's image-bearer. He gives man a choice which He has not given to anything else in our creation: *choose* to obey God. "Enjoy all of creation," God says, "do anything you want, and choose also to refrain from this one small activity." Such a small thing to ask, such an easy way to demonstrate how different man is from all other creatures.

We shall see in Genesis 3 that Adam does not drop dead on the day that he eats the forbidden fruit, so what do God's words mean? The warning refers to physical death, in that Adam would become subject to death the moment that he ate from the fruit. The processes of aging and decay began immediately, although it would take many years before his physical life finally came to an end. God's words may also refer to Adam's separation from God, a separation which is the very definition of spiritual death. We shall see that this aspect of death occurs on the very day that Adam eats. Yet His words do clearly refer to his physical death which will ensue "in the day that you eat of it." The author of Hebrews underscores this when he reminds us that "it is appointed for men to die once," the "appointment" being made when Adam ate.

So the Lord's dire warning here means that Adam will be placed under the authority of death if he eats, since in so doing he will be voluntarily trying to remove himself from the authority of the Lord of Life. To reiterate: this indicates that Adam was *not* subject to death prior to his fall; therefore, he must have been created immortal.

**18. Not good.** This is the first time that we hear God pronouncing something "not good"—yet, at the end of the day, He pronounces all things "very good" (v. 31). Obviously, there cannot be any element that is not good if God is to pronounce things "very good," so we must conclude that He did all these things—created all the animals, created man, planted a garden, watched man name the animals, and created woman—all on day 6!

Modern commentators, in standard fashion, have declared that this is impossible, it's just too much to ask. But that is the definition of a miracle, isn't it: something happening that is normally impossible. We shall see in Section 3 that this skepticism on the part of our modern commentators grows out of their refusal to believe in the miraculous; for now, we must recognize that this is the very meaning which the text conveys.

It also emphasizes how accelerated all things were during the first days of creation. It also demonstrates how intelligent Adam was, that he was able to study and discern and name all the animals of creation in one day. He was, after all, the perfect man, so it stands to reason that he was handsome, strong, witty, creative, and very intelligent. This again goes contrary to the doctrines of evolution, which teach us that mankind is growing smarter and better all the time—that he is evolving into some sort of demi-god. The Bible does not endorse this idea in any way; if anything, mankind is *devolving*, becoming less advanced as time passes, as the laws of physics demonstrate that all processes decay over time.

## Adam Gets to Work

God created man for two purposes (1:26): to be a special creature that reflects the image of God in creation, and to have dominion or stewardship over that creation. And, on the very day of his creation, God puts him to work. Man was made to be productive, and we have already seen that God calls upon all of His creation to take part in His work.

**19. God formed every beast of the field.** The so-called "higher critics" have tried to make the case that this verse contradicts the order of creation given in chapter 1—as though this verse claims that birds were made on day six. Others have suggested that this verse claims that God created a whole new set of birds and animals just so that Adam could name them. But that is not what the text is saying at all; Moses is merely reiterating here that God created the animals and the birds, even as he leads into the topic of Adam naming them. As I have stated earlier, there is no discrepancy between chapter 2 and chapter 1.

***God. . . brought them to Adam.*** If I had been inventing a myth, or a "narrative" (to use the heavily charged buzzword of modern commentators), I would have described how God led Adam around the Garden of Eden, introducing him to the many animals and birds so that he could observe them in their "natural habitat" before he set about giving them names. But this is not a mere narrative, it is an accurate description of something that literally happened—and God's ways frequently surprise mankind.

God brings the animals before Adam as a symbol of their subjection to his lordship. A sovereign does not go to his subjects; his subjects bring themselves before him out of respect for his role of headship. This can be seen in Job 1:6, when "the sons of God came to present themselves before the LORD." Yet God Himself, Lord over all creation, will surprise us on this by humbling Himself before His creation, as we shall see in chapter 3.

Adam sets about giving names to each of the species as they come before him, demonstrating another aspect of authority. A person who assigns a name to another creature is demonstrating his authority over that creature, as we have already seen in chapter 1. Giving something a name, however, also requires that the person in authority have a deep understanding of the creature that he is naming. In ancient times, a person's name was thought to somehow define the deepest essence of that person—such that, if someone knew your "true name," he gained some sort of mystical power over you, because he understood the deepest parts of your nature. In Judges 13, Manoah (Samson's father) asks the Angel of the Lord what his name is, and the Angel answers, "Why do you ask My name, seeing it is wonderful?"—the word "wonderful" meaning incomprehensible, beyond one's ability to understand.

So Adam must have been able to gain some degree of understanding of the creatures as they came before him, as the names that he gave them were intended to describe something about them that was unique to each. The name *platypus*, for example, is from the Greek words *platys*, meaning "flat," and *pous* (or *pod*) meaning "foot." A *woodpecker* is a bird that pecks wood. (A *woodchuck*, however, does not "chuck wood," regardless of any tongue-twisters you may have memorized.)

This business of naming something also brings with it a degree of accountability before God. The person who is naming has authority over the creatures being named, and this means that he also is responsible for that creature's welfare. God has placed Adam in the position of taking care of His creation, and any privileges which this brings—such as conferring names—also come with the burden of being held accountable before God for what happens to that creation. This fact becomes paramount in chapter 3, when Adam's sin causes dire ramifications to the very creation for which he is responsible.

Notice that Adam is doing this work by himself, as Eve has not been created yet. Most commentators will point out that God did it this way so that Adam could see for himself that there was no other creature that was "fit" to be his mate. Man has no counterpart in all of creation, being both "of the earth" and "of God." It is "not good that man should be alone," and there is a void in Adam's life, an emptiness that can only be filled by another creature that is like him. (And here again we encounter that word *void*, which Moses uses in chapter 1, and we must recognize once again that it does not carry any connotation of "chaos," as there is no evidence here of chaos or struggle or even lack of peace.)

But the fact that Adam is naming the animals alone also implies that the work which God has set for him is his alone; it is not a team effort which he shares with the woman. This concept goes against modern attitudes concerning "gender roles," attitudes which (like evolution) have subtly crept into and infused the thinking of modern Christians. Yet we shall see before we are finished with Genesis that God's original plan held very separate and distinct jobs for man and woman. (This must be balanced with the observation that God created "male and female" specifically to "have dominion" (1:26–27), which means that both work together to carry out mankind's purpose over creation. Specific jobs within that purpose, however, are not identical.)

*To see what he would call them.* Here is a fascinating comment. It appears that God Himself is "learning" from His creation, that He is curious about His own creatures. This is not to suggest that God "learned" in the sense that He lacked knowledge. It is more like a great inventor who has nearly finished his new machine, and is bursting with eagerness to watch it run. He knows what it will do simply because he designed it, yet he is still yearning to test it out. God is taking delight in watching His new creature do what he was designed to do.

Adam, for his part, is acting out his God-like image by caring for and taking authority over creation. He is doing what he was made to do, and he is imitating God in the process. God is watching, taking delight in seeing Himself reflected in the man, even as a father takes delight when he watches his son take an interest in the things which he himself enjoys.

Once again, we see the gentleness of God in His interactions with man and the rest of His creation. It is a ghastly misrepresentation to suggest that God would take delight in subjecting His creatures to suffering and death, yet this is the very charge that is leveled by Christian Darwinists when they claim that God used evolution to produce mankind. This is a lie which can only originate in the mouth of the serpent, as we shall see in chapter 3.

*That was its name.* Here again we have something altogether new: God entrusts Adam with his role of lordship over creation, and He trusts his decisions! God is not a micro-manager; He does not step in during the naming process with corrections or revisions, nor does He over-ride Adam's sovereignty over the animals. Whatever Adam names the animals, that becomes their names.

This sovereignty is actually a very sobering thing to recognize. It reminds us that God allows mankind to rule over His creation, and He also allows mankind to live with the consequences of his actions and decisions. Thus, Adam had better name well, since the name will become permanent. He had better be sure that he understands the creatures fairly intimately, since he will be accountable to God for them. This sense of seriousness will become all the more pronounced when Adam is called upon to bestow a name on woman. Modern man also takes a share in God's work, and we must not take that responsibility lightly.

**20. But for Adam there was not found a helper.** This word, "one who helps or succors," begins to provide specific insight into the role of woman, whom God is about to create. God deliberates with Himself in 1:26 on His plans for mankind, which includes both "male and female" (1:27). His intention, as we have seen, is that mankind have "dominion" over creation, so we can infer that mankind's dominion is not complete unless both male and female are involved. Thus, it is no surprise to find that Adam needs a "helper" in his role as steward. But we have just witnessed him naming the animals by himself, without any assistance from a helper. This suggests that the woman's part of the "dominion mandate," as it has been called, is not identical to that of the man's. No further insight is provided at this point, other than the fact that

God also commanded mankind to "be fruitful and multiply"—a function which Adam clearly could not fulfill by himself.

**Comparable to him.** As I've already said (see comments on 1:26), mankind is both "of the earth" and "of God." God commands the earth to "bring forth" animals, but God Himself reaches down and makes mankind from the dust with His own hands. Each animal is made "according to its kind," while man is made "according to Our likeness." A creature reflects the nature of its parents, so animals are "earthy" while man is both "earthy" and "godly." The Bible is adamant that man is unique amongst all of creation, but if man had evolved from the lower orders, then he would reflect *their* image, not the image of God.

Thus Moses reiterates that there is no other creature like man—no "Neanderthals" loping around dragging their knuckles, no "missing link" that is like man yet somehow not man. Adam has now met all the lower orders of creation, and there is nothing that comes close to himself. And this is not good, according to God's pronouncement; something is still missing to make creation complete.

## Building Man's Helper

Mary Baker Eddy, founder of the Christian Science cult, informs us that woman was created "last in the ascending order of creation."[6] Her applications of that observation are heretical,[7] yet the observation itself is valid—for woman "is the glory of the man" (1 Cor. 11:7), and her status as God's final creation "puts an honour upon that sex," in Matthew Henry's words. Indeed, Henry goes on to observe, "If man is the head, she is the crown, a crown to her husband, the crown of the visible creation."[8]

**21. One of his ribs.** Matthew Henry also comments that the woman was "not made out of [Adam's] head to rule over him, nor out of his feet to be trampled upon by him, but out of his side to be equal with him, under his arm to be protected, and near his heart to be beloved."[9] This aphorism has been widely quoted over the years, and it is valid insofar as it goes. But it strikes me that it is more valuable to ask "why a *rib*?" rather than "why not something else?" What exactly are ribs used for in the human body? This

---

6 Mary Baker Eddy, *Science and Health with Key to the Scriptures*, 508:21.
7 Christian Science, in fact, is another modern permutation of Gnosticism.
8 *Matthew Henry's Commentary on the Whole Bible*, vol. 1, 16.
9 Ibid.

question may help us to understand in some measure why God chose to use Adam's rib.

***Breathing:*** One of the primary functions of the rib cage is to enable a person to breathe. Muscles between the ribs expand and contract, forcing the rib cage to expand and contract like a bellows, forcing air into and out of the lungs.

Inhalation is akin to *inspiration*. I have already pointed out that the words "breath" and "spirit" are linguistically related, and the concept of a "breath" is that one is inhaling life or "spirit" (wind, air) into the body. The root word of *inspiration* is *spirit*;[10] thus, being "inspired" is to be "filled with spirit or breath." God "inspired" Adam when He "breathed into his nostrils the breath of life" (2:7).

Man's helpmeet, therefore, inspires him. In practical application, a godly woman will inspire her husband to take the spiritual lead in the home, perhaps encouraging him to lead in family devotions or to set an example of maintaining daily personal Bible study and prayer. She will inspire a man to strive for excellence in doing the Lord's work. It is easy for men to do "just enough," to slip into the habit of being content with mediocrity. I once worked at a shipyard that built nuclear submarines, and the standard saying there was "good enough for government work." A helpmeet encourages a man to go beyond "good enough." And, above all, she inspires a man to keep being filled with, inspired by, the Holy Spirit.

We must note at this point that Eve will fail in this regard.

***Chest:*** Ribs also give a man his upper body structure, his chest. Without a chest, a man would be grossly incomplete. He would also be severely weakened, for his most powerful muscle groups are his chest region and his thighs. Without a chest, a man could run away from danger, but he could hardly stand and fight. A man with a broad chest, conversely, is likely to be a powerful wrestler.

A good helpmeet helps a man to be strong, to wrestle against temptation, error, and other dangers. C. S. Lewis suggests, "Reason in man must rule the mere appetites," and he likens this to a man's body. "The head rules the belly through the chest—the seat. . . of emotions organized by trained habit into

---

10 The English word *inspiration* is drawn from the Latin *inspirare*, to breath, whose Latin root is *spiritus*, breath [*New Shorter Oxford English Dictionary*]. This concept becomes important when we address the false teachings of modern commentators in Section 2.

stable sentiments."[11] The chest, therefore, enables a man to keep control over his "lower passions," which are not limited to physical temptations—although Paul does address this when he suggests that, "if they cannot exercise self-control, let them marry" (1Co 7:9). Lewis further points out that this includes the ability to discern between truth and error,[12] and a helpmeet will encourage a man to be wary against all such temptations.

Once again, Eve will fail in this aspect of being a helpmeet, as it is she who tempts Adam to sin, not the serpent.

**Protection:** Ribs form a bone cage, protecting our heart, lungs, and other vital organs. Without the rib cage, a man's life would be in constant danger—the slightest impact could rupture his organs and kill him. A helpmeet provides a similar "cage" of protection by creating a safe home atmosphere.

Men need to have a "safe zone," a place to come home to that is characterized by peace and harmony. But a home characterized by strife and disagreement isn't safe—even singleness is better. Solomon tells us this in Proverbs: "Better to dwell in a corner of a housetop, than in a house shared with a contentious woman" (Prov. 21:9).

Once again, Eve will fail in this capacity. Rather than building a home for man and wife, she will go out and debate theology with a serpent.

**22. *The rib which the LORD God had taken from man.*** The creation of Eve cost Adam something. He literally had to give of his own flesh and blood in bringing her into existence. This is another example of God calling upon His creation to participate with Him in further creation. It also forces Adam to invest into the creation of his coming marriage, and into the sustenance of that marriage. She is literally part of his own body, and caring for her is the same as caring for himself. This is a basic principle of marriage which Paul will develop in more detail. Adam gave up something for his marriage, but Eve gave up nothing. This concept is further reflected in God's words when He declares that "a man shall leave his father and mother and be joined to his wife" (24).

***He made into a woman.*** What is the origin of the two sexes? Genesis tells us that God invented the concept, and that He created male and female versions of species right from the beginning. Evolution, on the other hand, offers no explanation for where the separation of genders came from. According to their tenets, the earliest forms of life were single-celled organisms that reproduced

---

11 C. S. Lewis, *The Abolition of Man*, 34.
12 Lewis refers to false teachers as "men without chests."

by splitting in two, with no requirement for another organism of any gender to get involved in the process. But if man evolved out of these little germs, at what point did the concept of sexual reproduction get evolved? And what sense would it make to evolve such an idea in the first place? Darwinists tell us, after all, that evolutionary changes take place in order to help a species survive, but reproduction by simply splitting oneself in half is certainly a lot easier and faster and more guaranteed for survival than going through some complicated "mating ritual" just for the rather unpredictable result of copulation. This method of reproduction is so much more complicated that it would actually *threaten* survival, not assure it.

This points out, once again, the utter absurdity of evolution. Who invented sex? Could an amoeba or a fish design eggs and sperm, and then *create* them so that they actually worked? And how would an amoeba or a fish then apportion them out to others, some getting eggs and others sperm?

For that matter, why would any creature want to reproduce in the first place? The more amoebas there are swimming around, the less food is available. The Darwinist will tell us that they have an instinctive "drive" for survival, wanting to ensure the future of their species. This is ridiculous. Why would any creature care what happens in the world after it dies? An amoeba cares only about keeping itself alive as long as possible and being comfortable and well-fed in the process. In truth, an amoeba cannot be said to "care" about anything, and such a creature is incapable of complex thoughts such as planning for its offspring's future.

No, the desire to reproduce is implanted within a creature, and once we admit to "implanted desires" we have acknowledged the presence of a Creator. Darwinists will switch their answer at this point, in the inconsistent and self-contradictory manner so characteristic of evolution, telling us that animals reproduce because it feels good. Yet this merely underscores the fact that God's creation is good, for He did not need to add pleasure to a creature's necessary survival activities. An animal will eat when it is hungry simply because it needs to, yet God also made eating pleasurable. There is no room for pleasure or joy within Darwinism; in that religion, everything is done from the compulsion to stay alive.

A Christian Darwinist might suggest that God intervened in His evolutionary creation, somewhere during the course of the evolutionary tool which He set in motion bazillions of years ago, and introduced gender and sexual reproduction. But that explanation would accomplish nothing whatsoever. If we're going to believe in some miraculous intervention on God's part, we may as well accept the miracles that are clearly described in Genesis. The irony is that the creation of Eve could easily be reinterpreted by our modern commentators to indicate that Eve evolved out of Adam—but that would then require that Adam also be taken from the rib of some lower animal, rather than built directly from the dirt by God Himself. We cannot mix and match, claiming that this verse is metaphor and the next verse is literal—yet this is precisely what modern Bible commentators try to do.

**He brought her to the man.** Notice that God brings the woman before the man, just as He did earlier with the animals. This concept will undoubtedly offend modern feminists (we shall see the origins of that heresy soon enough), yet it is here in Genesis and we do a disservice to ignore it out of some fear of offending people. God brings the woman before the man, because the man is the head of the woman—he is in authority, and she comes before him demonstrating her submission to that authority.

If I were going to write my own account of the creation of man and woman and marriage, I would probably have God standing in the middle of the Garden of Eden, inviting the man and the woman each to approach Him, probably one on His left and one on His right; and the two would pace slowly forward, gazing adoringly into one another's eyes, and then they'd be joined together in holy matrimony by God Himself.

This is not what happened. Once again, we have God surprising us with what He chooses to do; and once again, we have Moses writing something that we would not expect—something, indeed, which is not found in any ancient pagan writings.

**23. She shall be called Woman.** Again, Adam demonstrates his headship over his wife by conferring a name upon her.

## Pictures of the Last Adam

These things all serve to provide us with a picture of Christ, who is the Last Adam. Christ, of course, paid the ultimate price for His bride. Adam merely gave up a rib, while Christ died fully and was even separated from the Father. But while Christ thus "slept," His side was pierced, and out of that side flowed the lifeblood of His bride, the Church. We have done nothing, yet we gain all that we were created for in the person of our Groom. Like Adam, Christ will eventually give new names to His bride (Rev. 2).

There are many other ways in which Adam pictures the person and work of Christ—indeed, Christ *is* the Last Adam. Did Moses know and understand these things when he wrote Genesis? Of course not! Modern gnostic Bible commentators make much out of this question, nevertheless, telling us that we cannot presume that the "authors" of Genesis knew thus and such or understood this and that. This tactic is used to explain away many details in Genesis that demonstrate the book's divine inspiration, but when they come to Adam these same commentators put themselves into a pickle.

We will consider the importance of Adam in a future chapter, but for now it is important to recognize that the parallels between Adam and Christ point, at the very least, to the fact that Genesis is divinely inspired by God Himself. And once again, if Genesis is divinely inspired, then we must assume that its accounts of creation and the fall of mankind are accurate as written— they must not be rewritten to fit into modern evolutionary doctrines.

# 4
# Genesis 3

## The Fall of Our Father

This is one of the darkest hours in the history of mankind, comparable only to the crucifixion of the Last Adam.

## The Serpent

***1. More cunning.*** The Hebrew word for "cunning," or "subtle" as the King James puts it, is the same used for "prudence" in Proverbs 12:23: "A prudent man conceals knowledge, but the heart of fools proclaims foolishness."[1] We must remember that, at this moment in our text, the serpent is still perfect, so its subtlety and cunning are not negative qualities—yet. The serpent, apparently, was a prudent and resourceful creature, and must therefore have also been very intelligent. It was Satan who turned the serpent's prudence into a wicked shrewdness; and, in the same way, our own sinful natures can take our greatest strengths of character and turn them against us as sinful weaknesses.

***He said.*** The serpent speaks to Eve, and she does not appear to be startled by it. This certainly seems strange to modern readers, to say the least, and the image of a talking snake has led many to view this chapter as a fairy tale or metaphor. We must bear in mind, however, that this is before the fall of man, prior to the curse, and we really know very little of the state of creation during that brief time.

Man may have originally enjoyed a great degree of communion with the lower orders of creation. When he sinned, his communion with God was almost completely cut off, while communion with his wife was severely damaged (but not severed). As God's image-bearer, it stands to reason that man had at least some level of communication with the lower orders, just as God apparently held daily communion with him. Moreover, the severance of communication within the lower orders themselves was quite severe after man's sin—as animals suddenly turned upon one another and began killing and eating one another. It is not far-fetched, therefore, to surmise that some

---

[1] To understand a bit more of what "prudence" means, here is a quick word study from the book of Proverbs: 12:16, 23; 13:16; 14:8, 15, 18; 15:5; 16:21; 18:15; 19:14; 22:3; 27:12.

animals may have held greater communication with man prior to the fall than they do now. Also, the serpent was the most subtle of the creatures, a concept which suggests that the serpent had the ability to communicate on some level. How else can one be "subtle" except by communicating with others?

Regardless of these speculations, we do know that God gave the power of speech to Balaam's ass (Num. 22), so it is also possible that Satan counterfeited that by giving speech to the serpent. (Balaam registers no greater surprise at a talking ass than Eve does at a talking serpent.) It is also worth noting that one result of sin is the profound disruption of communication: man with God, man with wife, men with men (as at the Tower of Babel), and most likely man with animals.[2]

The important thing for us to remember is this: Genesis was written as a literal historical account of literal historical events, *not* as a word picture or metaphor or allegory of some abstract principles. We are certainly free to reject Genesis as false history because it features talking snakes, but we are not free to suggest that this passage is metaphor while other passages are literal history. To do so is to violate the most basic principles of reading.

**Has God indeed said.** Satan's first words to mankind are designed to cast doubt upon the word of God—the clearly stated and easily understood word of God. Mankind has imitated the evil one ever since, trying to rewrite Scripture to suit some private agenda. It is still happening today, as leading Bible scholars write commentaries that twist God's word into an unholy pretzel in an attempt to accommodate the religion of evolution. We shall hear the serpentine words of these men in Section 2: "Does Genesis 1 *really* say that God took six days to create the earth?"

However, this is not all that is happening in this conversation. I believe that Satan was not trying to cause Eve to doubt *God's* word primarily, but to doubt *Adam's* word. Remember that she was not present when God gave Adam the command regarding the forbidden fruit because she had not yet been created. Now, we must not build an argument from omission; that is, we cannot definitively conclude that God did not give that same command later to Eve simply because we are not told that He did. But as I pointed out in the last chapter, the command of God concerning the forbidden fruit was specifically for Adam, not for Adam and Eve.

---

[2] Man's relationship with animals changed radically after the flood (Genesis 9), so it is reasonable to suggest that it had also changed radically after Adam's sin.

It seems likely, therefore, that Adam had told Eve of the command since she had not been present when it was given; and thus, the serpent is actually asking Eve, "Are you sure that God really said that? After all, you have only Adam's word for it!" The devil was tempting Eve to distrust her husband concerning his reliability as the spiritual leader. This is the birth of the modern feminist movement.

*You shall not eat of every tree.* Satan now takes his tactic a step further by deliberately misquoting God. We will witness him using these same tactics thousands of years later when he tempts the Last Adam in the wilderness (Mtt. 4), first casting doubt upon God's revealed will ("If You are the Son of God. . . ."), then quoting Scripture out of context. Jesus, of course, will demonstrate the correct way of dealing with the Tempter: quote Scripture exactly as written, without any amendments; command him to leave.

Satan's attacks are indeed subtle and cunning, and in the Garden he attacks on two fronts: he impugns God, portraying Him as stingy and ungenerous; and, perhaps more importantly, he draws Eve into debate. This tactic of debating is one of the enemy's most effective strategies. He loves to lure God's people into debating foolishness, when he himself has absolutely no interest in the truth. This tactic permits Satan to define the battleground, as Eve now focuses her attention on correcting the serpent's "misconception," which only allows Satan to lure her in even further.

We see this same tactic at work today, but what is most disturbing is that the practitioners of these wiles are the very men who claim to be leaders in Biblical scholarship. They impugn Scripture as saying things that it does not say, drawing theologians into hair-splitting debates on ludicrous non-issues—such as whether "J" or "P" wrote a certain verse, or how the "*waw-infinitive*" is used in ancient Hebrew—and thus drawing future church leaders away from studying God's word with practical application in mind. In the end, these Gnostic theologians draw God's people away from God's word, killing their faith in the Bible as the inspired word of God.

## Eve Debates

**2. And the woman said to the serpent.** Satan deliberately targets Eve instead of Adam for his subtle temptations. His goal from the beginning of creation has been to turn God's created order upside down. He approaches Eve in hopes of luring her into his own sin: to usurp the authority of her head, even as Satan himself tried to do in heaven.

*We may eat.* Eve is immediately lured into debating with Satan (although she probably does not know that she is talking to Satan as opposed to a simple serpent), and in her first attempt she misquotes God. Compare her words with God's words:

*God (2:16):* "Of *every* tree of the garden you may *freely* eat" (emphases added).

*Eve (3:2):* "We may eat [not freely] the fruit of the trees [not 'every'] of the garden."

*God (2:17):* "but of the tree of the knowledge of good and evil."

*Eve (3:3):* "but of the fruit of the tree which is in the midst of the garden." This might imply that Eve did not know the name of the Tree of the Knowledge of Good and Evil, perhaps because Adam had not instructed her fully; or it may imply that she has added her own stipulation of avoiding that area ("the midst of the garden") altogether.

*God (2:17):* "you shall not eat."

*Eve (3:2):* "You shall not eat it, nor shall you touch it." This stipulation, whether added by Adam or Eve, was undoubtedly well-intended in hopes of avoiding temptation. Unfortunately, it also added man's rules to God's command, and this is the origin of legalism. We shall see that it also fails in its object, as the added rule did not help Eve or Adam to avoid temptation, nor did it strengthen them to do right when temptation did come.

*God (2:17):* "for in the day that you eat of it you shall surely die."

*Eve (3:3):* "lest you die." "You shall surely die" means that you shall most certainly die. "Lest you die," however, means "you will run the risk of possibly dying." It is unlikely that Eve deliberately tried to soften God's words—although she assuredly does fall prey to Satan's portrayal of God as a hard task master, so it is possible that she softens the sense here in order to make God seem less harsh. It is more likely, however, that she merely misquotes inadvertently, but the result of this whole conversation forces us to recognize how critically important it is to quote God's words accurately. We shall see in Section 2 how this injunction has been ignored by today's Bible scholars.

## Satan's Promises

**4. *You will not surely die.*** Notice that Satan knows God's actual words, "surely die," which underscores his deliberate attempts above to *misquote*

God.[3] This also demonstrates that Satan is not interested in learning truth—he already *knew* what God had said. His interest is only to draw Eve into debate so that he can confuse and distract her, ultimately seducing her to reject the word of God.

His words are also slightly ambiguous. His promise can be understood to mean, "you will not necessarily die—you might *not* die"; or to mean, "you certainly and assuredly will not die." This subtle ambiguity demonstrates the subtlety and deceptiveness of the evil one and his followers—yet, no matter how one understands his words, the end result is the same: they are a lie. Satan does not care what we think he means or what we believe, just so long as we reject the words and authority of the Creator.

**5. *For God knows.*** Satan now impugns God's character more openly, implying that God is deliberately oppressing Eve in some fashion, out of some unnamed fear that, if she should rise up and become independent, she shall become just like Him, and He will therefore lose some unnamed control and power over her. It is ludicrous as well as false, but common sense is not necessary in Satan's many lies. And in this moment, Satan and Eve will conspire together to invent the heresy of feminism.

Eve, after all, was not invited to the meeting between God and Adam. This puts her in the position of being forced to take Adam's word for what God said. Satan is, in effect, planting the seeds of doubt in her mind toward God *and* her husband. "Are you sure," the serpent hisses, "that your husband is competent to know God's will for you?"

***your eyes will be opened.*** This is the only part of Satan's promises which actually comes true, but not in the way which he implies. Eve takes it to mean that she will see more "good" than she does at present, that she will gain some sort of mystical insight which she currently lacks. What she ends up seeing, however, is only herself.

The benefits of sin which Satan promises to Eve are things that she already possesses. Ironically, those promised benefits are the very things that she and Adam will lose by submitting to the devil. Their eyes are already opened—to the point, even, of seeing God Himself face to face—but in the end they will become spiritually blind, and Jesus will spend much of His ministry restoring man's sight.

---

3 In Chapter 9, I will show how deliberately misquoting someone is the core of modern gnosticism, as explained by Harold Bloom, a self-described modern gnostic. By this definition, we must recognize that Satan was the founder of Gnosticism.

***You will be like God.*** But they already *are* like God! This is the crux of Satan's promises: he offers to give us what we already possess, then takes it away, leaving us only with evil.

Here again, Satan is implying that God and Adam are in some sort of conspiracy against Eve. Bear in mind that God gave the instructions concerning this fruit to Adam when Eve was not present, so she evidently has learned of the forbidden fruit from her husband. Satan is suggesting to Eve that her husband and God don't want her to be like them, that they are trying to "keep her down," to oppress her in some way by preventing her from discovering some "higher knowledge" which they are keeping secret. Again, this is the invention of the heresy which we call feminism.

The irony is that the true conspiracy is amongst Adam, Eve, and Satan against God—not the other way around. But Satan's goal is to turn the creation order upside down, and his lies are often mere inversions of the truth.

***Knowing good and evil.*** Eve already does know "good," as everything in creation is good at this point. But Satan's seductive words deceive her into believing that knowing evil will be "empowering" in some way, to use the modern feminist wording of the same lie. "Reach out," says Satan, "take what is being kept from you. It will bring you power, independence, enlightenment! Be a woman of courage: reach out your hand and *take*!"

And once again, Eve will actually *lose* her capacity to know good, as the presence of God will be removed from mankind. She will be left only with a knowledge of evil, and it will not turn out to be what she had envisioned.

## The Invention of Gnosticism

Several ancient heresies are invented in the Garden of Eden, including legalism, feminism, and the cult of self (as we shall see in a moment). But at the root we find the heresy called Gnosticism, a cult of "knowledge" which teaches that one can only understand God and His will by attaining some special, mystical, "higher knowledge" that is not available to the common man.

It is no accident that Satan has positioned himself beneath the Tree of Knowledge. His chief temptation of Eve is that she will gain knowledge by eating the forbidden fruit. He deceives her into believing that she is missing out on some "higher," more mystical level of knowledge, some form of "knowing" that is possessed by God Himself. In order to be like God, Satan assures her, she must first obtain this hidden knowledge. Once she has eaten, her "eyes will be opened" and she will "know."

This is the core of Gnosticism. It is a false religion which teaches that God is unknowable by the common man. Man must first attain to a higher level of some mystical knowledge, some vague secret "gnosis." It places the common man in the position of being forced to rely upon a cult of "priests" who possess that knowledge, false priests who dispense their false wisdom in impenetrable, obscure lingo.

This cult is still in practice today in many forms. We find it particularly at the root of modern scientific research and modern Biblical criticism. It is not a coincidence, after all, that modern Bible commentators refer to themselves as the "higher critics." But I will address this heresy in more depth in a later chapter.

## The Three Lusts

**6. *The woman saw*.** Satan has all but succeeded in his seduction of Eve, for she now turns her attention from his arguments to the forbidden object—which was the evil one's intention in the first place. Satan is not really interested in winning Eve's intellect, he is not concerned with fully convincing her of the truth of his assertions, he is interested solely in seducing her to commit sin. If one line of argument doesn't work, he will try another; his goal is to wear down a person's resistance and get him to start looking at the forbidden object. Once we focus our attention away from God's injunctions concerning sin, and onto the object of our temptation, we have nearly lost the battle of resisting.

John defines three types of temptation (1 Jn. 2:16): "the lust of the flesh, the lust of the eyes, and the pride of life." Eve experiences these the moment that she turns her attention to the forbidden fruit. She "saw that the tree was good for food," catering to the flesh. She saw "that it was pleasant to the eyes," catering to the lust of the eyes. She found that it was "a tree desirable to make one wise," flattering the pride of life. The final result is almost inevitable.

**She took of its fruit and ate.** God "took" (the same Hebrew word is used) of Adam's rib and *gave*, but Eve takes and gives to herself. This is the beginning of the ancient cult of self, which is so prevalent in modern Western societies.

**She also gave to her husband.** This is the last time that we shall see Adam and Eve giving anything to one another (with the exception of Adam's giving

Eve her name), but it is only the beginning of people giving evil to one another. Cain will demonstrate this more fully in Genesis 4.

***With her.*** The sense of "with" here seems to mean "beside," which suggests that Adam was standing beside his wife when she ate the fruit—quite possibly during the entire conversation with the serpent. Whether or not he actually listened in silence to the lies of the serpent, he most assuredly is now aware that his wife has eaten the forbidden fruit—and has evidently done nothing to prevent it.

Adam has failed completely in his role of protecting his wife. She is bone of his bones, and protecting her is to protect himself. He is her head, and has already demonstrated his understanding of this role by naming her "Woman" when God brought her before him. These things mean that he is also completely responsible for her welfare. But, instead of protecting her from the fruit of death, or at least running to find God once she had eaten, Adam voluntarily submits himself to his wife's headship. She tells him to join her in eating that which is forbidden, and he does so.

**7. *Then the eyes of both of them were opened.*** It is possible that the test of the forbidden fruit was a test for Adam alone, as I have already suggested. If we accept this passage at face value, then Eve's eyes are not "opened" when she eats, but only after Adam eats. God gave the instructions regarding the Tree of Knowledge to Adam alone, before Eve had even been created. We shall see from God's subsequent words that at least a part of his test involved his retaining headship over his wife, as his failure includes submitting himself to her. If this speculation is sound (and I am not being dogmatic on this), then it would follow that Eve's test involved a willingness to submit herself to the headship of her husband, trusting his word concerning the will of God. Either way, there is no doubt that the test involved simple obedience to what each understood of the word of God.

***They knew that they were naked.*** We are told in 2:25 that Adam and Eve were both naked prior to the fall, and that they were not ashamed. This suggests that they recognized already that they were naked—a rather silly thing to debate when one thinks about it. Yet here the sense seems to be that they *discovered* that they were naked once their eyes were opened, as though they hadn't known it before. The important "revelation," however, is not that they are not wearing any clothes, but that they have discovered shame.

Adam had previously seen Eve as complementary, but now suddenly he views her as different from himself. He had previously been accepting of her and had embraced her as part of himself, but now he is merely ashamed. What has happened is that Adam has discovered that *he* is naked. He has stopped gazing upon his wife and begun gazing upon himself.

Some commentators suggest that Adam became "self-aware" at this moment. This is not the case. Adam has already discovered that the lower orders of creation are not like himself, whereas Eve is. This revelation required that he be aware of his own unique status in creation. He even declares that Eve is "bone of my bones and flesh of my flesh," which indicates that he was aware of his own body. Adam has not become "self-aware," he has merely become self-obsessed.

***They sewed fig leaves together.*** Man discovers shame, and immediately tries to cover it himself. Once again, Adam should have run to God, but instead he relies upon his own efforts to cover his sin. This is the next step in legalism: once man's self-defined rules have failed to protect him from temptation and sin—and those rules always do fail—then he resorts to his own efforts to make atonement for sin.

This is also the first covering for sin in the sordid history of mankind. God will demonstrate shortly that man's sin did indeed need to be covered, but not by fig leaves. Man's efforts at atonement cannot cover his shame any more than his rules can *prevent* that shame. The fig leaves, furthermore, did not cost Adam and Eve anything except their own effort of gathering and sewing them. This is also true of legalism: man's efforts at making up for his sins may seem at the time to be quite costly, but in the eyes of God they are as futile and worthless as picking leaves off a vine. Man's sin requires a very costly sacrifice, as God will demonstrate later in this chapter, and the cost is ultimately too high for any man to pay himself.

***Made themselves coverings.*** Note that Adam and Eve each covers him*self*, they do not cover one another. Adam should have protected his wife by covering her disgrace; Eve should have supported her husband by making him clothes. Adam's number one priority was Eve, but in the end he only looks out for number one. We shall see, however, that it made little difference in the long run, for no man can cover his own shame or even that of another; only God can cover sin.

## Adam Hides But God Seeks

**8. *They heard the sound of the Lord God.*** The Hebrew word here can mean either "sound" (as New King James has it) or "voice" (as King James has it).

If Adam and Eve hear the *sound* of God in the garden, then it is a gentle, rustling sound, such as twigs snapping or leaves rustling.[4] Once again, we see the gentleness of God pictured here. He does not storm angrily into the garden, crashing through the underbrush. He is walking quietly, moving through His creation looking for His most beloved creature.

Yet that sound of snapping twigs, tranquil as it is, can still inspire fear under certain circumstances. A man in the woods, thinking that he is alone for miles around, might become quite nervous if he heard something man-sized moving unseen nearby. He might be well-advised to look around for his rifle and get ready to meet a bear. Adam is in such a predicament: he is filled with shame, knowing that he has disobeyed God's one small commandment, and he is filled with fear. Just yesterday, he would have been filled with joy at the same sound, eager to meet his Creator face to face. Today, he fears God's wrath and hides. This, too, is a result of sin and shame: "the sound of a shaken leaf shall cause them to flee; they shall flee as though fleeing from a sword, and they shall fall when no one pursues" (Lev. 26:36). "The wicked flee when no one pursues, but the righteous are bold as a lion" (Prov. 28:1).

If Adam and Eve hear the *voice* of God, then He is speaking gently. This is not the voice of thunder, the shouting voice of outrage; it is more like the "still small voice" which Elijah heard (1 Kings 19:12).[5] Whichever they hear, whether voice or sound, it is God approaching His creatures in gentleness—even after he has sinned! And here again, we witness God's gentle hand in creation, even fallen creation, rather than some chaotic conflict as claimed by the Christian Darwinist.

**Walking in the garden.** The sense here is that this is a frequent event, that perhaps God Himself was in the habit of entering the garden and walking about, talking with Adam face to face. He is approaching here as though it's just another of their regular "dates," as though nothing has happened. God knows full well what has happened, of course, but His approach here and His questions in the next verses indicate that He is behaving as though man has not sinned. This is not God putting on pretenses; it is God giving Adam the opportunity to come before him voluntarily.

**In the cool of the day.** Literally, "in the breeze of the day." This probably refers to the gentle, cooling breeze of a summer's afternoon. This is the same word that we discussed in chapter 1 which can mean "wind" or "spirit," as in

---

4 *BDBG*
5 *BDBG*

Gen. 1:2. The implication is that the entire garden is suffused with the Spirit and presence of the Creator. Yet Adam hides.

It is worth mentioning in passing that our Gnostic commentators use this Hebrew word in 1:2 to claim that a turbulent, chaotic wind was roaring above the unformed earth—then they turn around and tell us that it means "gentle breeze" in this verse.[6] Gnostic interpretations are generally driven by one's private agenda.

**Adam and his wife hid themselves.** It's each man for himself once again, as Adam and Eve each runs off and hides himself, neither evidently taking any effort to help the other. This is another of the surprising passages, as we would be more inclined to expect the couple to huddle together and protect one another at this time of threat. We certainly have countless examples of men and women who reach out to help others, even to the point of sacrificing themselves, during times of grave emergency. But this particular emergency is like no other, for the man and woman are fleeing "from the presence of the LORD God." The New Testament warns us that the day is coming when men shall once again flee from before God's face, and that time will in fact be characterized by chaos, when men shall imitate our first parents and concern themselves only with "number one."

Adam is hiding because he has now become unlike God, where he once was like Him. This is the opposite of what Satan promised Eve, but it scarcely matters since only Eve was deceived by those promises. Adam evidently knew all along that this would be the outcome. Yet it is still a tragic irony that he is hiding from the only one who can absolve him of his sin, and this has been true throughout history: sin causes men to hide themselves from the only Person who can save them. Here, then, is the true result of Gnosticism, feminism, legalism, "following your heart," and all the other lies that the world teaches: all lead a man away from God, not toward Him.

**9. God called unto Adam.** Here, amidst mankind's darkest hour, we discover a glimmer of God's grace, coming to him almost the very moment when he sinned. We also witness, once again, the gentleness and grace of God, as He "calls" to Adam rather than "yells."

Notice that God calls to Adam—not to Adam and Eve. God continues to hold Adam accountable for the welfare of his family—and of all creation. This also reinforces the speculation which I put forth earlier, that the test

---

6 E.g., Wenham, *Genesis*, 76.

of the forbidden fruit may have been only for Adam. God questions Adam about the Tree of Knowledge, but He makes no mention of it to Eve.

## God Asks Questions

**Where are you?** Why does God ask questions in this chapter, when He is omniscient? His question here does not imply that He does not already know where Adam is; rather, it implies that He is giving Adam the option of bringing himself before God. He is honoring Adam's free will, allowing him the right to choose to hide from God, to remain separated from Him. God has made the overture to man, humbling Himself by bringing Himself into Adam's presence (when it should by rights have been the other way around), but He will not take the final step of face-to-face confrontation unless Adam is willing. Adam could have chosen not to answer God at this point, and God would presumably have kept on walking.

**10. "I heard. . . I was afraid. . . I was naked. . . I hid."** Notice how self-centered Adam's response is: "I. . . I. . . I. . . I." His wife is cowering in the trees nearby—terrified, naked, and alone—but Adam hasn't a thought of her, only of himself. Here again we see the cult of self, as Adam looks out for number one.

And Adam is afraid. Here, then, is the end result of all our "-isms"—gnosticisim, feminism, legalism, and so forth. Man's religious systems lead him to fear the only one who can save him. Adam has lost his ability to trust God, even as Eve gave up her trust when she accepted the serpent's lies.

**11. "Who told you that you were naked?"** The answer to this question is simple: nobody! Nobody told Adam or Eve that they were naked, it was just self-evident. Adam's conscience has been awakened, and his focus has shifted to himself, turning him away from God and his wife. The first effect of sin was shame and guilt, and the first response was a cover-up. This trend in human nature is still with us today, as politicians are forever demonstrating. It is easier to cover up than to confess, as Adam is about to demonstrate.

We can read this question another way by placing the emphasis on "naked" rather than on "told": "Who told you that you were *naked*?" God is saying in part, "Why are you worried about being naked? We have some bigger, more serious things to discuss."

Adam and his wife had been naked from the beginning, but without shame. What has changed is not the nakedness but the *shame*. And Adam's behavior indicates that he is concerned, not with his nakedness, but with his overwhelming sense of guilt and remorse. He is experiencing that feeling which we all know, wishing that we could go back in time and do it over again. In other words, Adam is focused on his fig-leaf, his home-made covering, his own sense of shame and failure.

But God wants him to stop looking at himself and start looking at Himself. He wants Adam to address his *sin*, not how he *feels* about his sin. Adam needs to recognize the real ramifications of his sin: separation from God and subjection to death. His shame does indeed need to be covered, but it must be covered by God, not by Adam, and this cannot happen until some degree of reconciliation takes place between God and him.

**Have you eaten. . . ?** God continues to ask questions to which He already knows the answer. He knows full well that Adam has eaten the forbidden fruit, but He wants to hear it from Adam's mouth. He is trying to lead Adam toward a voluntary confession of his sin. Once again, God demonstrates His gentleness and His respect for Adam's free will by not shaking him and accusing him. It is important to recognize that the time for confession is *before* judgment, not after. Once the Judge has passed His sentence, it is too late to confess your guilt. God's sentence is coming, but He wants Adam to confess first in order to extend His grace.

**12. Then the man said.** Adam confesses that he did eat the fruit, yet he manages to avoid taking the blame upon himself. This is not a true confession, but God in His mercy evidently accepted it as such just the same.

Adam blames Eve. "The woman whom You gave to be with me" is literally "the woman whom you have set at my side."[7] Compare this attitude with his comments upon first meeting his wife: "This is now bone of my bones and flesh of my flesh." But Adam goes beyond blaming the woman (whom he should be protecting), and actually implies that it's all God's fault. After all, He made her and plopped her into his lap, making him responsible for her—without even consulting him first! "But indeed, O man, who are you to reply against God? Will the thing formed say to him who formed it, 'Why have you made me like this?'" (Rom. 9:20)

Adam does admit his guilt in eating the forbidden fruit, but admitting guilt is only half a confession. To truly confess our sins, we must also accept the responsibility for our actions, acknowledging before God that we are without excuse. David demonstrated true repentance after committing his sins with Bathsheba.

---

7 BDBG, 680.

## Section 1: Reading the Bible

David's sin began when he experienced lust of the eyes (viewing Bathsheba bathing), lust of the flesh (desiring her sexually), and the pride of life (using his influence as king to seduce her)—just as Eve experienced. Like Eve, David reached out his hand and took; he became one with Bathsheba, as Eve did with the fruit; he knew her, just as Adam and Eve came to know evil. David suddenly discovered that he was naked when he learned that Bathsheba was pregnant, realizing that his sin would be found out—so he resorted to a "cover-up," seeking to make amends for his sin by tempting Uriah to go home and lie with his wife. This scheme failed, as legalism and cover-up always do, leading David to further cover-ups and further sin.

So God came to David, since David was not going to God—just as He has done for Adam. God sent Nathan to confront David with the truth of his sin, yet Nathan did so in a gentle fashion: not raging at David, but allowing him to see the true nature of his own wickedness. But this is where David and Adam part company: David's confession was simply, "I have sinned against the LORD" (2 Sam. 12:13). He wrote in one of his psalms, "Against You, You only, have I sinned, and done this evil in Your sight that You may be found just when You speak, and blameless when You judge" (Ps. 51:4). On another occasion, "David said to the LORD, 'I have sinned greatly in what I have done; but now, I pray, O LORD, take away the iniquity of Your servant, for I have done very foolishly" (2 Sam. 24:10). This is the essence of true confession, acknowledging one's sin without proffering any excuses. It is also one reason that God called David a man after His own heart.

**13. *"What is this you have done?"*** Here we have the first recorded instance of God speaking directly to Eve. We cannot argue conclusively from omission, of course, which means that God may have carried on numerous conversations with both Adam and Eve which are not recorded. Yet the conversations that are recorded all have to do with obedience to God's will, both positive and negative—the things that God wants man to do, and those things which he must not do. In other words, the recorded conversations are centered upon headship, on spiritual authority—and it is significant that God has conducted those conversations only with Adam.

But Eve has usurped her husband's authority, and Adam has acquiesced by submitting to her headship; so, once again, God here honors man's decisions and turns to Eve as the temporary head of the family. Adam has passed on responsibility for his sin to his wife, and God now approaches her with accountability. She, however, follows Adam's model for confession, acknowledging her sin while denying her culpability, blaming the serpent instead.

*The serpent deceived me.* The Hebrew word for "deceived" is from a root word meaning "to carry or lift; to carry away." We have a similar sense in our modern expression, "he swept her off her feet." The serpent swept Eve off her feet, beguiling her with smooth speech and glorious appearance, fascinating and wooing her in much the same way that a seducer might steal the heart of a married woman. The lies of the evil one still have this effect today, seducing even the hearts and minds of those who are the Bride of Christ.

## Curse on the Serpent

**14. God said to the serpent.** God does not ask the serpent any questions, and He offers no opportunity for repentance. This is the condition of all creatures when their time of grace has passed—including man. Satan and his demons are outside of grace, and they are not given any hearing before God any longer. This is not true of mankind at present, yet the day comes for every man and woman when they seal their fate forever. The person who dies without repentance will pass beyond the bounds of God's grace, and will spend eternity with no hope of a hearing before the Almighty.

God also demonstrates for Adam and Eve the proper way of dealing with evil. The first step is to recognize Satan when you meet him, as he casts doubt upon God's revealed will, contradicts God's word, impugns Him with evil motives, and so on. Do not give the evil one an audience; do not be drawn into debates with the devil. "Did God really create?" Recognize the voice of Satan, and flee. The evil one demonstrated in the garden that he was not interested in discovering truth, only in causing confusion—and his tactic is the same today in dealing with God's written word. He should be given no opportunity to speak any further.

*On your belly you shall go.* Most modern commentators agree that the serpent did not have legs, and they generally point out that this "story" (as they call it) is not an "etiology" of why snakes crawl on their bellies.

I strongly disagree. Each of the curses which God pronounces declares that there will now be some reversal of previous conditions. There will now be enmity between serpents and "the seed of the woman," where no enmity previously existed. Woman will now bear children in much pain, and man will now till the earth by the sweat of his brow—the opposite of life in paradise. The serpent will now crawl on his belly, so the context suggests that he previously had other methods of moving about. In other words, the context does indeed appear to be presenting an explanation of why snakes crawl on their bellies.

Matthew Henry actually goes a step further by suggesting that the serpent may also have possessed wings, "a flying serpent, which seemed to come from on high as a messenger from the upper world."[8] The mythical figure of the winged dragon is universal, and universally pictured as a powerful foe of mankind, so this suggestion is not far-fetched. Most cultures, in fact, picture dragons ("that serpent of old, who is the Devil and Satan" [Rev. 20:2]) as having the power of human speech.

Once again, we do not know any of these details simply because we are not told. It does seem likely that the serpent at least had legs, but we cannot insist upon this, since it is not explicitly stated.

**You shall eat dust.** This is a colloquial expression which we still use today, "eat dust" indicating a most lowly and humiliating position. The phrase is used similarly in Micah 7:17, Ps. 72:9, Is. 49:23, among other references. This sense is probably self-evident to any honest reader, but it must be stated just the same since some modern commentators have suggested that the serpent is merely a metaphor of some sort—simply because real snakes don't eat dust.

Beyond that, this statement is probably also literally true. Snakes, as I understand it, use their tongues to gather information concerning their surroundings, and any creature that is crawling on its belly in the dust while sticking out its tongue is quite likely to be ingesting some dirt along the way. There is a poetic irony in this curse, for the serpent used its tongue to deceive Eve, making its tongue "dirty" by choice (if the serpent was given a choice on having Satan possess it—we are not told such details); now its tongue will be dirty by necessity, as it crawls on its belly for all time.

**15. Her seed.** This phrase, "the woman's seed," is quite striking, because women don't *have* seed. It appears metaphorical, "seed" meaning "offspring" or "descendents."[9] Yet why does God speak of the *woman's* seed, rather than of *Adam's* seed? This is, in fact, a prophecy of the virgin birth of Christ, for no man born of Adam could redeem Adam from sin.

---

8 *Matthew Henry's Commentary on the Whole Bible*, volume 1, 17.

9 To be more precise, this is an example of *metonymy*, a literary device which uses a part of something to represent the whole. "All hands on deck" means that all men should report on deck; "give us this day our daily bread" uses "bread" to refer to food in general.

Sin, Paul tells us,[10] is transmitted through the man. In some mysterious way, the man's seed carries the sin nature; the woman's egg, however, does not transmit the sin nature but does provide the human fleshly, corporeal element for offspring. Thus it was that God could implant holy seed, free from the corruption of sin and death, into a sinful descendant of Adam (herself untouched sexually by any man), producing the Son of God who was also the Son of Man. This underscores the fact that sin is transmitted through the seed of the man, a concept which proves to be more than a mere abstraction. We will consider Adam in more depth in a later chapter; for now, it is only important to understand that Adam is the literal, genetic head of the human race—not a metaphor of some theological concept.

Now, did Moses understand these mysteries? Of course not! Yet he wrote it down, recording it as part of God's curse on the serpent. This is yet one more demonstration of divine inspiration, and of Moses' faithfulness in recording what God revealed to him—whether or not he fully comprehended its larger theological (or scientific!) implications. Isaiah also prophesied of the virgin birth, yet could not himself have comprehended its full meaning. Once again, we are forced to state these obvious facts because modern commentators have claimed that Moses did not possess our modern understandings and therefore could not have meant what his words *seem* to mean. Modern theologians, in short, have rejected the divine inspiration of Scripture.

**He shall bruise your head, And you shall bruise His heel.** The Hebrew word translated "bruise" means to bruise, crush, grind, rub off.[11] The serpent's bruising or grinding of the man's heel (or, more precisely, The Man's heel—as the prophecy refers specifically to Christ) will cause some temporary discomfort. But the grinding of the serpent's head will eventually crush out its life (Rom 16:20; Rev 20:10).

## Curse on the Woman

**16. I will greatly multiply your sorrow and your conception.** The Lord now pronounces the curse which will befall the woman as a result of her sin. Both Adam and Eve have submitted themselves to the evil one, thus enabling him to invert the created order. The result of this inversion is that the very purposes for which man and woman were created are now perverted. Woman was created as man's "helper," and here we discover one of the central aspects of that help: bearing and raising children (1 Tim. 2:15).

---

10 E.g., Rom. 5:12ff.
11 *BDBG*, 1003

***Your desire.*** The Hebrew word for "desire" is from a root word meaning "to overflow, stretch out [as of overflowing water]." There is a sense here of the woman over-riding and overwhelming the man's headship, a desire for mastery or control. There also is the sense of hunger or craving present in this pronouncement. The same word is used in Gen. 4:7, where God is warning Cain: ". . . if you do not do well, sin lies at the door. And its desire is for you, but you should rule over it." This "desire" is a struggle for dominion, for dominance—sin vying for mastery of Cain, woman vying for headship with her husband. This element of struggle for supremacy is further underscored by the Lord's decree: "he shall rule over you."

Thus we find that another element of woman's created purpose has been perverted. She was created to support her husband as his "fit helper," but now sin has brought about a struggle for leadership between the two. It is important to remember that the concept of "headship" itself is not a result of the fall; rather, the *struggle* for headship came about because of Adam's sin. God had intended that man hold dominion over creation, assisted fully and willingly by the woman. But Adam chose to submit himself to her headship, removing himself from direct communion with his Creator and placing himself under the authority of sin and death.

## Curse on the Man

**17. Because you have heeded the voice of your wife, and have eaten.** Adam's sin is twofold: eating the forbidden fruit and submitting to his wife's headship. The Hebrew here can be punctuated and understood two ways: because you heeded your wife, therefore you have eaten; because you have heeded your wife *and* have eaten. If we punctuate it the first way, the suggestion is that Adam's submitting to his wife's authority led him into sin; punctuated the second way, it suggests that Adam sinned both by eating and by submitting. The end result makes little difference, however: the meaning is clear that God expected Adam to be the leader and to make his decision based upon God's command, not upon his wife's wishes or actions.

The word for "voice" here is the same used of God's voice in 3:8. Adam placed the woman in headship between himself and God, heeding her voice instead of His. This resulted in removing both of them—and all of their descendants—from the dominion of life and placing them under the authority of death. Once again, this removes any possibility (from the Scriptural perspective) of man's having evolved from lower orders.

***Cursed is the ground for your sake.*** Adam was created specifically for two purposes: to reflect the image of God, and to care for His creation. We have already seen that Adam's role-reversal and disobedience damaged his reflection of God's image. Now we discover that his role as care-taker is also damaged, that his work is cursed rather than blessed. All of creation will now fight against him, rather than willingly submitting to his headship, as Satan's upside-down plan for reversing the created order takes further effect. What was intended to be a source of joy for the man will now be a source of frustration, sorrow, and sweat—just as child bearing and marriage will be for the woman.

**18. *Thorns and thistles.*** Here we have another "etiology," explaining the source of thorns and other forms of natural protection systems. A perfect creature in a perfect world would not need to protect itself from death and predators but, when death entered creation, even plant life established methods of protecting itself from predators and competitors. This element of "adaptation" is one of the foundation stones of Darwinist theology—that life-forms adapted and evolved in order to survive. But a rose that grows thorns is still a rose, just as roses can be altered in appearance to create new colors—new colors of roses. The implication here is also that these changes—snakes going on their bellies, plants growing thorns—took place suddenly, not over millions of years.

It is important also to notice that the curse of the first Adam will eventually become the crown of the Last Adam, as Jesus took upon Himself the curse and wore the crown of thorns. He took upon Himself—voluntarily—the curse of Adam's race, literally becoming accursed for *our* transgressions. This is the way that God finally and ultimately clothed Adam's race and covered our shame: He turned the curse back upon Himself, thus neutralizing it and eventually ending it forever. Death is not what Darwinists believe it to be, the creative and immutable force of our universe; it is merely a temporary state, brought about by our first father but removed when we are born again into the Last Adam.

**19. *Till you return to the ground.*** Man will henceforth spend his whole life digging his own grave.

## Adam Names Eve

**20. *Adam called his wife's name Eve.*** This suggests that little time has elapsed since the creation of mankind on day six, since one would expect that Adam would have given his wife a proper name, not merely a genus name.

Married men don't generally refer to their wives as "woman," after all—not happily married men, anyway.

Feminists have claimed that this naming of Eve is an example of male dominance,[12] of patronizing patriarchy if I may suggest a more happy phrase for their use. But this would mean that anyone is being wicked who names a child, which is actually an expected element of one's responsibility as a parent. What we do discover, however, is that Adam's role of headship has not been revoked, despite his fall into sin, and he recognizes at least this one element of his responsibility toward his wife. God has not abandoned His plan of creation, even though man's sinfulness fights against it.

Here is another glimmer of hope in the middle of mankind's darkest day, showing that man and woman are not utterly estranged from one another—despite the ugly tensions which will now permeate relations between the sexes for the remainder of human history.[13]

Adam's name choice provides another point of encouragement, as he names her "Life" because she was destined to be "the mother of all living." It demonstrates that Adam has heard—and believed—God's promise of a future "Seed of the Woman." He names her "the mother of all living" out of faith that the human race will flourish in spite of death, and he (knowingly or otherwise) is looking ahead to the day when life shall be fully restored through the work of the promised Redeemer.

## God Covers Their Shame

**21. *God made tunics of skin, and clothed them.*** God Himself has now covered the shame of Adam and Eve, evidently discarding without comment the absurd fig-leaf loin-cloths which they had made for themselves. Man's best efforts at self-redemption are so absurd as to evoke no notice from the Lord. Yet even this covering, though created by God Himself, is inadequate and temporary. In fact, the nature of a tunic is that the person wearing it can choose for himself to remove it; it is not a permanent, unassailable covering for the shame of Adam's sin.

---

12 E.g., B. Vawter, *On Genesis: A New Reading*, 86; cited by Victor P. Hamilton, *The Book of Genesis, Chapters 1–17*, 206 n. 8. It is interesting that even the feminists recognize the element of headship suggested by Adam's naming his wife.

13 Interestingly, this is yet another "etiology," to use the gnostics' favored terminology. In this chapter, we learn the origins of the battle of the sexes. Feminism is a direct result of the fall—in fact, one of the factors which *led* to the fall—and contrary to the original plan of God.

Nonetheless, the skin tunic is better than a loincloth of fig leaves. The tunic covers almost the whole body, while the fig leaves covered only a small area. The tunic was a cloth garment, generally full-length, often (though not always) with long sleeves. It was the primary piece of clothing in the ancient Near East, worn next to the skin, with other clothing and accoutrements layered on top. This might suggest, if we are not pushing the symbolism too far, that God's sin-covering is the basic essential for a believer's clothing, with the additions of man and church added superfluously. Even the poorest person had a tunic.

In a later day, the Holy Spirit will provide the sons of the Last Adam with the armor of God (Eph. 6:11–18), covering the whole man from head to toe. This "garment" will do more than cover man's shame: it will actually serve to protect him from the attacks of the enemy, and even give him a weapon with which to fight back. Ultimately, the Last Adam, the Lamb of God, will Himself cover His children with white robes of righteousness (Rev. 19:8), paid for by His own sacrifice—and there shall finally be no further need for coverings of any kind.

The element of sacrifice is introduced into Scripture on the very day of man's sin, which occurred evidently soon after his creation. We have already seen that God calls upon His creation to participate in His creative work— He even called upon Adam to sacrifice a part of himself in the creation of the woman. But here we have a very different form of sacrifice, as at least one animal (probably one or two sheep) had to sacrifice their lives for the good of another: "skin for skin," as Satan himself says in Job 2:4. This time, also, the creation (of tunics) is remedial, not complementary (as with the creation of Eve). It is needed to cover an ugly flaw which has been ripped into the once-perfect order of creation, whereas all previous contributions from God's creatures have furthered the completion of that perfection. Notice also that God does not pronounce this act of creation "good." He knew, from before creation, that He Himself would ultimately provide the final sacrifice to cover Adam's shame.

### Paradise Lost

**22. *The man has become like one of Us*.** The Hebrew word for "man" is "adam," and it is sometimes used as the proper noun "Adam," referring specifically to the first human in creation, and sometimes used generically to mean "mankind." This pronouncement does not mean that Adam alone has gained a knowledge of evil, but rather that the whole human race has now been tainted. Once again, we are brought to see that Adam's sin transmitted his sin nature to *all* of his offspring—including Eve, who was taken out of his own body. This fact is reiterated throughout Scripture, and we have no option but to recognize the Bible's teaching that there was a literal "first man" named Adam who literally sinned by eating literal fruit.

As we've seen many times already, this fact alone prevents us from trying to fit "millions of years" into the six days of creation. If man evolved from the lower orders, then the Adam of Genesis becomes a mere metaphor of some kind, and Genesis 3 is myth rather than history. The only possible "wiggle room" which a Christian Darwinist might claim here is to suggest that God took millions of years to create everything *but* man—but what good is accomplished by arbitrarily rejecting all the miracles described in Genesis 1 except for this one? It is nothing less than dishonest scholarship to pretend that "day" is meant symbolically, while Adam's creation from dust and Eve's creation from his rib are meant literally.

***One of Us.*** Some have also suggested that God is speaking to the angels here. But angels are not "fallen" (unlike Satan and his demons), so one must ask whether angels can be said to "know evil." God Himself might be said to "know evil" only in the sense that everything—even Satan and death and hell itself—are under His dominion and sovereignty. Jesus "was in all points tempted as we are, yet without sin" (Heb. 4:15), and "He made Him who knew no sin to be sin for us" (2 Cor. 5:21). These things are a mystery, for how could Jesus "be sin" unless He "knew sin"? This is a tangent, and it is enough to recognize the mystery of God's sovereignty contained within this verse, but we cannot conclude that God is speaking to anyone here except Himself. God does not lump Himself together with any of His creatures; He is One, not "one of us."

***Lest he put out his hand and take.*** Eve reached out her hand and took the forbidden fruit, so now God takes steps to prevent Adam from reaching out and taking from the Tree of Life. It is significant that God says "lest *he* put out *his* hand," not "lest *they*" or "lest *he and she*." This is further underscored when God sends "him" out of the garden "to till the ground from which he was taken" (23), as Adam was taken from the ground but not Eve. It could be argued that this is a generic "he," referring to mankind as a whole, yet the context of chapter 3 has already strongly indicated that Adam's actions were affecting himself, his wife, and all of his descendants.

*The tree of life.* As discussed previously, it seems unlikely that the Tree of Life possessed any magical qualities of conveying immortality. It was more likely set apart by God as a ceremonial symbol, whereby God would bless man with an everlasting covenant and with the promise of eternal life—a ceremony consummated by Adam's eating of the fruit. After all, eating the forbidden fruit did not magically convey sin and death; it was his act of disobedience which brought death, and the fruit itself was merely serving the purpose of providing him with an opportunity to exercise his free will.

The obvious shortcoming of this view, however, is the Lord's concern that Adam might eat of the tree "and live forever." Those words do lend some weight to the possibility that there was some life-giving or life-sustaining power within the fruit itself—yet even just wording it that way goes against the teachings of Scripture, which teaches that only God is the source of life. Another possibility is that God would have chosen to honor His own ceremonial symbol if Adam had eaten from the Tree of Life. The Lord has already demonstrated that He will honor man's decisions, even when those decisions invert the entire order of creation, so it is not far-fetched to suggest that He would also have honored Adam's illegitimate snatching of eternal life at this point.

This is all mere speculation, of course, but it is clear from the text that Adam had *not* eaten of it prior to grasping the forbidden fruit—the opposite fruit, the fruit which symbolized death instead of life. It is self-evident today that the sons of Adam persist in reaching out for the many fruits of death, while refusing to eat of the Tree of Life.

It is also noteworthy that the Tree of Knowledge of Good and Evil does not exist in the New Jerusalem, while the Tree of Life flourishes there (Rev. 22:1–2). In fact, there are not one, not two, but at least *three* Trees of Life growing in eternity—and they stand beside the *River* of Life! And those trees produce fruit all year long, but not just one fruit: each produces 12 separate types of fruit perennially! Indeed, God is "able to do exceedingly abundantly above all that we ask or think" (Eph. 3:20), and there is no question that He is the God of Life, not the God of death. Would such a Creator willingly use the tool of death in producing His highest creation, mankind?

There is no coincidence that the Tree of Life grows in heaven, while the Tree of Knowledge does not. The Tree of Knowledge was finished, its purpose used up, when the Last Adam was Himself nailed to it like an owl nailed to a barn door.[14]

***And live forever.*** Adam was created immortal, but he has now voluntarily made himself subject to death. God's discussion with Himself here may appear vengeful at first glance, in that He does not want Adam to regain his immortality after his sin. But if we think it through, we recognize that this is His tremendous grace and love acting upon man's behalf once again. Eating from the Tree of Life evidently would have restored Adam's immortality in some fashion—but it would *not* have redeemed him from the curse of death. This means that, had he eaten, Adam would have lived forever in a body that was subject to decay, disease, the infirmities of age, and so forth. Imagine living to be 2,000 years old in a body that *looked* 2,000 years old!

This is also another indication of God's repugnance toward death, that He was not willing to have His creature live forever under its dominion. Adam has chosen to remove himself from communion with God and place himself under the headship of Satan and death, and God has allowed him to do so—temporarily. God has allowed the evil one to turn upside down the entire created order—temporarily. Yet even here, on the first day of the fallen order, God is setting in motion His plans for the redemption of mankind and the re-ordering of His creation. It was not God's will that death be present in His creation (contrary to the misguided beliefs of Christian Darwinists), but now that it is present He will not have life (immortality) commingled with death. Man's removal from the Tree of Life is necessary for the time being—but it, too, is only temporary.

Death is a dreadful curse, contrary to everything that God intended in His creation, bringing with it suffering and hardship and hatred and disease and every possible evil that the world has come to know—but it does have this one saving grace: it also brings eventual release. The curse of death includes the stipulation that "it is appointed for men to die once." God is demonstrating His grace here by not allowing Adam to become immortal again, since his immortality would be lived out in a body that is subject to the depredations of death.

---

14 Nobody knows the location where the Garden of Eden stood, but in eternity we may learn its location. Perhaps it stood near Jerusalem. I shall not be surprised if we learn in eternity that the center of Eden was at Golgotha. Eden, after all, appears to be a hill, as the rivers flow out of it. If this should prove true, I am fully confident that the cross stood where the Tree of Knowledge once grew.

**24. *So He drove out the man.*** The Hebrew for "drove out" means also to divorce or put away. This "spiritual divorce" is surely part of what God was warning Adam of concerning the death which he should die on the day that he ate of the forbidden fruit—yet it is not the whole of it. We who have been born again into the Last Adam have been delivered from this spiritual death, and the "divorce papers" were nailed to the cross of Christ; but we are not delivered from the curse as long as we occupy our mortal flesh, and we still groan under the laws of death while we remain on earth—the laws of death which were instituted *after* Adam sinned, but not before.

# 5
# SELECTED NEW TESTAMENT PASSAGES

## Let the Bible Interpret the Bible

So far, we have been restricting our study for the most part to the book of Genesis. We have, however, touched upon certain concepts that can only be fully understood from the New Testament, such as the Triune nature of the Godhead. It will be worthwhile, therefore, to look at a few passages more closely from the New Testament, passages that impinge upon our central question of whether the Bible can endorse any elements of Darwinian theology.

This is by no means an exhaustive study on the Bible's view of evolution; it is merely a look at a few highlights. We'll take the passages one at a time, and consider what they have to say concerning creation and evolution.

## John 1

> In the beginning was the Word, and the Word was with God, and the Word was God. He was in the beginning with God. All things were made through Him, and without Him nothing was made that was made. In Him was life, and the life was the light of men. And the light shines in the darkness, and the darkness did not comprehend it. . . . He was in the world, and the world was made through Him, and the world did not know Him. He came to His own, and His own did not receive Him.
> —John 1:1–5, 10–11

**1. *In the beginning.*** John begins his gospel by deliberately taking us back to Genesis 1:1. This is no accident; John is making a deliberate connection between Jesus and Adam—a connection which Paul will develop further, as we'll see in another passage. John is letting us know, in a sort of metaphysical shorthand (which he develops more fully throughout the gospel and in his epistles and Revelation), that Christ ushered in a new creation, and that He fulfilled the law and removed the curse—that Christ did all the things which Adam failed to do.

Thus we find that our view of Genesis will affect our understanding of Christ. If we have treated Genesis as a "narrative," a mere story which teaches some abstract principles about God, then we will be forced to view Christ in the same way, as a man who was a good teacher or a really nice guy. But John begins his gospel by claiming that Jesus is more than a mere man—much, much more. In fact, Jesus is both man and God!

**The Word.** John informs us that there was only one agent of creation: the Word. Genesis shows us the Word in action: "God said . . . and it was so." John underscores this when he tells us further that "the Word was with God." If there had been any other creative agent involved in making the heavens and the earth, any other agent which brought life to the planet and brought man to life—then that creative agent would also have been "with God."

Christian Darwinists might try to wiggle out of this by suggesting that God gave the command for fish, then Jesus as His Lieutenant went out and sub-contracted the work to Death. "God wants fish, so go kill something and make fish happen." This is worse than absurd; it is actually blasphemous to the character of God, as we shall see shortly. Death is a tool which God will not touch.

**Was God.** This is one of the major passages which teach the deity of Christ.[1] The Word, as we will soon discover, is Jesus. As we have already seen, whoever created mankind is mankind's God, by default. John demonstrates this principle here: before he gets into the subject of creation, he makes it clear to us that Christ is God incarnate.

**3. All things were made through Him.** Christian Darwinists try to claim that God used evolution to create mankind. God decided to create man, so He set in motion certain "laws of evolution" which brought that about. But here John reiterates that there was only one agent of creation, only one "tool" that was used: the Word.

**Without Him nothing was made that was made.** Nothing was created by any other agent or "law" whatsoever; God did not turn over His creation work to any other force or agency—including His own laws! God did command the earth to bring forth living creatures (Gen. 1:24), but John assures us that God Himself—the Word—was the creative agent.

---

1 This passage so clearly teaches that Jesus is God that the Jehovah's Witnesses, who deny the deity of Christ, have added the word "a" into the verse in hopes of denying John's teaching (the article is not present in the Greek): "In [the] [sic] beginning the Word was, and the Word was with God, and the Word was a god" (John 1:1, *New World Translation of the Holy Scriptures*).

The Christian Darwinist will leap up in great excitement at this point and exclaim, "Aha! Now it is *you*, Benoit, who are being arbitrary! You claim that God is the creative agent when He commands earth to bring forth animals—so why not read that verse as 'God said, "Let the earth *evolve* the living creature"'?" I will acknowledge that I cannot completely explain the process by which the "earth brought forth" land animals; I tried to suggest one picture in chapter 1, but it is only surmisal, since we simply are not told. It is unquestionably a miracle, since the earth does not of itself burp up cats and dogs any longer.[2] But the element here of God using the Word to create underscores the miraculous component of Genesis 1, where God *speaks* and that which He commands instantly becomes reality. John is emphasizing this aspect of God's creative power: He simply spoke "the Word," and it was so. There are also many other important reasons why we cannot read "let the earth evolve the living creature" into Genesis 1, which we will consider as we go along. It is sufficient at this point to emphasize what John is trying to communicate: that God *spoke* and it became so—instantly.

**4. In Him was life.** God is life. Life and death cannot co-exist any more than light can co-exist with darkness; where one is, the other is absent by default. Shadow is the absence of light; death is the absence of life. Here we have another answer to the Christian Darwinist's claim that God used evolution as His creative tool. If He had used death to create life, His hand could not have been involved in the operation—for where His hand is, there is life; and where life is, there is *not* death.

Death is repugnant to God. Consider some of the laws which God instituted in the Old Testament concerning the treatment of dead bodies. God commanded that any person who even touched a dead body was defiled and unclean (Num. 19:11). God made His "dwelling" in the camp of the Israelites during their journey out of Egypt, and He commanded that anyone who had touched a dead body should be put outside the camp (Num. 5:2). God would not allow even a hint of the taint of death to be anywhere near His holy presence. A man who had touched death was not permitted even to *approach* God's presence.

Would God, therefore, choose to touch death Himself? Yet this is precisely what Christian Darwinists are suggesting when they claim that God

---

2 The doctrine of evolution, incidentally, claims that evolution is still happening today, which is yet another doctrinal element of that false religion which Christian Darwinists fail to wrestle with.

used evolution to create life! We must come to terms with these basic facts: 1) God hates death; 2) evolution in any form requires death; 3) whatever "tools" God may have used to create required that He "touch" them Himself, for we are assured at every turn that God is a "hands-on" Creator. This simple bit of logic forces us to recognize that God would not have touched a tool which was repugnant to Him—especially not when He was creating something which He would declare "very good."

Christian Darwinists of all stripes are claiming that God used evolution and death to create life on earth. This is a slander to God's character; He would never choose to touch something which He commands His people to avoid.

***The life was the light of men.*** John tells us in verses 5–9 that Jesus is actually the Light spoken of in Genesis 1:3. God's command "let there be light" does not mean that Jesus was created at that moment. It means that, in that moment, God shared—exposed—His life force which animates all creation. This is why mankind cannot create life, even though (being in God's image) we can create nearly everything else. Life itself is found only in God, and cannot be forged or created.

John reiterates yet again that life and death are as mutually exclusive as light and darkness. Yet Darwinism is actually a religion of darkness, not of light. True Darwinism (not the adulterated Christian-Darwinist amalgam preached by modern commentators) teaches that evolution is a series of random events that happen mostly by chance. There is no guiding hand in evolution because there is no God who exists *outside of* the natural cosmic order. True Darwinists are naturalists, believing that there is no supernatural power, no Creator who exists outside of His creation. Their god is the force within our cosmos which drives all change: the force of death and survival.

Darwinism is utterly inconsistent with the character of God. God subjected His son—our Creator—to death in order to *free* mankind from death. This was a tremendously costly sacrifice, and it makes no sense to suggest that He would first choose to subject mankind to death, just for the opportunity of later sacrificing His Son to ransom mankind *out of* death. Man's subjection to death, as Genesis teaches us, is man's own fault.

Christian Darwinists would have us believe that God subjected His creation to millions of years of death—untold millennia of suffering; millions of years of disease and war and famine and fear and pain—generation upon generation, millions and billions of His precious creatures suffering and dying—just to produce mankind?! Then, once mankind was fully evolved, God said, "You are free from death now, after 50 billion years—unless, of course, you eat a piece of fruit from that tree over there." Upon which, He immediately cursed man and placed him right back under the jackboot of death.

Darwinism is darkness, and we must not attempt to commingle it with light.

**5. *The light shines in the darkness.*** A candle burning in the noonday sun seems very weak and dim, but that same candle burning in the darkest cave is blindingly brilliant. So it is with God's word: when a nation knows and more or less believes the creation account of Genesis, it seems self-evident and obvious and not worth writing books about. But when that same nation has gone blind, has been deluded by the darkness of evolution, then suddenly the good news[3] of Genesis shines brilliantly clear with a startling account of man's origins that is the exact opposite of the nation's received religion. John is letting us know that Jesus is the One who is prophesied in Genesis 3, that He is the Last Adam, that He has come to lead mankind out of the darkness of death and false religions into the Light of God's glory.

This is one of the more serious charges which I will bring against modern theologians, for they have cheated our generation of the knowledge of the truth, cheated us of a major doctrine which distinguishes Christianity from the paganism around us. A person who is searching for truth, for some understanding of the world and of life which transcends the bleak hopelessness of the world's teachings, will be drawn to the Scriptures for that very reason—the Bible has something unique to offer, something which is radically different from the teachings of the world. But if we continue to allow our modern gnostics[4] to adulterate God's word, then there will remain nothing to distinguish the Bible from the evolutionist paganism of the world around us.

---

3 Literally, the gospel of Genesis. The first three chapters of Genesis give us much more than a simple account of the world's creation; they lay the very foundation for Christianity. They tell us where death came from, and why men suffer, why we have war and disease and hatred. And, more importantly, they also give us the first gospel of Jesus Christ, as God prophesies of the coming Messiah, "the seed of the woman" (Gen. 3:15) who will crush the head of Satan—who will ultimately defeat death and remove the curse.

4 I will demonstrate more fully in a later chapter that most modern theologians—certainly those writing commentaries on Genesis—are modern manifestations of the ancient heresy of Gnosticism.

***The darkness did not comprehend it.*** We use the English word "comprehend" to mean "understand." This use is certainly true in this verse, in that the world has never fully understood the person, works, and teaching of Jesus. Similarly, the darkened mind of the Darwinist simply cannot understand the faith of the creationist—cannot recognize that he himself is taking a truly colossal leap of faith by believing in evolution.

Yet the Greek word translated "comprehend" (some versions have "apprehended" or "overcome") means more than a mere intellectual understanding. It means "to lay hold of so as to make one's own, to take into oneself."[5] Even our English word "comprehend" literally means "to seize or grasp completely."[6] Here are two other passages which use the same Greek word (which I am highlighting with added emphases):

> "And wherever it [a demon] *seizes* him [a boy], it throws him down; he foams at the mouth, gnashes his teeth, and becomes rigid."
> —Mark 9:18

> "Not that I have already attained, or am already perfected; but I press on, that I may *lay hold of* that for which Christ Jesus has also *laid hold of* me."
> —Phil. 3:12

John is warning us that the forces of darkness desire to seize, to lay hold of, to absorb the truth of Jesus Christ—in the same way in which a demon was seizing a young boy in his death-grip. The forces of darkness have failed, John tells us, yet they continue to try. This is precisely what Satan is attempting to do when he stirs up Christians to adulterate the Bible with the false teachings of evolution.

**10–11. *The world was made through Him, and the world did not know Him. He came to His own, and His own did not receive Him.*** God created the world through Jesus, as we have already seen. Yet mankind has continued to reject Him as their creator, preferring to embrace silly fables of atheism. But what is far worse than this is that many Christians, who claim to be Christ's followers, have also rejected Him as their Creator, preferring to embrace silly fables of atheism.

---

5 *The New Thayer's Greek-English Lexicon of the New Testament*, Jay P. Green, ed., 332.
6 *Shorter OED*.

Evolution rejects Christ as the Creator. By what right, then, do Christ's followers go about making compromises with that false religion? These Christians tell themselves that they are being faithful to the Bible *and* modern science, but modern science teaches us that mankind was brought about through the agency of death and survival of the fittest. Those who embrace the teachings of science actually embrace the heresy that God used the tool of death to create His world.

If Jesus is the agent of creation, as John tells us, then death cannot be the agent of creation. If we tell people that God used death (evolution), then we are in effect refusing to receive Him as our Creator. This is the very definition of heresy.

## Hebrews 1 and 11

> God, who at various times and in various ways spoke in time past to the fathers by the prophets, has in these last days spoken to us by His Son, whom He has appointed heir of all things, through whom also He made the worlds; who being the brightness of His glory and the express image of His person, and upholding all things by the word of His power, when He had by Himself purged our sins, sat down at the right hand of the Majesty on high. . . . Now faith is the substance of things hoped for, the evidence of things not seen. For by it the elders obtained a good testimony. By faith we understand that the worlds were framed by the word of God, so that the things which are seen were not made of things which are visible.
> —Hebrews 1:1–3; 11:1–3

***1:2. Heir of all things.*** This phrase alludes to the role of Christ as the Last Adam, which we will look at in more depth in the next chapter.

***He made the worlds.*** The author of Hebrews reiterates John's assertion that Jesus is the agent of creation. Once again, we must remember that the Creator of mankind is mankind's God, by default. This is another passage, therefore, which teaches the deity of Christ. Christian Darwinists, however, unwittingly claim that God created the world through the agency of Jesus, who carried out creation through the agency of death (which they call "evolution"). Death, therefore, is a demigod of Christian Darwinism, and the *only* god of Scientific Evolutionism (since true evolutionists remove Jesus and the Father from the equation altogether).

**1:3. When He had by Himself purged our sins.** Would God deliberately subject mankind to death in order to *create* him, then send His own Son to die on the cross in order to *remove* that subjection? What is worse, would God subject man to death in order to create him, then *blame mankind* for that very subjection to death? Yet this is precisely what is taught by Christian Darwinists, because Scripture is adamant that man's sin is what brought death into the world, while death (according to Darwin) is the agent of evolution.

When considered this way, in fact, we are confronted once again by the absolute absurdity of the Christian Darwinist position, which claims that God used evolution to create mankind (or at least the lower orders of creation) which requires the presence of death to be possible, the death itself brought about by the sin of man—the man who is being *created* by death! It is as dizzying to consider as a drawing by M. C. Escher.

**11:1. Faith is the substance of things hoped for, the evidence of things not seen.** Faith is the act of choosing to believe certain things that we cannot see. It is an act which we all commit daily, when we cross a bridge in faith that it will not collapse, when we accept on faith things that we are told by people around us.

Darwinists place their faith in the teachings of modern science, believing the words of the "priests" of Darwinism—paleontologists, archeologists, sociologists, astronomers, and (most treacherous of all) modern theologians. No man ever witnessed evolution, and the average man cannot hope to test the veracity of the claims and studies of highly specialized modern scientists. This is an act of faith. It comes down to choosing whom one believes, since neither source (science nor the Bible) can be ultimately proven fully reliable. The bottom-line question is this: Do we place our faith in modern science, or in the written word of God, the Bible? (That is, the written word of God *as written*—not as rewritten to accommodate a false religion. We will begin to confront the rewritings of modern theologians in Section 2.)

Faith is also the "substance of things hoped for." Hope is the confident assurance that something will come to pass in the future. Again, we all exercise hope every day, as we have a confident assurance that the sun will rise tomorrow—things that we simply take for granted. Christians set their hope in the resurrection, that we will one day rise from the dead and see our

Creator face to face. Darwinists, however, have no hope, for in their religion death reigns supreme. Death is the final authority in evolution; once death has spoken, there is nothing else to say. There is no after-life in Darwinism, no resurrection. Death cannot be defeated. Death is god.

Christians, however, know that God is supreme, mightier even than death itself. Jesus, in fact, has *defeated* death; He has destroyed forever the false god of evolution. Here, in fact, is the true "dualism" of gnosticism,[7] the true element of the yin/yang symbols in Eastern Mysticism: the struggle of Life versus Death. The act of mixing evolution into the Bible is an attempt by men to reconcile these two irreconcilable forces of death and life. This combat, however, came to its climax on the cross. The Christian places his faith in the fact that Jesus rose from the dead, thereby defeating death; the Darwinist places his faith in the fact that Jesus died, but he disbelieves in the resurrection—thereby making death the final victor. The two religions are mutually exclusive, and simply cannot be commingled—in Genesis or anyplace else in the Bible.

**11:3. By it the elders obtained a good testimony.** The "elders" are the great heroes of the faith—Abraham, Moses, David, and many others who are singled out in this chapter of Hebrews—who "obtained a good testimony" by their faith. The men and women listed in Hebrews 11 all have one thing in common: each chose to place his faith in the word of God, accepting His word at face value and believing that it was true.

Faith is a deliberate act of one's free will, generally involving a conscious choice to act upon—or believe in—one word of testimony over another. Sometimes this faith requires that the believer act on God's word against overwhelming opposition. That opposition might be threats of physical death, such as the prophets faced; or it might simply be the assumptions and presuppositions and deep-rooted beliefs of the world around. Consider Abraham, who chose of his own free will to believe that God would resurrect his son Isaac from the dead, believing at a time when the world around him scoffed at resurrection. It is this choice to believe what God has said, in the face of tremendous opposition from the world, which made these men and women the heroes of our faith.

This matter of faith is of tremendous importance—faith in God's written word, faith concerning the Biblical testimonies of creation and "origins of

---

7 See chapter 9 for a fuller discussion of Gnosticism.

the species"—for it is only by our faith that we can hope to "obtain a good testimony" before the world. There is certainly more involved in faith than what we believe about creation, but we have already seen (and will see yet more in the next chapter) how critically important the doctrine of creation is to our Christian faith. This is not a matter to take lightly, to treat as a mere "difference of opinion" within Christian thought, on a level with the question of immersion baptism versus baptism by sprinkling. Our beliefs on creation will affect our entire approach to the person and work of Jesus Christ.

It is also worth noting that many of the heroes of the faith lived in a world which embraced the religion of evolution. Moses himself lived in a world which believed in an ancient version of the same duality which we today call evolution. The ancients used myths and stories to explain their theories, while today we use gnostic systems of thought, but the basic premise was the same.

***The things which are seen were not made of things which are visible.*** Genesis, as we have seen, teaches that God created all things from nothing—*ex nihilo*. Modern evolutionists are presently teaching that all matter came from a Big Bang. (I say "presently" because scientists are constantly changing theories, discovering new "facts," disproving the very "facts" that yesterday were incontestable, and so forth.) Creationists, in other words, believe in creation out of nothing, while Darwinists believe in destruction of something—some thing, some chunk of "matter," which went Bang and created life and planets and solar systems and water and energy and all manner of wonderful things. As though explosions actually *created* things rather than destroying them.

But what *was* this "mass of matter" that exploded? What, exactly, went bang? And where did it come from? How did this mass of matter get in outer space? And where did the very space itself come from? Even empty space, after all, is an entity—as is time. The concept of "space" implies that something else lies around its perimeter—otherwise, it would not be "space."[8] And where exactly did time come from—who invented it? The concept of time itself requires that there be an entity or power that exists *outside* of it. This is the larger meaning of "the things which are seen were not made of things which are visible," the recognition that our entire cosmos had to be created by some entity which exists outside of our universe.[9]

---

[8] I am being only slightly facetious here. The evolutionist believes that the universe is all that exists; that there is nothing beyond. For him, the term "space" means "all that exists."

[9] For a much fuller treatment of this concept, see *Miracles* by C. S. Lewis.

Evolution can only explain the existence of the created order back to a chunk of inert matter. It has no explanation for where that matter came from, nor how that inert matter came to life. Ironically, at this point the evolutionist exercises the same act of faith as a creationist, believing that somehow these things came to exist—this lump of matter and life itself—out of nothing. The evolutionist has no explanation for his faith because he wants to believe that there is no God outside of the cosmos; while the creationist believes that "the things which are seen were not made of things which are visible," but were created out of nothing by the Word of God. Alas, the Christian Darwinist wants to believe both theologies, and is left with nothing but double-mindedness and confusion.

## 2 Peter 3

> . . . knowing this first: that scoffers will come in the last days, walking according to their own lusts, and saying, "Where is the promise of His coming? For since the fathers fell asleep, all things continue as they were from the beginning of creation." For this they willfully forget: that by the word of God the heavens were of old, and the earth standing out of water and in the water, by which the world that then existed perished, being flooded with water. But the heavens and the earth which are now preserved by the same word, are reserved for fire until the day of judgment and perdition of ungodly men. But, beloved, do not forget this one thing, that with the Lord one day is as a thousand years, and a thousand years as one day. The Lord is not slack concerning His promise, as some count slackness, but is longsuffering toward us, not willing that any should perish but that all should come to repentance. But the day of the Lord will come as a thief in the night, in which the heavens will pass away with a great noise, and the elements will melt with fervent heat; both the earth and the works that are in it will be burned up. Therefore, since all these things will be dissolved, what manner of persons ought you to be in holy conduct and godliness, looking for and hastening the

> coming of the day of God, because of which the heavens will be dissolved, being on fire, and the elements will melt with fervent heat? Nevertheless we, according to His promise, look for new heavens and a new earth in which righteousness dwells. Therefore, beloved, looking forward to these things, be diligent to be found by Him in peace, without spot and blameless....
> —2 Peter 3:3–14

**3. Scoffers will come in the last days.** The context here is that scoffers will mock the promised return of Christ. But notice the condition which brings this mockery to pass: the scoffers will mock because they willfully forget "that by the word of God" all things were created. As I have been saying throughout this book, our views of creation will affect all that we believe about the person and work of Christ. To reiterate yet again, it is impossible to believe that God created all things by His Word *and* to believe that He used evolution as His creative tool. The two are mutually exclusive.

Those who attempt to rewrite Genesis to incorporate Darwinism will ultimately come to deride the teachings in the New Testament concerning the imminent return of Jesus Christ. Peter warns us, furthermore, that this condition will be a sign of "the last days." If we do not rebuke those theologians in our midst who are adulterating the word of God with the lies of evolution, this result will surely follow.

**5. They willfully forget.** The King James says that these scoffers are willfully ignorant, that they deliberately choose to ignore that the heavens and earth were created "by the word of God." The basic concept of evolution—that a fish can grow lungs and feet just because it decides to—is so illogical and impossible and absurd that it requires a deliberate abdication of common sense and logic to place one's faith in it.

People choose to believe in evolution—with an emphasis on *choice*—because they do not want to be accountable to a Creator who exists outside of time and space. This is understandable, though not excusable, when it is unbelievers who are making that faith choice. It is, however, utterly unconscionable when done by Christians—and *beyond* unconscionable, to the point of blasphemous heresy when done by Christian theologians, because Christians have the very hope which the world is desperately seeking: the hope of transcendence, the hope of defeating death. If we change the text

SECTION 1: READING THE BIBLE

of our sacred Scriptures to *accommodate* this lie, we cheat the unsaved of any hope for transcendence.

**7. *Reserved for fire until the day of judgment and perdition.*** When I was younger, I had a favorite saying: "It's all gonna burn!" We must remember this, that this entire creation is destined for destruction—and that those among us today who die without Christ shall face judgment and eternal perdition. Believers in Christ must recognize that the Darwinist has no hope. Unless he submits to his Creator, this world is all he gets! And how can he hope to submit to his Creator, when he has not heard? And how shall he hear, when those responsible for *telling* him are too busy trying to fit evolution into the Bible?

Again I ask: By what right do Christian theologians water down the creation message of Genesis? They will answer, "We are trying to make the gospel relevant to today's scientific knowledge, trying to show the world that we are not afraid of science, that the Bible actually *supports* science." The problem, however, is not whether or not Christians are willing to grapple with science—the problem is that modern evolutionary science has parted company with the Scriptures, taking a divergent road which the Bible does not tread: the road of naturalistic atheism. And modern theologians are trying to make the Bible go scampering along right behind! In doing so, these theologians are making it even more difficult for the unsaved to find their way to salvation.

"Woe to you lawyers! For you have taken away the key of knowledge. You did not enter in yourselves, and those who were entering in you hindered" (Luke 11:52).

**8. *One day is as a thousand years, and a thousand years as one day.*** Christian Darwinists love to quote this verse as proof that Genesis really means "thousands of years" (by which they themselves really mean "millions and billions of years") when it says "a day." Peter, of course, is not referring back to creation here, but is looking ahead to the second coming of Christ, answering those scoffers who say, "He hasn't come after all these years, so therefore we conclude that He's not ever coming." Yet the principle might still be applicable in addressing the "days" of creation described in Genesis 1.

Christian Darwinists of all stripes, including those calling themselves "Progressive Creationists" (a gross misnomer which we will address in Section 2), use this verse to claim that God actually took a million years at each "stage" or "day" described in Genesis 1. Yet here we have another example of willful ignorance: these theologians willfully ignore the second part of that phrase—that a thousand years is equal to a day. In other words, we can just as easily say that God accomplished in one day what we would have expected to take a thousand (or a million billion bazillion) years.

The true scholar will read this passage and compare it to Genesis 1, concluding that the two support one another, recognizing that this passage confirms that God can accomplish in one day what should take thousands of years. The propagandist, however—men such as our "higher critics" who have an agenda—will use this passage to justify *rewriting* Genesis 1. "Genesis 1," say our theologians, "disagrees with my beloved gnostic sciences when it says 'day,' so I want to rewrite 'day' to mean a million years.... and *here* is my proof text!"

Others, more honest than our modern theologians, will ask a sincere question: "What difference does it make whether it took six million years or six days—it's all the same to God!" Well, it matters first of all for the simple reason that the Bible *says so*! Genesis tells us that it took six days, so it must be important from God's perspective that we know that it took six days.

But second, the order of creation is very important. We have already seen that the serpent's objective was to invert the created order. Part of putting the created order rightside-up again is to stop changing the word of God to fit the teachings of men. The order of creation—including the *timeframe* of creation—is of vital and absolute importance. If God took a billion years to create animals, then He used evolution in the process—He included death in the process. It cannot be otherwise: you cannot claim that God made animals suddenly appear out of the dirt *and* have it take place over millions of years. Extending the timeframe of creation beyond the six days stated in Genesis is, *de facto*, to introduce the elements of death and evolution into God's creative work.

Thus, Christian Darwinists choose to believe that God needed 1,000 years to create, but He called it a day; while the creationist believes that God created in one day what the world thinks took millions of years.

# 6
## First Adam and Last Adam

*Take the snake, the fruit tree and the woman from the tableau, and we have no fall, no frowning Judge, no Inferno, no everlasting punishment—hence, no need of a Savior. Thus the bottom falls out of the whole Christian theology. Here is the reason why in all the Biblical researches and higher criticisms, the scholars never touch the position of woman.*
—Elizabeth Cady Stanton[1]

Elizabeth Cady Stanton, a pioneer of the modern "women's rights" movement, viewed the downfall of "the whole Christian theology" as a desirable goal, since Christianity was seen by early feminists (and most of their modern offspring) as the root of western patriarchy and oppression of women. We have already seen in Genesis 3 where this heresy originated. Yet Stanton has a clearer comprehension of the critical importance of the early chapters of Genesis than modern theologians exhibit—that is to say, she recognizes that our understanding of Adam and his sin sits at the very foundation of all our Christian beliefs. Take away Adam, and down crashes "the whole Christian theology."

The simple fact is this: if we have no original Adam, then we have no original sin. If we have no original sin, then we have no sin nature. If we have no sin nature, then we have no need of a Redeemer. If we have no first Adam, we have no Last Adam.

If one claims that creation took millions of years, then one is also claiming that evolution occurred. There are a few theologians who claim that they don't believe in evolution, yet they still cling to the idea that the word "day" in Genesis 1 actually means millions of years. But this cannot be. That would mean that God created fish simply by the power of His command—

---

1 From a letter to *The Critic*, quoted in Elizabeth Cady Stanton, *The Woman's Bible: A Classic Feminist Perspective*, xi. Stanton and her cohorts relied heavily upon the German "higher criticism" movement and other forms of modern Gnosticism in her own eye-opening rewriting of the Scriptures. Anyone having doubts about the true roots of modern feminism might peruse this book for enlightenment.

that God "created great sea creatures and every living thing that moves" (Gen. 1:21) in an instant—then left them to swim and fly around the globe for a few million years before getting around to the instantaneous creation of land animals—not to mention the sun, moon, etc. Such a scheme gains nothing, for why bother arbitrarily reading "day" to mean a million years while simultaneously taking the miraculous creation literally? It also defies common sense, since for example plants could not have survived millions of years without the sun.[2] And why would God have fish and birds and land animals exist for millions of years without man, when He specifically created man to be their overseer?

We are not permitted by the rules of reading to claim that "day" means millions of years, then to turn around and claim that God created man in one 24-hour day. Day either means 24 hours or it means millions of years. If it means millions of years, then God did not create man instantaneously on "day six," because "day six" is millions of years long. This scheme requires that we understand the creation of man to have taken a great period of time. There are scholars, however, who try to interpret "day" to mean "an age" while simultaneously telling us that God created Adam in one 24-hour day, thus reading the same word two different ways within the same context. These writers are either inept or dishonest.

The so-called "progressive creationist" invents his own brand of evolution, not endorsed by either modern science or the Bible, whereby he decides that evolution actually took place within various species—creating a wide variety of "cats," for example, including (presumably) great lions and tigers as well as my pet cat. I say "presumably" because these "theologians" are careful not to explain their theories in detail for the simple reason that they are so ludicrous. And once again, nothing is gained by such a compromise. If God is going to miraculously intervene at any point, then we may as well accept the miraculous interventions just as they are described in Genesis 1 and 2—that God created every existent species instantaneously on specific, literal 24-hour days, in the exact order that is described.

But what is more important in our discussion, and what we must address in this chapter, is that any evolution whatsoever will impinge on the person of Adam. As I've already said, nothing is gained if we suggest that God used evolution to create the lower orders, then miraculously intervened on "day

---

[2] Although these silly pretend-theologians also tell us that the order of days in creation is all mixed up. Each modern theologian invents whatever scheme is good in his own eyes.

6" (regardless how the arbitrary theologian chooses to describe "day") in the method described in Genesis 2 to create Adam and Eve. Such a reading is arbitrary because these theologians are flagrantly rejecting the literal reading of the first five days (and of the very word "day" itself), then arbitrarily deciding to read the creation of mankind literally—while *still* arbitrarily saying that it took a million years to *complete* day six! This is not merely arbitrary, it is downright dishonest and incompetent.

If God used evolution to create Adam, then we have no literal Adam. If He created Adam from dust, as literally stated in Genesis 2, then we must also read the rest of the creation account that way: literally. This includes creating Adam *and* the land animals on day six. Again, if we claim that animals evolved over the course of "age six," then we must also have mankind evolve. And if mankind evolved, then who was Adam?

Derek Kidner at least has the honesty to wrestle with the implications of these absurd misreadings. In his commentary on Genesis, Kidner embraces the gnostic claim that the word "day" means "a long period of time," then goes on to posit a theory on who or what Adam was.

> The answer may lie in our definition of man.[3]

> ... [T]he intelligent beings of a remote past... may yet have been decisively below the plane of life which was established in the creation of Adam. If, as the text of Genesis would by no means disallow, God initially shaped man by a process of evolution, it would follow that a considerable stock of near-humans preceded the first true man, and it would be arbitrary to picture these as mindless brutes. ...

> On this view, Adam, the first true man, will have had as contemporaries many creatures of comparable intelligence, widely distributed over the world. One might conjecture that these were destined to die out, like the Neanderthalers (if indeed these did), or to perish in the flood, leaving Adam's lineal descendants, through Noah, in sole possession. Against this, however, there must be borne

---

3 This brings to mind eerie echoes of Bill Clinton: "It depends what the meaning of 'is' is."

> in mind the apparent continuity of the main races of the present and those of the distant past, already mentioned, which seems to suggest either a stupendous antiquity for Adam . . . or the continued existence of 'pre-Adamites' alongside 'Adamites'.
>
> If this second alternative implied any doubt of the unity of mankind it would be of course quite untenable. God, as we have seen, has made all nations 'from one' (Acts 17:26). Genetically indeed, on this view, these two groups would be of a single stock; but by itself that would avail nothing, as Adam's fruitless search for a helpmeet makes abundantly clear. Yet it is at least conceivable that after the special creation of Eve, which established the first human pair as God's viceregents (Gn. 1:27, 28) and clinched the fact that there is no natural bridge from animal to man, God may have now conferred His image on Adam's collaterals, to bring them into the same realm of being. Adam's 'federal' headship of humanity extended, if that was the case, outwards to his contemporaries as well as onwards to his offspring, and his disobedience disinherited both alike.[4]

Poor Kidner twists himself into a theological pretzel trying to fit evolution into Adam's lineage. He nicely demonstrates the method of arbitrarily (he even uses that word!) reading one part of Genesis metaphorically and another part literally. He takes literally the account of Noah and the flood, as well as the creation of Eve from Adam's rib and Adam's "fruitless search for a helpmeet," while simultaneously insisting that the creation of Adam from dust is mere metaphor. He tries to work out the conundrum of who this Adam was, and how he fit together with those "lesser beings" from whom he evolved, and why God arbitrarily chose him to be His image-bearer while rejecting all of his forebears, and just what exactly became of those "lesser beings" who were his contemporaries, and just who is the father of the human race anyway, and so on and so forth.

---

4 Derek Kidner, *Genesis: An Introduction and Commentary*, 28–29.

This is probably why our contemporary gnostic commentators are careful not to spell out exactly how God used evolution to create mankind, knowing that any efforts to do so will merely show the world the absurdity of their gnostic views. Kidner has barely scratched the surface in dealing with some of the implications of mixing evolution (including "day/age" and other man-made theories) into the Genesis account of creation, so let us take a closer look ourselves at some of these implications. Doing so, I think, will make clear the absurdity of Christian Darwinism—more, it will demonstrate the tremendous danger to the church of permitting our leading theologians to continue churning out this heresy.

## Who Cares?

Why should we even care if Adam was a literal man or not? Does it really make a difference?

We first and foremost come back to the question which we have been asking all along: if chapter 1 of Genesis is metaphorical, at what point does the book *stop* being metaphorical? If we treat one portion of Genesis as metaphor rather than literal history, then we must treat the entire book as such. There is no point at which Moses changes his tone or approach to what he is writing, switching from a metaphorical "story" or "narrative" (to use two of our theologians' favorite, loaded words) into a historical account of literal human beings. So if we make Adam non-literal, then we must do the same for Noah, Abraham, Isaac, Jacob, Joseph, and everybody else in the book.

But this, as I have already said, is the least of our worries. Because if we don't have Adam, we don't have Christ.

## Jesus Christ, the Last Adam

We have already considered God's pronouncement of the curse on woman in Genesis 3:15, and we have seen that His comments concerning "the seed of the woman" are a Messianic prophecy, foreshadowing the work of Christ at Calvary. (See comments in chapter 3.) Some theologians, however, claim that this prophecy does not refer to any specific individual but rather to the offspring of Adam and Eve in general.[5] This is false.

The church has viewed "the seed of the woman" as a reference to Christ for most of the church age. Women, after all, don't have seed; only men

---

[5] E.g., Keil and Delitzsch, *Commentary on the Old Testament*

carry seed. The "seed of Adam" would have referred to Adam's offspring in general, but "the seed of the woman" is a direct reference to a very specific individual—to the only individual in human history who could claim to be born of "the seed" of a woman—that is, a virgin birth.

This prophecy also helps us to understand the importance of the virgin birth of Christ. Jesus, after all, is both fully God and fully man; He is born of a woman, but He has no earthly father. His human form—his flesh—was imparted by the woman (Mary), but His divinity—His divine nature or "Godhood"—could only be imparted by God Himself through the agency of the Holy Spirit. It was imperative that Christ not be born of the seed of man, because He would then have received the spiritual inheritance of Adam. This is a mystery, but evidently the Adamic sin nature is passed through the seed of man, while the fleshly, corporeal elements of our human bodies are imparted through the woman.

If Christ had inherited Adam's sin nature, then He would have been a sinner by default, just as all other humans are. This, of course, is the logical continuation of the doctrine of creation, that like begets like—that a fish brings forth a fish, not a semi-humanoid creature. A sinner can only bring forth a sinner; mankind is not evolving into godhood.

If Christ had inherited the sin nature, then He would have been subject to the curse—it would have been "appointed" for Him "to die once." If that were true, then He would have been ineligible to die for the sins of others, having His own debt to pay. But Christ was "without sin" (Heb. 4:15), which means that He was not under the curse, not doomed to die. Thus, He was able to die for *my* sins, since He had no debt to pay.

This is why we "must be born again," as Jesus told Nicodemus: "Unless one is born again, he cannot see the kingdom of God. . . . That which is born of the flesh is flesh, and that which is born of the Spirit is spirit" (John 3:3, 6). We are all born of the first Adam, inheriting the sin nature and the curse—but we can choose to be born again to the Last Adam, inheriting His sinless nature. We put to death the old Adam (symbolized in baptism) with his "corruptible seed" (1 Pet. 1:23) and take on that which is "incorruptible" through Christ as our Last Adam.

Let's look at a few passages in more detail to gain more insight into this concept.

## Matthew 4

> Then Jesus was led up by the Spirit into the wilderness to be tempted by the devil. And when He had fasted forty days and forty nights, afterward He was hungry. Now when the tempter came to Him, he said, "If You are the Son of God, command that these stones become bread." But He answered and said, "It is written, 'MAN SHALL NOT LIVE BY BREAD ALONE, BUT BY EVERY WORD THAT PROCEEDS FROM THE MOUTH OF GOD.'" Then the devil took Him up into the holy city, set Him on the pinnacle of the temple, and said to Him, "If You are the Son of God, throw Yourself down. For it is written: 'HE SHALL GIVE HIS ANGELS CHARGE OVER YOU,' AND, IN THEIR HANDS THEY SHALL BEAR YOU UP, LEST YOU DASH YOUR FOOT AGAINST A STONE.'" Jesus said to him, "It is written again, 'YOU SHALL NOT TEMPT THE LORD YOUR GOD.'" Again, the devil took Him up on an exceedingly high mountain, and showed Him all the kingdoms of the world and their glory. And he said to Him, "All these things I will give You if You will fall down and worship me." Then Jesus said to him, "Away with you, Satan! For it is written, 'YOU SHALL WORSHIP THE LORD YOUR GOD, AND HIM ONLY YOU SHALL SERVE.'" Then the devil left Him, and behold, angels came and ministered to Him.
> —Matthew 4:1–11

Adam was born into a perfect world where everything and everyone lived together in peaceful harmony. Jesus, on the other hand, was born into a fallen world where He was hated and resisted at every turn. Adam had an abundance of food and comfort, but Jesus had not eaten for 40 days. So right from the start we have Christ in a position that is far less favorable for obedience than the situation faced by Adam—yet Jesus faced similar temptation as both Adam and Eve and came through unscathed.

Notice Satan's words in verse 3: "If You are the Son of God." Satan begins his temptation of Jesus in the same way that he began tempting Eve: by casting doubt on God's words. Notice also that he *knows* God's word—and that he quotes it to his own advantage.[6]

Satan's main focus on his temptations of Christ is to question His deity, and he takes the same approach to his task that he took with Eve. He appeals to Jesus' flesh (v. 3)—"You're hungry? Well, if you really *are* God, prove it! Turn these stones into bread and satisfy your flesh." He tries to seduce Him into spiritual pride in verse 6: "No? You won't feed your flesh? Well then, mortify it completely! Show us that you are who you claim to be: throw yourself down and let your mighty angels catch you!" But the Lord meets these seductions by quoting Scripture, even as Eve attempted to quote what God had said concerning the forbidden fruit—except that Jesus quotes God correctly.

Finally, the devil appeals to the one thing that might have "frightened" Jesus: the pending separation from His Father. Satan says in verse 9, "Here, I'll give you the world—it can be yours again, if you really *are* the God who created it! And, what's even better, you won't have to die to get it! All you need to do is acknowledge me as the world's master, and I'll give it right back to you!" This is exactly where Adam fell, because he chose to make the devil his master and reject the headship of his Creator. Jesus recognizes the devil's lies for what they are: a rejection of the Creator as Lord of the universe. His response demonstrates exactly what Adam should have done, as He tells the devil to leave Him.

In this passage, then, we see Christ taking on the role of the first Adam, facing the same tests which Adam faced but passing them without sin.

## Romans 5

> Therefore, just as through one man sin entered the world, and death through sin, and thus death spread to all men, because all sinned (For until the law sin was in the world, but sin is not imputed when there is no law. Nevertheless death reigned from Adam to Moses, even over those who had not sinned according to the likeness of the transgression of Adam, who is a type of Him who was to come. But the

---

6 Satan chooses to read literally this Messianic passage from Psalm 91, while conveniently ignoring the very next verse: "You shall tread upon the lion and the cobra, the young lion and the serpent you shall trample underfoot" (Psalm 91:13).

free gift is not like the offense. For if by the one man's offense many died, much more the grace of God and the gift by the grace of the one Man, Jesus Christ, abounded to many. And the gift is not like that which came through the one who sinned. For the judgment which came from one offense resulted in condemnation, but the free gift which came from many offenses resulted in justification. For if by the one man's offense death reigned through the one, much more those who receive abundance of grace and of the gift of righteousness will reign in life through the One, Jesus Christ.) Therefore, as through one man's offense judgment came to all men, resulting in condemnation, even so through one Man's righteous act the free gift came to all men, resulting in justification of life. For as by one man's disobedience many were made sinners, so also by one Man's obedience many will be made righteous.
—Romans 5:12–19

In this passage, we begin to understand why the issue of headship, the issue of the created order, is so vitally important to our Christian faith. Paul tells us that Jesus came to fulfill everything that Adam was created to do (see 1 Corinthians 15:45 also); He came to stand in Adam's place as the head of the new creation.

Adam was created to be the head of the entire human race, and in that role he stood in our place as our figurehead. His disobedience in Genesis 3 was imparted to all mankind; his sin became *our* sin, because we are descended from him. Once we are born of Adam's lineage, Adam's heritage of sin and death becomes *our* heritage, and both sin and death are inescapable. But once we are born *again* into the Last Adam, we inherit Christ's heritage, a heritage of eternal life and righteousness. And this new heritage is as solid and immovable as that of the first Adam; once we are reborn into Christ, we can no more lose His heritage of salvation than we could have escaped death under the curse of the old Adam.

When we are born anew to the Last Adam, His obedience is imparted to us—it becomes *our* obedience, just as the first Adam's sin became our sin. Christ, like the old Adam, stands in as the figurehead for all believers. He is our Head, and He stands in our place before the throne of grace. Even as the old Adam was thrown out of paradise, and his children were prevented from ever returning to paradise—even so, the children of the Last Adam are permitted to enter the presence of God, and we can never again be separated from the love of the Father.

Paul also makes it clear that death did not exist in our world prior to Adam's sin. He states it unequivocally in verse 12: "through one man sin entered the world, and death through sin". He reiterates it in verse 14: "through one man sin entered the world, and death through sin". This implies that death did not reign prior to Adam's sin, which would include the animal kingdom.[7] The reason for this is that Adam was the titular head over all creation (excepting the angelic orders, of whose creation we know nothing), and his sin was imparted to all those orders of creation over which he had headship. This included his offspring, as we have seen, as well as the lower orders of creation for which he was designed to be the steward. Paul expands upon this theme in 1 Corinthians 15:21–22: "For since by man [Adam] came death, by Man [Christ] also came the resurrection of the dead. For as in Adam all die, even so in Christ all shall be made alive."

## Revelation 21–22

> Now I saw a new heaven and a new earth, for the first heaven and the first earth had passed away. Also there was no more sea. Then I, John, saw the holy city, New Jerusalem, coming down out of heaven from God, prepared as a bride adorned for her husband. And I heard a loud voice from heaven saying, "Behold, the tabernacle of God is with men, and He will dwell with them, and they shall be His people. God Himself will be with them and be their God. And God will wipe away every tear from their eyes; there shall be no more death, nor sorrow, nor crying. There shall be no more pain, for the former things have passed away." Then He who sat on the throne said, "Behold, I make all things

---

[7] James Boice [*Genesis: An Expositional Commentary*, vol. 1, 77] makes the case that the animal kingdom was subject to death prior to Adam's sin, in an attempt to argue that the animal world evolved while mankind did not. Besides the gross offense to common sense of such an absurd position, these verses make it clear that Adam's sin affected all the created orders over which he had headship—including his offspring *and* the lower orders of creation.

new." And He said to me, "Write, for these words are true and faithful." And He said to me, "It is done! I am the Alpha and the Omega, the Beginning and the End. I will give of the fountain of the water of life freely to him who thirsts. He who overcomes shall inherit all things, and I will be his God and he shall be My son. . . . But I saw no temple in it, for the Lord God Almighty and the Lamb are its temple. The city had no need of the sun or of the moon to shine in it, for the glory of God illuminated it. The Lamb is its light. And the nations of those who are saved shall walk in its light, and the kings of the earth bring their glory and honor into it. Its gates shall not be shut at all by day (there shall be no night there). And they shall bring the glory and the honor of the nations into it. But there shall by no means enter it anything that defiles, or causes an abomination or a lie, but only those who are written in the Lamb's Book of Life. And he showed me a pure river of water of life, clear as crystal, proceeding from the throne of God and of the Lamb. In the middle of its street, and on either side of the river, was the tree of life, which bore twelve fruits, each tree yielding its fruit every month. The leaves of the tree were for the healing of the nations. And there shall be no more curse, but the throne of God and of the Lamb shall be in it, and His servants shall serve Him. They shall see His face, and His name shall be on their foreheads. There shall be no night there: They need no lamp nor light of the sun, for the Lord God gives them light. And they shall reign forever and ever.

—Revelation 21:1–7, 22–27; 22:1–5

Finally, John takes us ahead for a glimpse at the restoration of Paradise, to the New Jerusalem where Christ the Last Adam shall stand in headship over all His offspring. Adam's bride was taken from his side, as we learn in Genesis 2, and the Bride of Christ (the church) has similarly been taken from His side—the side that was opened by the centurion's spear, flowing forth the life-giving blood and water of Christ. Eve was brought before her husband in Genesis 2, and in the same manner the Bride of Christ shall be brought before the Last Adam (21:2). Conversely, God brought Himself before Adam in the Garden of Eden, as we saw in Genesis 2 and 3, and He will do so again forever in the New Jerusalem as He comes among His children and dwells with us forever. This time, however, we shall never again be driven out of His presence, for the Last Adam has completed God's will once and for all.

Never again shall the tempter enter Paradise (21:27). Nor shall God's children ever again face temptation or testing, as there is no longer a Tree of the Knowledge of Good and Evil in Paradise. Evil no longer exists there, so how could we be tempted to know it? What does exist in Paradise is Life— "life more abundant and free!" Notice that the Tree of Life *does* exist in the New Jerusalem, and it is 36 times more fruitful than it was in Eden. There are not one but three Trees of Life there, and each one produces fruit 12 times a year. What's more, these Trees of Life grow, not in the center of the garden as they did in Eden, but beside a River of Life. God is, without question, the God of Life, not the God of death, and His generosity is super-abundant to all His children.

## Resurrection of Christ

> Jesus answered and said to them, "You are mistaken, not knowing the Scriptures nor the power of God. For in the resurrection they neither marry nor are given in marriage, but are like angels of God in heaven. But concerning the resurrection of the dead, have you not read what was spoken to you by God, saying, 'I AM THE GOD OF ABRAHAM, THE GOD OF ISAAC, AND THE GOD OF JACOB'? God is not the God of the dead, but of the living."
> —Matthew 22:29–32

> Jesus said to her, "I am the resurrection and the life. He who believes in Me, though he may die, he shall live. And whoever lives and believes in Me shall never die. Do you believe this?"
> —John 11:25–26

Paul, a bondservant of Jesus Christ, called to be an apostle, separated to the gospel of God which He promised before through His prophets in the Holy Scriptures, concerning His Son Jesus Christ our Lord, who was born of the seed of David according to the flesh, and declared to be the Son of God with power according to the Spirit of holiness, by the resurrection from the dead.
—Romans 1:1–4

Or do you not know that as many of us as were baptized into Christ Jesus were baptized into His death? Therefore we were buried with Him through baptism into death, that just as Christ was raised from the dead by the glory of the Father, even so we also should walk in newness of life. For if we have been united together in the likeness of His death, certainly we also shall be in the likeness of His resurrection, knowing this, that our old man was crucified with Him, that the body of sin might be done away with, that we should no longer be slaves of sin. For he who has died has been freed from sin. Now if we died with Christ, we believe that we shall also live with Him, knowing that Christ, having been raised from the dead, dies no more. Death no longer has dominion over Him.
—Romans 6:3–9

Now if Christ is preached that He has been raised from the dead, how do some among you say that there is no resurrection of the dead? But if there is no resurrection of the dead, then Christ is not risen. And if Christ is not risen, then our preaching is empty and your faith is also empty. Yes, and we are found false witnesses of God, because we have testified of God that He raised up Christ, whom He did not raise up—if in fact the dead do not rise. For if the dead do not rise, then Christ is not risen. And if Christ is not risen, your faith is futile; you are still in your sins! Then also those who have

> fallen asleep in Christ have perished. If in this life only we have hope in Christ, we are of all men the most pitiable. But now Christ is risen from the dead, and has become the firstfruits of those who have fallen asleep. For since by man came death, by Man also came the resurrection of the dead. For as in Adam all die, even so in Christ all shall be made alive.
> —1 Corinthians 15:12–22

The resurrection of Christ from the dead is the central tenet of the Christian faith. Paul explains in Romans 1 that Jesus is fully man, "born of the seed of David according to the flesh," inheriting His human flesh through the humanity of Mary; and fully God, "according to the Spirit," inheriting His deity by virtue of being born of God rather than of a human father. I have already explained why it was necessary that Christ not be born of the seed of Adam: Adam's seed automatically inherit the sin nature, the curse, the bondage to death.

Christ, according to Paul, has proven His deity by rising again from the dead. As God, He has defeated death once and for all. This death, we are told throughout Scripture, came upon mankind—came upon all of creation—through the sin of Adam. If Adam did not exist as a unique man, instantly created from dust as described in Genesis 2, then his sin is also non-existent, and man's bondage to death cannot be broken. There is, in other words, no possibility of resurrection from the dead.

Christians understand that we are baptized into Jesus' death *and* into His resurrection. It is upon this teaching that we base all our hopes of eternal life. If we remove Adam from the equation, however, we also remove our only hope of eternal life through the resurrection of Jesus Christ. "For if we have been united together in the likeness of His death, certainly we also shall be in the likeness of His resurrection" (Rom. 6:5).

If we teach that God took millions of years to create mankind, then we are forced to believe that mankind evolved, forced to recognize that there was no Adam, and forced to remove all hope of Christ's resurrection. "We are of all men the most pitiable.... For since by man came death, by Man also came the resurrection of the dead. For as in Adam all die, even so in Christ all shall be made alive" (1 Cor. 15:19, 21, 22).

If creation took longer than six days, then death existed prior to the creation of man—*de facto*. If there was death, then mankind evolved from the lower orders—*de facto*.⁸ If mankind evolved, then we have no Adam. If we have no Adam, then we have no resurrection, and Jesus Christ never rose from the dead. In short, any who claim that creation took longer than six days are, by default, claiming that Jesus Christ has not risen from the dead, and those who believe that lie are, of all men, most to be pitied.

This is an inexorable chain of logic. If you start with the first point, that creation took longer than six days, then you are forced by the flow of logic to reach the conclusion that Jesus Christ did not rise from the dead. You cannot start with the first point—claiming that creation took longer than six days—without finding yourself (if you are honest enough to follow the logic through) driven inexorably to this conclusion. You cannot come in on one of the middle points of this chain of logic—claiming that God used a mixture of evolution and miraculous creation, for example—without being driven back to the first point that creation took longer than six days, and without being driven just as inexorably by the chain of logic to the final conclusion that Jesus Christ is not risen from the dead. It is one unbreakable chain of logic.

If God used evolution to create any element of creation, even different types of cats, then death was present prior to the creation of mankind, death being necessary for evolution to work. And if death was present before mankind, then Genesis 3 cannot be taken literally; it becomes some kind of allegory on the origins of sin. But what's worse than that, Genesis chapters 2 and 3 are *completely wrong*, because they claim that sin is the root cause of death, whereas death (according to Christian Darwinists) existed prior to sin.

Sin requires the ability to choose between right and wrong, because sin is the deliberate choice of wrong and the repudiation of right. An amoeba, and probably even a fish, is not capable of such thought processes; there is no "right" and "wrong" for an amoeba; an amoeba does what it was created to do, it does not make moral choices. Therefore an amoeba is incapable of sin—yet amoebas were subject to death, according to evolution, because death was required to be present if the amoeba was to evolve into a higher order. So therefore we must conclude that sin is not the root cause of death, and Genesis 3 is wrong, according to the Christian Darwinist's scheme.

---

8 I have already shown numerous times that we accomplish nothing whatsoever by claiming that God used evolution to create the lower orders, then intervened with a miraculous creation of Adam from dust. Nor can we claim that He created each level of life miraculously, then made them sit around for a million years waiting for the *next* miraculous creation. It is one or the other: six-day instantaneous creation by God's word alone, or else death and evolution. No middle ground exists.

And things get worse still as we follow the logic of Christian Darwinism to its unavoidable conclusion. If sin is not the root cause of death, then Jesus' death on the cross accomplished nothing for me. According to this heresy, Jesus' payment for my sins does not give me victory over death, because sin is not the root cause of death. Furthermore, Jesus' sinless life also accomplished nothing for Him if sin is not the root cause of death; He would also have been subject to death despite His sinless state. He would have died anyway, because living a sinless life did not give Him freedom from death—if sin is not the root cause of death. So Christian Darwinism leads inevitably to this conclusion: Jesus was subject to death, and would have died anyway, and His resurrection (if it happened at all) was meaningless.

Or perhaps a Christian Darwinist would suggest that Jesus was a more highly evolved form of mankind who had evolved beyond the need for death—He had reached godhood and was no longer subject to death because He had evolved out of death. In which case, of course, He could not have been put to death in the first place, because He had evolved outside of death's reign and was not able to put Himself back under the reign of death out of which He had evolved any more than a man can put himself back under the domain of water out of which *he* allegedly evolved.

Christian Darwinism under any name is a heresy. Admitting any of its claims at any stage of creation will lead inexorably and unavoidably to these absurd and heretical conclusions.

## Taking Away the Key of Knowledge

These doctrines of the Adamic sin nature and of Christ's role as the Last Adam are obviously central to our beliefs as Christians. But it is absolutely imperative that we recognize this: that the New Testament treats Adam as a literal man whose literal sin brought death to the whole world, and if we pretend that there was no literal Adam we lose the entire reason behind our need for salvation.

The teachings of evolution rob us of the literal Adam who was the literal father of the entire human race, they rob us of any meaning behind "original sin," rob us of the inherited sin nature, and finally rob us of the only Person who can ever bring redemption to mankind. Christians who try to adulterate the Bible with any element of evolution are actually robbing mankind of any hope for eternal life. Woe to these men!

# Section 2:
# Rewriting the Bible

# 7
# REWRITING GENESIS 1

It is time now to turn our attention more fully to the works of modern Bible commentators, focusing on those books which interpret Genesis. There are many commentaries available on Genesis, but I will look closely at those which are the most popular and influential works. These range from the "scholarly" works of theologians such as Gordon J. Wenham to the more "popular" commentaries of writers such as James Montgomery Boice. The vast majority of these works have been colored by Gnosticism, which I will address in more depth in Section 3, and most attempt to incorporate some element of evolution into the teachings of Genesis.

In the following chapters, I will not go verse by verse through the chapters of Genesis, as I did in Section 1, but will focus instead upon some of the major points of error which are espoused by modern commentators. Some of these commentaries, such as that by Gordon Wenham, are so full of error that it would require a whole book to address them all. Therefore, I will attempt to address some of the more glaring examples which impinge most closely upon the heresy of Christian Darwinism. I will not attempt to debunk the J-E-P fairy tale[1] here, since it is so patently absurd as not to warrant careful attention. In fact, the J-E-P nonsense is already coming into a long-overdue disrepute even amongst modern gnostic commentators; we will leave it to them to hash out the heretical aspects of their German "higher critic" fathers.

## Chaos and Wind

**2. *Without form and void.*** The phrase translated "without form and void" in Genesis 1 is a translation of the Hebrew phrase *tohu wabohu*. This is an unusual Hebrew expression, the two words appearing together only

---

[1] In a nutshell, there is a widespread school of commentary which claims that Genesis (and the entire Pentateuch) was not written by a single author, but rather was compiled and edited and added to by a series of "redactors" over a period of centuries. These mythical persons are labeled as "the Jahwist" (J), "the Elohist" (E), and "the Priestly group" (P) based upon fictional distinctions which the "higher critics" pretend to find in the subtle Hebrew wording of Genesis. The fairy tale was the invention of certain Germans who called themselves "higher critics" during the mid-1800s.

three times in the Old Testament.[2] The first word, *tohu*, means "formlessness, confusion, unreality, emptiness," with the major senses being "formlessness" and "emptiness."[3] The second word means "emptiness,[4] void."[5]

The sense of the two words together provides a double emphasis, literally "empty void" or "barren emptiness." This is actually an example of a literary device known as *hendiadys*, a phrase in which a single idea is expressed by two words, often connected with "and." "It is nice and warm today" is a hendiadys expressing the idea that the weather is exceptionally temperate. A hendiadys frequently also uses two words which express the same concept, making the meaning more emphatic by virtue of repetition. "It is freezing cold today" uses the duplication of ideas to underscore that the weather is exceptionally cold.

In this Hebrew phrase, it is easy to see that the two words work together to underscore a concept, and the fact that the two words have similar meanings ought to make that concept quite apparent. Both words carry the sense of "emptiness" or "formlessness," so it stands to reason that the phrase is doubly emphasizing the concept of emptiness. This, of course, is the reason that virtually all modern Bible translations render this as "formless and empty" or some similar permutation. But clear reasoning is not a requirement for modern Bible commentators. These theologians insist that the true meaning, the "hidden meaning" which only the highly educated and initiated can discern, is "chaos."

The word *tohu* by itself is used 20 times in the Old Testament.[6] Modern Bible translations render it as "confusion" three times, all in Isaiah.[7] Deuteronomy 32:10 is translated as "waste howling wilderness" in most translations, which is the one time which conveys the sense of "chaos." All other 16 uses of the word, including in Isaiah, are translated to mean either "empty" or "unmolded."[8] The word *bohu* or *wabohu* appears three times in the Old Testament[9], translated as "emptiness" or "void" in all three.

---

2  Gen. 1:2; Is. 34:11; Jer. 4:23.

3  BDBG, 1062.

4  BDBG, 96.

5  James Strong, *Dictionaries of the Hebrew and Greek Words*.

6  Gen. 1:2; Deut. 32:10; 1 Sam. 12:21; Job 6:18; 12:24; 26:7; Ps. 107:40; Is. 24:10; 29:21; 34:11; 40:17, 23; 41:29; 44:9; 45:18–19; 49:4; 59:4; Jer. 4:23.

7  Is. 24:10; 34:11; 41:29.

8  The New King James Version translates *tohu* in the remaining passages as follows: empty; nothing; nowhere; empty space; without form; wilderness; empty words; worthless; useless; in vain; for nothing.

9  Genesis 1:3; Isaiah 34:11; Jeremiah 4:23

## SECTION 2: REWRITING THE BIBLE

Yet modern commentators persist in claiming that the two words placed together take on the new meaning of "chaos," despite the overwhelming Biblical usage to the contrary, despite the fact that all modern translations (produced by teams of highly educated linguists) render the phrase as "formless and empty." They justify this by choosing the least likely translation of *one* of the words in the phrase (*tohu* as "confusion") which is used with the least frequency both in the Old Testament and in other ancient literature. They insist upon this unlikely rendering because they have a large case to construct: the case that Genesis actually *teaches* evolution.

They use circular logic to support this mistranslation. Ancient pagan myths, such as the *Enuma Elish*,[10] teach that creation came about as the result of chaos, the gods fighting against one another or against chaos itself. These modern commentators claim that the "editors" and "redactors" who allegedly wrote Genesis took their ideas from pagan myths, cleaning them up to be palatable to the Jews. Therefore, our commentators argue, since pagan myths taught the concept of chaos, we must conclude that the phrase *tohu wabohu* means "chaos." Then they turn around and say that, since the word "chaos" appears in the Genesis account of creation, we must conclude that the "editors" and "redactors" used pagan myths as their source material. Once again, we have a dizzying Escher-like description where one hand is drawing another hand which is drawing the first hand.

Chaos is demonic, an element of hell or Pandemonium, as Milton so beautifully pictures in *Paradise Lost*. What modern commentators have actually demonstrated is that the *Enuma Elish* and other pagan myths are

---

10 The *Enuma Elish* is a Babylonian poem which praises one of the Babylonian gods (see Appendix 1). It exists on cuneiform tablets which were written somewhere between 750 and 200 BC, and nobody can say for certain just when the poem itself was first composed. Gnostic scholars, in standard fashion, assume whatever is most threatening to the Bible, and claim that the myth was in great circulation prior to the writing of Genesis—even though Genesis was written 1,000 years earlier! (This is comparable to claiming that Augustine was influenced by *Huckleberry Finn*.) They accomplish this claim in part by insisting that Genesis itself was written after the time of David, which is one of the reasons that the J-E-P fairy tale is so vitally important to these charlatans. The *Enuma Elish* has long been exalted as the actual source for the "Genesis narrative" of creation, but this fiction is also coming to be discredited. The story that it tells bears virtually no resemblance whatsoever to Genesis, containing such fascinating insights as the god Marduk killing a goddess, cutting her body in half, and stretching it above the earth to serve as the sky. One reason that the modern gnostics continue to insist that this blasphemy is the source of Genesis is that they are bent upon proving that "chaos" existed prior to creation—and chaos is the foundation of evolution.

merely cloaked demon worship, while Genesis gives us an account which is radically different. God is not pictured in Genesis as struggling with anything whatsoever; on the contrary, the entire creation process is effortless: God merely speaks and it becomes so. There is an aura of peace and gentleness which pervades the entire creation—the peace and gentleness which are of God—as opposed to the struggle and rage and chaos purported by the pagans. Chaos is of the devil, while God is the God of order.

Furthermore, this whole system of false interpretation focuses on one minor meaning of *tohu*, ignoring the more common meanings, *and* it completely ignores the meaning of the second word in the phrase, *bohu*. This word appears three times in the Old Testament, and in all three cases it appears together with *tohu*.[11] The meaning of the word is usually "emptiness" or "void," and is translated as such in all three uses. Now, a less-common meaning of *bohu* is "waste," so one might try to make the case that the phrase means "place of chaos and waste." Isaiah 34:11 speaks of the day of God's vengeance, when He shall lay waste to the earth in His wrath. If ever there was a place for *bohu* to mean "wasteland," this is it. Yet in verse 10, Isaiah uses the more common Hebrew word for "waste" (*charab*), while in verse 11 *bohu* is rendered as "emptiness" in nearly all modern translations.[12]

The fact is that the phrase *tohu wabohu* does not include any suggestion of chaos or conflict. It means exactly what it has always been translated to say: that the earth was without form and empty. But once again, modern "higher critics" have elected to ignore common usage of the phrase (if one can call it "common" of an uncommon phrase), the essentially unanimous opinion of vast bodies of translators, and the usage within the Old Testament itself—to ignore this in favor of arbitrarily insisting upon the most obscure and least-common usages.

Logic, furthermore, compels us to understand this phrase just as it has always been translated, to mean "without form and void." A void is an empty space, and an empty space cannot contain chaos. Chaos is brought about by a struggle between two or more entities. It can mean a conscious conflict between two intelligent beings, or simply a conflict of inanimate forces, such as powerful winds and surging waves. Something that is empty, however,

---

11 Gen. 1:2; Is. 34:11; Jer. 4:23

12 NIV translates it as "desolation," Holman Christian Standard has "destruction and chaos." New King James, ASV, RSV, NAB, NASB, ESV, and other modern translations all render *bohu* as "emptiness" in this verse.

## Section 2: Rewriting the Bible

cannot contain chaos or struggle simply because it is empty—there are no entities present to *have* a struggle.

Now, we do know that the earth was not entirely empty; it was covered with water. Furthermore, there is an intelligent force "hovering over the face of the waters"—the Holy Spirit. (Ironically, our modern theologians attempt to mistranslate this as well, as we shall see in a moment.) So, if there *were* any element of chaos present, it would have been simply the wind of the Spirit stirring up the waters which covered the earth. Yet even then, "chaos" would suggest that the winds were howling, the seas raging, thunder and lightning—a hostile and deadly environment. Genesis 1, however, emphasizes the gentleness of God's creative work, as I have tried to demonstrate in Section 1. The Spirit of the Lord is shown as hovering gently; the word picture which Moses uses of the creation implies a potter gently massaging his lump of clay. Even the gnostic commentators acknowledge this![13]

This Hebrew phrase, *tohu wabohu*, indicates that the creation material was ready to be molded, but was as yet unshaped. Even the phrase "face of the waters" suggests gentleness and placidity. This is a literal transliteration of the Hebrew words. If the seas had been raging, Moses would more likely have told us that "darkness ruled over the tempestuous waters" or something to that effect.

The word "face" is an important word in Genesis, used frequently in reference to the presence of God and the inner workings of the hearts of men. For example, Adam will hide himself from the "face of the Lord"[14] after he sins. Cain will remove himself from the face of the Lord after he murders his brother.[15] The wickedness of mankind will "come before the face of God" during Noah's day.[16] The sense of "face of the waters" implies the open countenance of the earth during its early stages of creation, a time when all creation was working in harmony with God.

Simple logic also dictates a gentle approach to creation. Moses pictures God as the Great Potter, hovering above His unshaped lump of clay, but a

---

13 E.g., Hamilton, *The Book of Genesis*, 114; R. Kent Hughes, *Genesis: Beginning and Blessing*, 21–22; Kenneth A. Mathews, *The New American Commentary: Genesis 1–11:26*, 136; Waltke, *Genesis*, 60.

14 Gen. 3:8. The Hebrew word in this verse is usually translated "presence," but is the same word translated "face" in Gen. 1:2.

15 Gen. 4:16. See above comment.

16 Gen. 6:11 uses the same word "face": "the earth also was corrupt *before* God," suggesting that man's wickedness was "in God's face."

potter does not wantonly sling his clay about the room when he is making something. A woodworker might use tools that cut or tear, but his overall approach to his creation is one of tender care.

Chaos is actually the one thing which is *lacking* during the creation week. God blesses His creation. He sets things in order, dividing and separating and establishing boundaries. His tender love is abundantly evident in Genesis 1 through 3—even after man sins against Him. Chaos is the opposite of all these elements.

In fact, the chaos theory implies that earth pre-existed, that there was a chaotic globe existing along with God, and He put His hand to it and brought order out of the chaos. This is pagan heresy, yet it is actually the unspoken assumption of many modern Bible commentators!

Why does this matter? Because "chaos" requires conflicting forces; if there are not at least two forces struggling together, there cannot be chaos. To insist that there was chaos prior to creation is to insist that there were forces struggling against God prior to creation, and this is actually the very element of "duality" upon which Gnosticism is founded.[17]

If we force this phrase to mean "chaos" here, we leave ourselves only two options: create hurricane conditions around the unformed planet, or introduce Satan into the creation scheme. The simple reason is that one cannot have chaos without at least two forces in competition, as I have already stated. The early Gnostics, as we shall see in Chapter 9, inserted chaos into Genesis because they also intended to insert Lucifer as co-creator of mankind, but this is not an option for Christians—God alone is the Creator, and there was no other entity involved in any way, either positively or negatively, actively or passively (apart from the created material itself, when the Lord commands the earth to bring forth living creatures).

This then forces us to assert that there was conflict between wind and wave, creating a chaotic, destructive storm. Some modern commentators have attempted to make this conflict plausible in Genesis by removing the Spirit of God from creation and replacing Him with Mighty Wind or Wind of God, deliberately revising Genesis 1:2 to read "the Wind of God hovered

---

17 One might argue that the fall of Lucifer demonstrated the presence of two conflicting forces prior to the creation of the earth, but the creation account of Genesis is eloquent in its silence concerning any creative force apart from God. Indeed, Gnosticism is founded upon the heresy that Lucifer participated in the creation of mankind, as we will see in Section 3. By changing "formless and empty" into "chaos," modern gnostics are laying the foundation for introducing that heresy into Christianity.

over the waters."[18] But even if Mighty Wind is "hovering" above the waters instead of the Spirit of God (and would one really refer to a hurricane wind as "hovering"?), we are still prevented from wreaking chaos here by the context of Genesis 1. Whatever is "hovering" over the water—Spirit or Wind—is doing so *gently*. Further, there is no sense of resistance or conflict anywhere during the creation week; all elements of creation are in perfect harmony, fully cooperative with God's hand and will, even going beyond cooperation to "bring forth" fish and birds and plant life. Beginning this week of cooperative harmony with a catastrophic hurricane is both illogical and out of context.

And adding a hurricane to Day One also accomplishes nothing, since Pharaoh's magicians do not have any storms or other natural phenomena in mind when they read "chaos" into the Hebrew here—if, in fact, they have anything in mind at all. For some of the "scholars," sad to say, seem to be merely mimicking Gordon Wenham or Gerhard von Rad or some other gnostic mentor without stopping to assess for themselves whether the points are true. The original "higher critics," however, did have an agenda in their "chaos theories," and that agenda was to imbue the creation account with dualistic theologies—i.e., gnosticism.

I will take this matter deeper in Chapter 9, but for now I will point out that "chaos" is an important concept in the ancient Gnostics' accounts of creation. Chaos or the Abyss is the abode of the "highest deity" in the Gnostic theology—the Fallen One, the Thrown-Down One, the god of light (Lucifer means "Light Bearer")—and this Gnostic god is above and beyond Jehovah. Jehovah (going by a different name) is still the creator in the ancient Gnostic system, but his creation takes place amidst chaos in ancient Gnostic literature. This ancient Gnostic mindset, this modern gnostic approach to Scripture, is the foundation upon which our "higher critics" have built their house of cards; the tricks of the ancient Gnostics are the same ones used today by Pharaoh's magicians.

***The Spirit of God.*** As I mentioned in Section 1, the Hebrew word which is translated "Spirit" (*ruach*) can also mean "breath" or "wind." The Hebrew phrase in Gen. 1:2, translated "Spirit of God," is *ruach Elohim*. The word *Elohim* is actually the name of God,[19] and the phrase literally means "the

---

18 Wenham, *Genesis 1–15*, 2; cf. Mathews, *Genesis 1–11:26*, 135–44. Some commentators translate *Elohim*, meaning God, to mean "mighty" or "extremely powerful," thus rendering the Spirit of God as "Mighty Wind."

19 It is written as "God" in most translations, as opposed to "Lord God," which indicates the name *Jehovah Elohim*.

Spirit of the Lord" or "the wind of the Lord" or "the breath of the Lord." Some modern commentators try to remove God's name from this phrase, claiming that it should be translated "a mighty wind," using the name *Elohim* to suggest power and might. This absurdity was endorsed widely for a time, but has since fallen into the disrepute which it deserves. The Old Testament *never* uses God's name to mean "something really strong"—even Gordon Wenham, one of the most highly regarded of modern "higher critics," does not dare to go this far in his translation.[20]

This word *ruach* does sometimes mean "wind" or "breath." For example, God walks in the garden in the "cool" of the day (Gen. 3:8, literally "the *ruach* of the day," the breeze of the day), and the Lord sends a wind to bring plagues in Egypt (Ex. 10:13, 19) and to open the Red Sea (Ex. 14:21). Moses tells us that God sent the "blast" of His "nostrils" to part the Red Sea (Ex. 15:8). Each of these examples uses the same word *ruach* to indicate "wind" or "breath," and their respective contexts supports that translation. Even so, one would not go far wrong to translate *ruach* to mean "spirit" even in these passages; for example, "You blew with Your *Spirit*, the sea covered them; they sank like lead in the mighty waters" (Ex. 15:10). But never does *ruach* appear together with God's name *Elohim* without the sense demanding that *ruach* mean "Spirit."

What difference does this make? Apart from the circularity of reasoning which our "higher critics" exercise ("We know that *tohu* means 'chaos' because *ruach* means 'wind,' and we know that *ruach* means 'wind' because *tohu* means 'chaos'!"), there is a more vital, more sinister motive behind these mistranslations. The so-called "higher critics" grew out of a flock of German theologians in the 1800s who rejected the existence of miracles. These theologians set about disproving all that is miraculous in the Bible, the most important element being the concept of divine inspiration, and they

---

20 Wenham translates Gen. 1:2 this way: "Now the earth was total chaos, and darkness covered the deep and the Wind of God hovered over the waters" [*Genesis 1–15*, 2]. As an example of the way in which these commentators use circular reasoning, Wenham explains (17) that translating *tohu* ("without form") as "chaos" demands that we also translate *ruach* ("Spirit") to mean "wind." As I have already demonstrated, there is no justification for translating *tohu* as "chaos," but Wenham does so anyway—then turns around and uses that mistranslation to justify *another* mistranslation. This demonstrates why we simply cannot allow modern theologians to take one false step, lest they use that false step to justify running completely into Gnostic heresy.

Incidentally, it is worth noting that the Jehovah's Witnesses translate Genesis 1:2 nearly the same way, rendering *ruach* as "God's active force."

rejected wholesale the possibility that the books of the Bible were written through men by the Holy Spirit.

Not all modern theologians have embraced the heresies of these men, but many have. Even those who reject the J-E-P fairy tale[21] still have been poisoned with the insidious subterfuges of the gnostics, while others have embraced the foundational heresies, including the rejection of the Bible as the inspired, inerrant Word of God. For these theologians, it is essential to reject any element which suggests that Genesis was written by God Himself through the pen of Moses.

Having the Spirit of God involved in the creation week makes it impossible to reject divine inspiration, because it impinges on many other elements in Genesis which point in that direction, as we shall see as we go along. For example, when God refers to Himself as "us," the gnostics are adamant that He cannot be referring to Himself in the plural, because the "authors" of Genesis could not have been aware of God's triune nature. But if those alleged "authors" were not aware of that doctrinal truth, then it becomes very inconvenient to modern gnostics to have the Holy Spirit hovering about (since it demonstrates that God is the true author of Genesis), so they work backward to verse 2 and insist that it isn't the Spirit of God but merely a strong wind.

It is for this reason that I am harping upon what is generally viewed as a small difference of opinion. Most theologians treat these translational tricks as insignificant degrees of pedantry, as though two scholars disagreed over some small nuance of meaning. But it is upon these false premises that an entire heresy has been constructed, and it is essential that we reject every sleight of hand trick which has been played by the "higher critics," by these Magicians of Pharaoh who pull theological rabbits out of their seminary mortarboards.

## Night and Day

**3. *There was light*.** There is much that we are not told about the creation of our cosmos. We are not told, for example, when the earth began rotating on its axis, nor when it began revolving in its orbit. Was the earth already orbiting empty space prior to day four, when God created the sun? This seems likely from the text, as the earth presumably needed to be revolving

---

21 See Note 1 above.

on its axis by day one in order to produce "evening and morning." (The light of the first day was provided by the Spirit of God, presumably, as He hovered above the waters.) If this was the case, then the earth was orbiting in empty space without its moon. Day four saw the sudden brilliance of the sun beaming down upon earth plus the sudden appearance of the moon, instantly beginning its own orbit about earth. Evidently, day four also introduced the other planets which share our solar system, each instantly taking its place in the heliocentric rotation.

It will sound outlandish to 21st Century westerners to suggest, but it must be said: science might one day discover that all our assumptions are incorrect concerning the planets and their rotations and so forth. Who can say? We have just recently decided that Pluto is not really a planet.[22] Science believed for millennia that the sun orbited the earth; might we not one day meet another Galileo who proves that planets do not orbit as we presently think they do? A new Einstein may come forward with some dramatic new theories which force us to completely revise our currently held assumptions. The next genius may discover that light travels at varying speeds or that the universe is not as big as we presently believe. Science is merely the aggregate of man's learning, and man makes mistakes. It is a false and deadly presumption to assume that science is infallible.

The important thing to understand from verse 3 is that God called forth the *entity* of light on day one; He did not (as far as we are told) create a *source* for light. But modern commentators refuse to recognize this concept, insisting that there cannot be light without a material source, such as the sun. Thus, Ronald Youngblood treats the creation of light as a metaphor of "the spiritual light that illumines [sic] the hearts of believers in Christ."[23] Bruce Waltke tells his readers that the text is not actually chronological (a widespread lie that we shall deal with in more detail later), and that "the narrator" is putting this statement early in the creation account so that we can learn that "God is the *ultimate* source of light," and also because "the narrator" is actually trying to disprove pagan myths (another falsehood to be dealt with later).[24] James Boice goes so far as to claim, "It is not said that these [sun, moon, stars] were created on the fourth day; they were created in the initial creative work of

---

22 Interestingly, Pluto is named for the pagan god of Hades or Hell—a fitting planet to have fallen from grace.
23 Ronald Youngblood, *The Book of Genesis: An Introductory Commentary*, 27.
24 Waltke, *Genesis*, 61.

## Section 2: Rewriting the Bible

God referred to in Genesis 1:1."[25] I don't know what Bible Boice is reading; here's what mine says of day four: "Then God made two great lights: the greater light to rule the day, and the lesser light to rule the night. He made the stars also. . . . So the evening and the morning were the fourth day" (v. 16, 19).

Of course, I have already suggested that there may well have been a source for the light: God Himself, as His Spirit hovered above the waters. But one of the tricks that is commonly played by modern commentators is to pretend that the only light which can shine upon earth is light from the sun or the stars. This is an absurdly childish stance to take, pretending that the sun is the world's only source of light, and it is likely that the commentators themselves don't really hold such naive ideas. They insist upon it here solely because they wish to introduce "problems" and "mysteries" and "difficulties" into the text of Genesis in order to bewilder the average reader, leading us to believe that we cannot understand the *real* meaning of the creation account without their "higher knowledge" elucidating it for us.

**5. *The evening and the morning were the first day.*** Having been allowed to claim that there cannot really be any light shining on earth prior to the sun's appearance, our gnostics go on to point out that we cannot hope to have a "morning" and "evening" without the sun to define it for us. They tell us that we cannot have "day" without having "daylight"—by which they mean sunlight. They essentially claim that we cannot even have a 24-hour period of time without the sun to measure it by! They pretend to think that the sun *creates* time, as though time itself would come to a standstill if their watch stopped ticking. The sun is used to measure time, not to create it or even to define it. Twenty-four hours would still be 1,440 minutes and 86,400 seconds long whether the sun existed or not.

I have already addressed this ridiculous quibble in Chapter 1, pointing out that any source of light hovering above the earth would produce the phenomenon of "morning" and "evening" as the earth rotated. This, in fact, lends further credence to the suggestion that the Spirit of God unveiled His light upon the unformed earth on day one, producing a morning and an evening as the watery globe rotated upon its axis.

But the modern gnostics argue over "morning" and "evening" and "day" because they have a bigger agenda in mind. It is their goal to adulterate

---

[25] James Montgomery Boice, *Genesis, vol. 1*, 75.

God's word with the false teachings of evolution, and they are desperate to devise some method of forcing Genesis—even against its will—to embrace Darwin. One recent method of this traduction has been to claim that a day is not really a day, that the word translated "day" does not mean a 24-hour period of time but rather a great age, a millennium. This has been called the "day/age theory."

This is the foundation of Christian Darwinism—at the present moment, anyway. (The Christian Darwinists are constantly shifting ground, inventing new absurdities the moment the last one has fallen into mockery.[26]) Evolution requires billions of years to accomplish the impossible, and having God create the world in six days simply will not permit fish to become humans. Therefore, our "higher critics" must reinterpret Genesis to make room for millions of years of death and destruction.

This "day/age theory" claims that the word "day" does not mean a 24-hour period of time, but rather means an indefinite period of time. The argument used to prove this is that the Hebrew word *yom*, translated "day" in every English Bible, can also mean an indefinite period of time. The commentators who endorse this fiction invariably point to Genesis 2:4, where Moses says "in the day that the LORD God made the earth and the heavens." In that verse, "in the day" obviously means "at the time," so therefore it means the same thing in chapter 1.

This reading, of course, completely disregards the context in which the word is used, since Moses specifically stipulates that the "days" of creation included one "morning" and one "evening." The "day/age theory" was ludicrous from its first advent, and Bible critics are now gradually acknowledging that the text cannot support it. Yet they are loathe to stand courageously against modern scientific scoffers, and now are doing some quaint theological footwork to hold the same position while simultaneously acknowledging its impossibility within the Genesis text. They are developing a new nuance on the "day/age" nonsense, calling the "day" merely a literary device. Yes, Moses did mean a 24-hour long day, and yes he clearly does underscore it repeatedly by insisting that each "day" was "evening" and

---

26 This habit of changing tactics can be seen when one considers the so-called Gap Theory, which was widely endorsed in the early part of the 20th century. It was ridiculous from the beginning, asserting that one could discover a huge gap of time between the first two verses of Genesis if one read *between* the verses. Today the gnostic commentators speak snidely of the Gap Theory, even while purporting an equally absurd contention that "day" means millions of years.

"morning"—but he really didn't *mean* a literal day because that disagrees with modern science, which we know to be infallible. No no, he was just using a literary device—speaking figuratively, you see—because ancient man was too stupid to comprehend it if he had said "in the second epoch, God divided the waters." We're smarter than they were, so God has revealed this truth to us after 10,000 years of pretending otherwise.

This, as always, forces us to arbitrarily decide when Moses *stopped* speaking figuratively and started being literal.[27] It forces us to assume, further, that Adam and Eve were mere literary figures—a position which cannot be tolerated if we are to retain a sound basis for New Testament theology, as I have already pointed out in the previous chapter.

These so-called scholars are like an adulterer caught in the act, who pushes his consort away and promises to be faithful in the future—and then immediately turns to embrace her again. They confess that the "day means an age" idea is utterly unsupported in the text, then immediately insist that Moses *speaks* of a literal 24-hour day but actually *means* millions of years. They pretend to have abandoned their illicit theory while continuing to consort with her under a new tryst, disguising this infidelity under a new name: the "framework hypothesis."[28]

The context of Genesis 1 demands that we read it literally. Moses is telling us that God created the entire cosmos in six literal, 24-hour days. We certainly are free to reject that as impossible. We are free to say that modern science has proven the claim false, and that the earth is not really 10,000 years old as Moses claimed. We are equally free to say that modern science is wrong, and that the earth is not billions of years old. But we are *not* free to say that Moses is telling us in some secret code, some gnostic "higher knowledge," that creation took any longer than six days. We are not free to say that Genesis 1 is metaphorical, while reading subsequent chapters as historical. We are not free to ignore the context of words or verses, and we

---

[27] The "higher critics" do not deny, for example, that Abraham and Isaac and Jacob were real people and that the events recorded of them in Genesis really happened. They acknowledge, in this way, that the latter half of Genesis was intended by the author to be read as literal history—while simultaneously insisting that the first half of Genesis was *not* intended to be read as literal history. They do not, however, explain where the transition takes place in the book from metaphor to historical document.

[28] This trick of renaming old ideas is becoming quite prevalent, as many commentators are now calling themselves "progressive creationists" to disguise their embrace of the framework hypothesis.

are not free to invent our own alleged "sources" that *might* have existed when Moses was writing to prove that he really means something other than what he says. The fact that our modern theologians are playing these very tricks demonstrates that they are not to be trusted, that they have betrayed their sacred calling as shepherds of the flock.

**16. God made two great lights: the greater light to rule the day, and the lesser light to rule the night.** Moses tells us that God created the sun on day four, the day *after* He had created plants. Now, one day without the sun does not present any problem to plant life. It only becomes a problem when a theologian desperately wants to capitulate to the Darwinists, because plants could not have survived waiting around for a billion years while God figured out how to get the sun turned on. Furthermore, evolution itself teaches that the sun came into existence billions of years *before* any plants appeared on earth, so even the false chronologies do not fit together.

This teaching of Genesis is contrary to the doctrines of evolution in every way, and by this fact alone we should be forced to recognize that the Bible cannot be melded together with Darwinism. But the Christian Darwinist is less concerned with Biblical integrity than he is with his worldly reputation, so if one of those elements must suffer it will invariably be his reading of the Bible.

How do our gnostic commentators resolve this discrepancy? By rewriting Genesis, of course. At this point, even their dishonest reinterpretation of the word "day" falls apart, because a million-year long "day" will not accommodate plant life without a sun. Therefore, they conclude (quite arbitrarily) that the creation account in Genesis is not given in chronological order!

And how do they prove this assertion? Well, the Hebrew doesn't actually say "*the* fourth day," it says "*a* fourth day!" That's right, it was just *a* fourth day—any old fourth day. It might have been the fourth day of the first year or the fourth day of the billion-and-first year or the fourth day of whatever year fits your latest theory—any fourth day will do.

In this outrageous bit of sophomoric scholarship, our critics are suggesting that "the editors" of Genesis are merely enumerating different things that God created at different times, using the concept of a "day" to represent some indefinite stage of creation—*and* they're just doing it in a random order, jotting down nifty stuff that God did as it pops into their minds. Some might even go so far as to suggest that "the editors" restricted their creation myth to six "days" because they wanted to justify their observance of the Sabbath.

## Section 2: Rewriting the Bible

The critics who commit this scandalous act of sophistry do not tell us what *other* days are out of chronological sequence. This is a nice show of foresight on their parts, as it allows them the flexibility to rearrange the entire week at will any time a new evolutionary theory comes along.

And, to add some flavor to the fun, our "higher critics" have invented a new word for this phenomenon: the text, they tell us, is actually *dischronologized*! Nearly every one of them uses this cool word,[29] and each uses it off-handedly in a way which suggests that the word has been a standard literary term for millennia—on a par with other standard literary terms such as *farce* and *satirical fiction* and *buffoon* and *outright dishonest scholarship*. Nobody ever defines it, of course, because that might spoil the magical spell which they hope to cast over the innocent reader; much better to use the term as though it is a widely recognized literary technique used to tell a story which purports to be chronological but which really isn't. Needless to say, no such literary technique exists except in the minds of our modern theologians. The ancient Gnostics also practiced this trick, inventing strange new jargon to clothe their heretical teachings, jargon that would sound mystical and learned to the common man.[30]

Once again we ask, "does it really matter?" Is it really all that important what *order* God created things in? The modern gnostics calmly assure us that it doesn't, patting our heads in their best patronizing manner. "There there, common man," they purr, "don't worry your pretty little head over these big questions. All that matters is that the Bible teaches that God is sovereign over creation; leave the details to your betters to figure out." Their words sound oddly familiar, and one can detect a serpentine sibilance whenever they wag their forkéd tongues. Because, you see, the created order *does* matter—it

---

29 E.g., Matthews, *Genesis 1–11:26*, 110, 148; Youngblood, *The Book of Genesis*, 26; Waltke, *Genesis*, 61. Waltke, in a stroke of doubly creative genius, even claims that the dischronologization is proof that Genesis is a polemic!

30 Boice does not directly claim that the creation account is not given chronologically, but his ludicrous assertion that the sun was created prior to day four comes close. It is worth noting that his capitulation to Darwinism on this issue accomplishes nothing whatsoever. Science claims that the light of the stars takes billions of years to reach earth, so rewriting the obvious chronology of the creation account still will not satisfy the claims of science, still will not harmonize Darwinism and creation. The only result is that, once again, the gnostics have managed to destroy the credibility of Scripture without gaining any credibility in the scientific community. Truly, these gnostic Christians are to be pitied, for they have sacrificed their credibility within the Christian community in hopes of gaining it in the scientific community, only to make themselves an even greater object of derision amongst unbelievers.

matters a very great deal. Satan himself entered the garden for the express purpose of upsetting the created order. Adam's sin was at least partly that he inverted the created order. *The created order is of utmost importance!* Modern theologians are doing the serpent's work when they attempt to rearrange the given order of creation.

A moment ago, I accused modern theologians of adulterating God's word, and I want to state clearly that I am not using my words lightly. The creation in Genesis 1 is so patently described in chronological order that this claim of "dischronologization" can be categorized in no weaker terms. There is utterly no evidence whatsoever to indicate that the chronology of creation should be understood in any order other than the order in which it is presented, yet the gnostic "scholars" make their accusation in a casual, off-hand manner as though it were self-evident. This is nothing short of a bold-faced lie, and the reason that modern theologians have become so brazen in their tricks is that they have not been called to account for previous ones. It is time that this changed, and in Section 3 we will hold them accountable for their sleight-of-hand tricks, their scholarly posturing, their forthright lies, and their breath-taking arrogance.

**20. Let the waters abound with an abundance of living creatures, and let birds fly above the earth.** I pointed out in Chapter 1 that practically everything about the Genesis creation account flies in the face of modern science. We delude ourselves when we think that we can somehow harmonize Genesis with any element of modern theories of origins. Places where the two schemes coincide are minor and often coincidental, as modern science draws conclusions from those observations which completely contradict what the Bible teaches. We need to recognize the utter futility of trying to reconcile scientific theories of origins with the Genesis account. It's a shame that they disagree, but everyone—*everyone*, including the most learned scientist—must take a step of faith no matter *what* he chooses to believe about the origins of life on earth. Christians must come to grips with the fact that we are being called by God Himself to "choose for yourselves this day whom you will serve, whether the gods which your fathers served... or the gods of the Amorites, in whose land you dwell" (Josh. 24:15).

This utter incompatibility becomes evident on day five, for example, when the Bible teaches us that fish and birds were created on the same day—and that day came *after* the creation of plant life. As I said in Chapter 1, evolution preaches that plant life came after the appearance of fish, and that mammals and birds both evolved *out of* fish. So our theological magicians might attempt to delude us with their sleight-of-hand tricks by saying that day five is actually dischronologized, that Moses doesn't really mean that fish were created after plants (day four); the order is actually reversed because modern science says so. But even that theological adultery does not accommodate modern science, because fish and birds are still shown in Genesis as appearing at the same time, *and* shown as having no inter-relationship to one another—they are separate species entirely, according to Genesis, not one leading into the other.

I cannot emphasize enough how utterly futile this whole game is—worse than futile, it is destructive to the Christian faith. Our leading modern theologians—Gordon Wenham, Victor Hamilton, Bruce Waltke, R. Kent Hughes, Ronald Youngblood, and many others—are selling out their birthright like Esau and getting *nothing* in return. Even Esau had sense enough to get a bowl of pottage, but this sell-out leaves the Christian community devoid of any credibility in the eyes of the world while also stripping away the very truth of the Bible which is intended to set men free.

**24. Let the earth bring forth the living creature according to its kind.** The Bible blatantly teaches that like brings forth like, that a creature can only give birth to its own kind of creature—that existing life forms do not evolve into new life forms. If the gnostic "higher critics" had been honest with Scripture from the start, they would either have been hot enough to refrain from rewriting the Bible or cold enough to convert to atheism and abandon Scripture altogether. Either option would have been better than their present lukewarm approach.

And now we have a sub-group of Christian Darwinists who assure their readers that they do not embrace evolution on any level, then turn around and tell us that God used evolution *within* some species but not *outside* of the species—that cats evolved into different cats, but not into humming birds![31] This is the natural result which we should expect of a gnostic approach to Bible interpretation, where each man does that which is right according to his own agenda. Some theologians are quite comfortable admitting that they worship at Darwin's altar, while others evidently fear that they will lose face with their "constituency" if they openly make that confession—so they attempt to deny it while fully embracing the religion's false teachings.

---

31 E.g., Boice, *Genesis, Volume 1*, 75–76.

Once again, these men succeed only in offending all parties concerned, because their homemade Darwinism is not true to the doctrines of the Darwinist church, nor are they true to the Word of God. The sad fact is that the Darwinists are the ones who openly mock these lukewarm theologians, rejecting their ludicrous attempts at compromise, while the church of Christ sits silent and allows them to publish books and poison future generations of Bible teachers.

In this verse we also have a most entertaining irony: our modern commentators love to tell us that Genesis is a "polemic," a book whose sole purpose is to refute the claims of some other book. Needless to say, this claim is as false as all their other claims, as I will demonstrate in Section 3, but here in verse 24 our gnostics at least have the opportunity of proving their thesis—and they (for one blessed moment) actually keep silent! If Genesis truly is a polemic, if Moses really is writing this book in order to refute the pagan teachings of his day, then assuredly that is what he is doing here! Remember that evolution is not a new idea; it was the basic religious system of ancient Egypt and other nations during the time of Moses. So why not view this verse as a deliberate refutation of evolution? If there is any place in Genesis 1 that could be viewed as polemical (and there actually isn't, because Genesis is *not* a polemic), that place would be here, where Moses is telling us very clearly and in no uncertain terms that like begets like—that the donkey brings forth the donkey, and that donkeys do not evolve into higher critics, despite appearances.

And why don't these theologians mention "polemic" in this verse? For the obvious reason that, if we view this verse as polemical, then we are confronted once again with the most painfully, blatantly, self-evident fact that the Bible does not endorse evolution! Our gnostic commentators do not want us to notice that fact, so they deliberately stop braying "polemic! polemic!" when they get anywhere near a verse that might actually be seen as *being* polemical.

Like begets like. This is what the Bible teaches, and it means exactly what it says. It is essential that we recognize and accept this doctrine, because it sits at the very foundation of the role of Jesus Christ as the Last Adam. If one creature can evolve into another creature—even another type of the *same* creature—then there is the hope that Adam's offspring will one day evolve into sinless human beings. The Bible makes it painfully clear that Adam's children *have no hope*! We will *not* evolve ourselves out of our Adamic nature;

we will *not* evolve ourselves into sons of the Last Adam; we will *not* evolve ourselves into godhood.[32] This was the belief of Lucifer, for which he was cast out of heaven. It is a severely serious offence to be teaching this within the church—it is, in short, heresy.

**26. Let Us make man in Our image.** In Chapter 1, I addressed some of the "problems" which Pharaoh's magicians, our modern commentators, have magically created with this verse. As I said before, it should be self-evident to any honest reader of Genesis 1 that God is addressing Himself here, particularly since Moses has already told us that God's Spirit is hovering above the waters. This, of course, is the very reason that Pharaoh's magicians also magically made the Spirit disappear and replaced Him with a "mighty wind" in verse 2. So, having dispensed with the Spirit of God from verse 2, our magicians are now free to make "us" in verse 26 refer to anyone they want. Here are some of the reinterpretations offered by our gnostic "scholars" for this verse:[33]

1) Chapter 1, not being written by Moses as they so painfully try to prove, is actually a direct copying of some pagan myth. It doesn't matter that no such pagan myth exists; Pharaoh's magicians are never hindered by facts—they just *surmise* that one existed which the original "redactor" copied. And the later "editors" who compiled and reformulated the book which we call Genesis evidently forgot to correct this bit of residual paganism. (I'm not making this up!)[34]

2) On second thought, the later "editors" actually *did* catch this bit of residual paganism, but they *liked* it because the other "gods" that were being addressed were actually angels. So when God says "let us create," He is actually getting the angels to help Him with the arduous task of creating mankind.[35]

3) God is a king, and kings refer to themselves in the royal "we." So that's what is happening here: God is referring to Himself as *we* and *us*, as any self-respecting monarch always does.[36]

---

[32] James Boice: "But there is a sense in which those who know God are enabled to evolve increasingly into that image of what he would have us to be, and we rejoice in that" [*Genesis, vol. 1*, 79].

[33] See Wenham, *Genesis 1–15*, 27–28; and Hamilton, *The Book of Genesis*, 133–34 for this synopsis.

[34] "Thus this text is a remnant of the earliest form of the story that somehow escaped the editor who removed from his borrowed tale any pagan elements that would be offensive and unacceptable to monotheists" (Hamilton, *The Book of Genesis*, 133).

[35] "The image of God means that in some sense men and women resemble God and the angels" (Wenham, *Genesis 1–15*, 38).

[36] E.g., *The NIV Study Bible*, 7, note 26. And here is a real gem from one of the most

4) If that sounds too grand and self-inflated, then we'll just have God thinking out loud. It's not that He's being pompous, but rather that He's somewhat indecisive about creating man (as well He might have been, foreseeing how some of them would pervert His word in the 21st Century). "Let's see, now," says God, "to make mankind or not to make mankind, that is the question before us."[37]

God is not speaking to any other part of creation here, for the simple reason that He says "let us create mankind together." God is the sole creator of all that exists; no person or thing or entity helped Him.[38] Furthermore, man is not created in the *image* of any entity except God alone. We are not made in the image of angels,[39] nor are we made in the image of earth. As I pointed out in Chapter 1, man does have some degree of duality in that we are both *of* earth and *by* God. By this I mean that our earthy part is our flesh, while our Godly part is our *image* or *likeness*—those many elements of man's nature which comprise God's image. God did use earth to create us, it is true, but only as a raw material, not as a creative co-agent. The potter alone is the creator of a vessel, even though he might use clay in producing it. The clay has no more part in the creative process than the earth did in verse 26.

---

influential commentaries on Genesis: "No other explanation is left, therefore, than to regard it as *pluralis majestatis*, —an interpretation which comprehends in its deepest and most intensive form (God speaking of Himself and with Himself in the plural number, not *reverentiae causa*, but with reference to the fullness of the divine powers and essences which He possesses) the truth that lies at the foundation of the trinitarian view, viz., that the potencies concentrated in the absolute Divine Being are something more than powers and attributes of God; that they are *hypostases*, which in the further course of the revelation of God in His kingdom appeared with more and more distinctness as persons of the Divine Being" (C. F. Keil, *Commentary on the Old Testament*, Vol. I, 62). It will be interesting to note, when we look more closely at Gnosticism in Section 3, that the early Gnostics loved to refer to the godhead as *hypostases*.

37 "This would be comparable to an individual who might say to himself: 'Let's see, should I walk to work tomorrow or take the bus?'" (Hamilton, *The Book of Genesis*, 134). One of the most damning facts facing these gnostic charlatans is that scholars who openly reject Jesus Christ actually *quote them* to prove that Christians themselves don't believe in Him! See, for example, *http://www.outreachjudaism.org/genesis1-26.html*, where an Orthodox Jew quotes these very theologians to demonstrate that God is not a Trinity.

38 When God called upon the earth to "bring forth" living creatures, He was not asking the earth to work together with Him in the creative process; He was commanding His creation to do what it was created to do: be fruitful and multiply. The Christian Darwinist might try to claim that God was instituting the process of evolution at that point, but the context of Genesis 1 demands that we recognize this to be a one-time act of creation.

39 "The image of God means that in some sense men and women resemble God and the angels" [Wenham, *Genesis*, 38]. This statement is heretical, and has its roots in ancient Gnosticism.

He is indeed speaking to Himself, but not in some silly "royal we" manner nor in some wishy-washy "gee, what should I do now" manner. Moses has already introduced us to the Spirit of God, and it is self-evident that God at least has a dual nature—that the Godhead is composed at least of God the Creator (or God the Father, as we now understand it) and God the Spirit.

Notice that this verse also presents a major problem for Pharaoh's magicians. They point out that Moses could not have been familiar with "Trinitarian theology," using that argument to further confuse a straightforward reading of Genesis 1. They then tell us that Moses plagiarized ancient pagan myths to produce his own account of creation (an absurd lie which I will address in Appendix 1), claiming that later "redactors" and "editors" worked to remove any hints of pagan polytheism. Yet if such a make-believe "editor" were in fact changing what Moses wrote, he would certainly have removed such a glaring reference to polytheism—since, according to the scheme of Pharaoh's magicians, the Old Testament Jews did not understand the triune nature of Jehovah. If Genesis 1 were in fact stolen from pagan myths and later revised to be palatable to the Jews, then such later "editors" would have made God say, "I will make man in my own image" rather than "let us make man in our image."

An honest scholar at this point would question his own theory, confessing that he might be wrong about his idea that Moses used pagan myths as his source for a polemic to refute those myths. An honest critic would say to himself, "gee, maybe this book of Genesis really *is* inspired by the Holy Spirit! After all, who would know about Trinitarian theology better than God Himself?"

A critic with an agenda, however, will not make such a confession. Admitting that Genesis is divinely inspired forces a reader to recognize that its creation account cannot be melded together with modern science. So, rather than acknowledging the problems within their own theories, these sham scholars set about "discovering" the various "problems" in the Genesis text.

One group tries to suggest that God was talking to the angels—but this quickly lands them in a heretical quagmire. Another group claims that God is trying to encourage Himself: "Yeah! Go, Me, go! We're doing great, God—now let's create man!" Evidently God suffers from a poor self-image, according to this line of thinking. A few of the "higher critics" have been bold enough to suggest that God is addressing Himself simply because the godhead *is* plural—but this view has been persistently rejected by the likes of Gordon Wenham because of its implications of divine inspiration.

It is astonishing to wade through volumes of in-depth, highly technical literary analysis of Genesis, only to find that none of Pharaoh's magicians has noticed the most glaring parallel construction in this chapter. God says to Himself in verse 26, "Let us create man in our own image." Then in verse 27 we are told that "God created man in His own image... male and female He created them"—thus referring to mankind in both the singular and plural. The magicians, of course, divine huge problems and difficulties in understanding why God refers to Himself in the plural, and they distract our attention away from the obvious truth with their usual sleights of hand. God is addressing Himself in the plural because He *is* plural, as demonstrated by the fact that His Spirit hovered over the waters during creation. Moses underscores this mystery by pointing out that mankind himself is a duality, both male and female. If the magicians are genuinely so fascinated by the literary techniques of Genesis 1, how have they missed one so painfully obvious?

The answer is that they miss it because they *choose* to miss it—they ignore this parallel emphasis in these two verses because it is one of the countless features in the passage which give the lie to their heretical scheme. God's plural reference to Himself is prophetic, after all, telling His people, thousands of years before Christ, of His own Triune nature. Acknowledging this fact, however, requires that a theologian believe in divine inspiration, and that is the stone of stumbling for our "higher critics."

Many of our modern commentators, whom I'm lumping together as Pharaoh's magicians, are the theological descendants of the German "higher critics" of the mid-1800s. Those German theologians openly rejected the existence of miracles, including the idea that the Bible is the divinely inspired Word of God. Their modern descendants do not openly state that they reject the divine inspiration of the book of Genesis, but that presupposition lies behind every word printed on every page of most of these modern commentaries.

This is the reason that Pharaoh's magicians are so rabidly determined not to permit any hint of God's triune nature in this chapter—removing His Spirit from verse 2 in favor of a "big wind," having God speaking to the angels in verse 26 rather than to His Spirit—because if they admit that the doctrine of the trinity has its roots in this chapter while also telling us that Moses could not be expected to know of the trinity, then they are forced to confess that the words which Moses is quoting are in fact *the very words of God Himself*. Admitting that would also entail their admitting that Genesis is divinely inspired; and if Genesis is divinely inspired, then all their wretched schemes and tricks and dishonesties come to naught because we are forced to recognize that it is God Himself who is telling us plainly how He created heaven and earth, and no further discussion is possible concerning evolution.

# 8

# REWRITING GENESIS 2

## The Sabbath

***2. And on the seventh day God ended His work which He had done.*** I have been demonstrating a few of the countless ways in which modern commentators rewrite Genesis, choosing to interpret "day" in chapter 1, for example, to mean "a long period of time," and so forth. Ironically, when these same commentators arrive at chapter 2, they suddenly switch from reading hidden meanings into the text to reading it in a straightforward manner. Thus, they stop (temporarily) looking for ancient pagan texts from which the "authors" stole their ideas and treat the Sabbath material as being God's words.

This is one of the gnostics' favorite tricks: making up their own rules of literary interpretation as they go along, applying one set of rules to one verse, and an entirely different set of rules to the next verse. They choose to understand the Lord's words concerning the Sabbath rest as literal, because they want to use those words as proof that "day" cannot be interpreted literally in Genesis 1. Their argument is that God's use of "the seventh day" is open-ended; there is no "morning" and "evening" formula applied at the end, suggesting that the Sabbath day is still on-going today. This, in turn, "proves" that the other six days are not literal 24-hour days, either.

Yet the fact that Moses does not use the "morning/evening" formula at the conclusion of the seventh day actually indicates that the seventh day is different in some way from the preceding six. In this case, the commentators are actually correct (in spite of themselves) in suggesting that God's Sabbath rest is still continuing today—that is, that God completed His creative work at the end of day six, and He is no longer creating new life forms on earth. They are incorrect, however, when they attempt to force this reading back upon Genesis 1, for the simple reason that day seven is *different from the preceding six days*. Moses underscores this in his wording, while our modern charlatans are attempting to twist that meaning to fit their own evolutionary agenda.

## SECTION 2: REWRITING THE BIBLE

## "The Generations Of"

**4. *This is the history of the heavens and the earth when they were created.*** In Chapter 2, I explained that Moses uses a formula to change his topics within Genesis, known as the "*toledot* structure," *toledot* being the Hebrew word which is generally translated as "generations of" or "history of" such-and-such a person. I also addressed the "problems" which have been invented by our "higher critics" to obscure the straightforward understanding of Genesis 2:4–7. I will begin by quoting these verses in two different modern translations—the New King James and the New International—to illustrate the issue.

### New King James:

> This is the history of the heavens and the earth when they were created, in the day that the LORD God made the earth and the heavens, before any plant of the field was in the earth and before any herb of the field had grown. For the LORD God had not caused it to rain on the earth, and there was no man to till the ground; but a mist went up from the earth and watered the whole face of the ground. And the LORD God formed man of the dust of the ground, and breathed into his nostrils the breath of life; and man became a living being.

### New International:

> This is the account of the heavens and the earth when they were created.

> When the Lord God made the earth and the heavens—and no shrub of the field had yet appeared on the earth and no plant of the field had yet sprung up, for the LORD God had not sent rain on the earth and there was no man to work the ground, but streams came up from the earth and watered the whole surface of the ground—the LORD God formed the man from the dust of the ground and breathed into his nostrils the breath of life, and the man became a living being.

Pharaoh's magicians, our so-called "higher critics," have built careers upon arguing over how to "properly understand" this simple literary device. Some critics argue that the "authors" of Genesis used this device to conclude a section; others argue that the "authors" used it to begin a new section. Why does it matter to the "higher critics" whether this formula concludes one section or begins another, you may well ask. And the answer is that, in fact, it doesn't. The "higher critics" are not actually interested in discovering the truth, they are solely interested in obscuring the Word of God. It is their contention that the book of Genesis is not God's inspired word but merely the literary efforts of some invented band of "redactors," as I have been saying so frequently. They use these *toledot* passages, such as the one here and in chapter 5, to claim that the "authors" had access to some ancient tomes (which the "higher critics" have invented out of thin air), documents that give pagan accounts on creation and genealogies and the flood and practically anything else that they feel the need to fabricate. Of course, any ancient documents concerning the genealogies of Adam, if they were legitimate, would have been lost in the flood, so it's doubly unlikely that Moses had any such books in his possession.[1]

The critics boost their careers by writing lengthy diatribes arguing that the "generations of" device in Genesis proves that the "authors" were copying some ancient pagan writings, and that they were either ending one pagan writing at Gen. 2:4 or beginning another. It does not really matter which view wins, because they have accomplished their hidden agenda once they have caused modern theologians to focus their attention on Moses' "sources" rather than on the fact that Genesis is God's inspired word to mankind. And why is this agenda so vital? Because it prevents people from asking themselves, "What does this mean to me today? How can I apply these principles in my life? What does God want from *me*?" This, as I shall address in Section 3, is the very case with modern commentaries in Genesis, most of which offer little or no practical application of the Word of God to their readers.

The straightforward and honest reader, however, will quickly recognize that the *toledot* structure is used for both an introduction *and* a conclusion:

---

[1] Henry Morris posits this claim, that Moses may have possessed ancient documents written by Adam himself. It is possible, of course, but that would presuppose that Noah had them on the ark. It is far more likely that Moses did not have any ancient writings with him during the wilderness wanderings—and he *certainly* was not lugging around stone tablets of pagan myths!

## Section 2: Rewriting the Bible

Moses concludes one section and introduces his next section by summarizing what he has said previously and leading forward into what he is going to discuss next.

This is precisely what he does, for example, in Gen. 5:1–5:

> This is the book of the genealogy of Adam. In the day that God created man, He made him in the likeness of God. He created them male and female, and blessed them and called them Mankind in the day they were created. And Adam lived one hundred and thirty years, and begot a son in his own likeness, after his image, and named him Seth. After he begot Seth, the days of Adam were eight hundred years; and he had sons and daughters. So all the days that Adam lived were nine hundred and thirty years; and he died.

Moses here summarizes what he has already told us: that God created man in the likeness of Himself, both male and female, and that He blessed them and called them "mankind." We already knew this information; it is a mere short-hand summary of what Moses has already been telling us. Then he moves on to give us some new information about Adam: that he was 130 years old when Seth was born, and that he had "sons and daughters" besides the ones that we have already met in chapters 1 through 4 (Cain, Abel, and Seth). Finally, Moses moves on with entirely new information, concluding the life of Adam at 930 years of age and introducing us to his offspring. This is the "genealogy" part, where Moses lists the various people who lived between Adam (subject of the previous section of Genesis) and Noah (subject of the next section). In this simple way, Moses both concludes the previous section (Adam) and introduces the next (Noah).

Moses is using his *toledot* structure, his transitional device, in Genesis 2:4–7, as well. He begins by summarizing what he has already told us in chapter 1: "I have now finished telling you of the history of the heavens and the earth and how they were created—how God created the earth back before there were any herbs or plants in the fields."

Then he adds some new information: "Back in that day, the Lord had not yet caused it to rain, and there was no man created yet to till the ground—instead, a mist went up and watered the ground."

Finally, he makes the transition into his new topic: "Then the Lord created man from the dust of the earth, breathing into him the breath of life, and man became a living being. Then God planted a garden for him. . . ."

But now take a look at the translations above, and notice how the punctuation within the verses radically alters the meaning of those verses. The New King James' punctuation makes the verses read essentially as I have just paraphrased: that God created the earth before there were any plants, before rain had fallen, before man had been created to till the ground (summary), but then God created man (transition to new material).

The New International, however, punctuates the verses quite differently, even making the second half of verse 4 into a new paragraph. The NIV translators used dashes to make the information about the timeframe (no shrubs, etc.) come *after* man's creation. In other words, their use of punctuation now makes the verses mean this: "This is the history of how the heavens and the earth were created. Now, it so happened, that back before plants had appeared—before it had ever rained on earth and streams watered it instead, back before there was a man to till the ground—at that time, the Lord created man."

This way of punctuating the verses actually suggests that God created man prior to day three, that He created Adam *before* He created plants. But that cannot be right, because it disagrees with what we are told in chapter 1, that God created man on day six, *after* He had created plant life.[2] A person reading the NIV, then, might well scratch his head and wonder why there seems to be a discrepancy between the chronologies of chapter 2 and chapter 1.

This conflict, however, is purely one of modern English punctuation; it is not a conflict in the original Hebrew text. The original Hebrew text does not contain any sort of modern English punctuation, such as commas or dashes. We need to have those punctuation points put in if we are to make sense of the text in modern English, and one of the responsibilities of the translators is to ascertain how to correctly punctuate the verses. But herein lies the crux of our dilemma: the punctuation as given in the NIV creates a conflict

---

2 The New American Standard further complicates the issue by translating the Hebrew word "and" as "now" at the beginning of verse 5. This, too, is a rather arbitrary translational choice, as the Hebrew word more frequently means "and" than "now," and the use of "now" creates a conflict which does not need to be present. As with the punctuation, this is a purely arbitrary choice.

between chapters 1 and 2, while that used in the NKJV (and most other modern translations) does not. If there is no punctuation in the original and a translator needs to add it, then one of the first things that translator will do is to examine the context—because context is king, as I've said repeatedly—to ensure that any added punctuation does not contradict the rest of the text. This is a very basic rule of literary interpretation.

It is not my purpose to argue the merits of one modern translation over another, and there may be a valid reason why the translators of the NIV chose to punctuate this passage differently from most other modern translations.[3] The big issue for us to address is the fact that the "higher critics" are the ones who essentially *invented* this punctuational dilemma. Their agenda, as I have been suggesting, was to undermine the credibility of divine inspiration, to invent ways of proving that Genesis is merely the work of fallible men and not to be trusted as the inspired Word of God.

They accomplish this using one of their favorite magicians' tricks: circular reasoning. The gnostics claim that the traditional (and sensible) punctuation is wrong and that the verses opening chapter 2 should be punctuated in a way that causes the verses to contradict what has come before.[4] Then they turn around and claim that the re-punctuated verses, which now contradict chapter 1, prove that the book was not written by one author but by three or more imaginary redactors! This is the basis for the J-E-P fairy tale: "Chapter 2 contradicts chapter 1 because we want it to; and now that Chapter 2 contradicts Chapter 1, we must explain how it happened—so we'll conclude that the two chapters were written by two different people, whom we will arbitrarily name E (the *elohist*) and J (the *jahwist*)."

Let me reiterate: there is absolutely no contradiction between the creation account of chapter 1 and the transitional summary of chapter 2. The apparent contradiction comes only when one punctuates 2:4–7 incorrectly, "incorrectly" being any punctuation which causes those verses to contradict their context—because there *is no punctuation in the Hebrew*. If a translator or theologian chooses to insert English punctuation into those verses which contradicts their context, he is doing it by choice.

---

[3] Having said this, I must frankly state that I suspect these punctuation choices to be driven by agenda. The "higher critics" invented this non-existent "conflict" 150 years ago, long before the NIV or any other of our most modern translations were created. As I say above, there is no reason whatsoever within the Hebrew text to punctuate the verses as the NIV does as opposed to the NKJV, but the implications of these little punctuation points are immense.

[4] They provide no basis whatsoever for this invention, as far as I can discover.

**17. You shall surely die.** In Chapter 2, we examined the fact that Adam was created as an immortal being, not subject to death. I also pointed out the fact that our modern commentators insist that he was *not* immortal when created; that he was subject to death in some manner that the commentators never deign to specify. They don't specify how their scheme works out practically, of course, because they do not want to let the reader see that their logic is utterly unsupportable—that making Adam subject to death in some way *prior to* eating the forbidden fruit nullifies the curse of sin and death that his eating brought upon mankind. But it is essential in the gnostic scheme to make Adam mortal when created for the simple reason that it is necessary if they are to worm evolution into the creation account.

These gnostics invariably cite 1 Timothy 6:16 as their sole bit of Scripture to support their claim. As usual, our Bible commentators take their supporting verses out of context, so here is the context of 1 Timothy 6:16:

> Fight the good fight of faith, lay hold on eternal life, to which you were also called and have confessed the good confession in the presence of many witnesses. I urge you in the sight of God who gives life to all things, and before Christ Jesus who witnessed the good confession before Pontius Pilate, that you keep this commandment without spot, blameless until our Lord Jesus Christ's appearing, which He will manifest in His own time, He who is the blessed and only Potentate, the King of kings and Lord of lords, who alone has immortality, dwelling in unapproachable light, whom no man has seen or can see, to whom be honor and everlasting power. Amen.
> —1 Timothy 6:12–16

Paul tells us that God dwells in "unapproachable light," that "no man has seen or can see" Him, and that God "alone has immortality." Yet in Genesis we see God Himself walking in the Garden of Eden, speaking face to face with Adam. Clearly, prior to man's sin, God chose to leave His "unapproachable light" and descend to earth for the express purpose of allowing mankind to see His face. It is only after man's sin that God has removed Himself from mankind, so it is equally possible that mankind was once immortal.

Furthermore, Paul tells Timothy in the same paragraph to "lay hold on eternal life," while also telling him that God alone is immortal. How are we to harmonize this evident contradiction? And what about the angels, who are also immortal? The simple answer is that God alone "gives life to all things," and all life flows from Him. Without God, no life would exist, and in this sense it is God alone who is completely above and apart from death.

It is really not necessary, however, to explicate these verses in order to understand that verse 16—"[God] alone has immortality"—does not have anything to do with Adam in the Garden of Eden. Yet here is what some of our favorite gnostics have to say regarding Adam's immortality:

> **Victor Hamilton:** "Yet another alternative is that 2:17 means 'on the day you eat of it you will become mortal.' This approach assumes that God created man immortal, a fact that is not explicitly stated in Genesis and seems contrary to 1 Tim. 6:16, which states that deity alone has immortality. Indeed, in no OT passage does the phrase *mot tamut* mean 'to become mortal.'"[5]

> **Kenneth Mathews:** "There is no suggestion from the passage, as is assumed by some, that Adam was created immortal but subsequently forfeited immortality by his sin. There is a difference between man's creation, in which he receives life by the divine inbreathing (2:7), and the perpetuation of that life gained by appropriating the tree of life (cf. 3:22). Immortality is the trait of deity alone (1 Tim 6:16)."[6]

> **R. Kent Hughes:** "Here we must note that this passage does not suggest that Adam was immortal and that, had he not sinned, he would live forever in the garden.[7] There is a difference between man's creation when he received life

---

5 Hamilton, *The Book of Genesis*, 173.
6 Mathews, *Genesis 1–11:26*, 211–12.
7 I should point out in passing that I am not suggesting what God had planned for Adam and Eve, had they not sinned. Nobody knows what would have happened if Adam had not sinned, and I am not claiming that Adam "would live forever in the garden." I *am*, however, claiming that Adam would have lived forever.

by God's inbreathing (2:7) and the perpetuation of that life by appropriating from the tree of life (cf. 3:22). Adam was not intrinsically immortal. Only God is immortal (1 Timothy 6:16).[8]

Notice Hamilton's sleight of hand trick in his last sentence, "Indeed, in no OT passage does the phrase *mot tamut* mean 'to become mortal.'" The phrase *mot tamut* is the Hebrew translated "you shall surely die," and it is used elsewhere in the Old Testament.[9] And of course it doesn't mean "you shall become mortal" in other passages! In order to *become* mortal, a person would first need to be *immortal*! The only place in the entire Bible where a man was immortal is in the Garden of Eden; whenever the phrase is used elsewhere, the person being addressed is *already* mortal! The phrase does not mean "you shall become mortal," it means "you shall surely die"—as it is translated in every appearance in the Old Testament. God told Adam that he would "surely die" on the day that he ate of the forbidden fruit—but he *didn't* die on the day that he ate of that fruit, he became *subject to death* on that day. Prior to that day, Adam was *not* subject to death, he was immortal.

Notice also the way in which our gnostics parrot one another, referring to God as "deity," citing the same Scripture passage to support the same absurd allegations, copying one another's high-flown phraseology. Hughes seems to have lifted Mathews' words wholesale, without even citing him in his footnotes. In fact, both Mathews and Hughes go on at this point to quote the same passage from John Calvin. The word for this is "plagiarism."

One of the favorite tricks of Pharaoh's magicians is to insist upon a literal reading of one verse—of one phrase *within* a verse, even—while simultaneously insisting upon a metaphorical reading of the words and verses surrounding it. Here we have an example of this trick, as our magicians demand that we read Paul's words literally here (out of context, of course) while simultaneously demanding that we *not* take literally Paul's teachings that death entered the world through the sin of Adam.

Rather than taking this one verse, in context or otherwise, to prove that Adam was not immortal, we need to consider the great body of New Testament teaching which insists that death came into the world as a result of Adam's sin. This doctrine demands that we recognize that Adam was *not*

---

8 Hughes, *Genesis: Beginning and Blessing*, 55.

9 E.g., Genesis 2:17; 20:7; 1 Samuel 14:44; 22:16; 1 Kings 2:37, 42; 2 Kings 1:4; Ezekiel 3:18; 33:8, 14; Jeremiah 26:8.

subject to death prior to eating the forbidden fruit. If this does not prove that he was "immortal," I cannot think what will.

But, as I have said previously, modern "higher critics" are not actually concerned about discovering truth, they are merely concerned about forcing their agenda on the church. Part of this agenda is to seduce Christians into believing in evolution, and we help them to further that agenda if we allow them to get away with their many sleight of hand tricks. We must hold these theologians accountable for every false word they write, and one of these falsehoods is their insistence that Adam was not created "immortal."

# 9
# GENESIS 3 AND ADAM

## Why We Need Adam

I feel that it is necessary to underscore the gravity of suggesting that creation took more than six days. Christians tend to think that it is a mere matter of opinion whether one reads Genesis 1 as teaching that God created the cosmos in six literal days or six figurative millennia. This is not the case. It is nothing short of heresy to suggest that God took millions of years to create the earth, and those who try to play games with the text of Genesis 1 are heretics.

These sound like strong words, but when we come to the person of Adam we find ourselves in a tight bind if we have tried to "metaphorize" Genesis 1. As I have said already, if we insist that creation took millions of years, then we are also insisting that evolution took place. Whether or not we confess that fact, it is a necessity.

We essentially have two choices regarding the origins of life on earth: either God created all things out of nothing in six literal days, or else He used some form of evolution over an undefined period of years. We gain absolutely nothing by insisting that "day" (*yom*) means "millions of years," then claiming that God created life instantly from nothing as the text states. Nor can we legitimately claim that millions of years went by as God gradually coaxed various life forms into existence *without* using evolution; if we believe that He created *ex nihilo* as the text claims, then we must also believe that He did it in six days as the text claims. We cannot arbitrarily mix and match our favorite portions of creation and evolution; the options are either all evolution or all creation

If God used evolution, then we do not have a literal Adam in Genesis 3. You must have a literal Adam if you are going to have a literal Christ. Jesus is the Last Adam, but what becomes of Him if you have no First Adam? You have no need of a Redeemer if you haven't sinned, and sin, like the human race, must have an original parent—there has to be an original sin if there is to be a present generation of sinners. In other words, there has to be a literal Adam who committed the first literal sin which introduced the sin nature into all of his descendants; otherwise, you have no need of Jesus Christ.

Paul also tells us (Rom. 5:12–21) that Christ has brought eternal life to mankind in just the way that Adam brought death. But if we have no Adam who brought death, then how shall we have a Christ who brings life?

Some might argue that, just as Christ is not the literal father of His off-spring—that is, Christians—so also there was no literal Adam who has fathered all men. They might point out that the "headship" of Christ as the Last Adam is a sort of mystical or titular role, that He was raised to this position by God as a result of His obedience. They will then infer that the same might be true of the First Adam: that the story in Genesis 3 is merely an allegory of some sort, Adam representing the "common man" who falls short of God's standards.

Others might even go farther out on this rotted limb by suggesting that there really was a literal Adam, a man who had reached a certain stage of evolution which God deemed to be showing forth the "image of God," and that this man was then dubbed the "father of mankind" or some such thing—thus ascribing his sinfulness to all in the same way that the righteousness of Christ is ascribed to all believers.

Now, I must first state that I have not actually encountered anyone quite so deranged as to make these claims, but I have tried to think through any way that a person might claim that Adam evolved while still holding to the New Testament teachings on Christ. These positions of Adam as a "titular head" of the human race are untenable on a number of levels, but we will consider only the Scriptural, theological aspects.

First, Paul tells us clearly that death entered the world through the sin of "one man" (Rom. 5:12), which has been understood traditionally as meaning that death did not exist in the world at all prior to Adam's sin—not even in the animal kingdom. Many modern theologians, however, actually do claim that death existed prior to Adam (in order to accommodate the theology of evolution), and that Adam's sin somehow conferred death upon his descendants—or else deprived his descendants of the right to eat from the Tree of Life, which would have conferred immortality.[1]

---

[1] I am forced at this point to fill in the blanks for these theologians, since few of them have the honesty to carry their "day/age" evolutional theology out to the point of Adam. They tell us that the earth evolved over billions of years because Moses really means "millions of years" whenever he says "day," but they suddenly switch to a literal reading of Adam, with no explanation as to where Moses changes from metaphor to history. They also do not address the questions of how we can have a literal Adam who evolved from muck—yet they essentially rewrite Genesis 1 and 2 in order to accommodate that very evolution.

The implication of this contorted theology is that the new human race, which had finally evolved into the image of God (as though even an *image* of God can evolve out of death), would now be set free from the bondage of death, under which they had suffered for millions of years, and be granted immortality by virtue of the high evolutionary attainments of Adam. This wonderful emancipation was unfortunately cancelled when our newly evolved Adam decided to eat a piece of magical fruit, and God changed His mind about allowing him to eat a *different* piece of magical fruit which would have made him immortal.

Derek Kidner is one of the few theologians who is honest enough to wrestle with the insurmountable problems that such a theory poses.[2] He points out that, if man had evolved into God's image from lower orders, then there would still be many "Neanderthals" living alongside Adam. Did Adam's sudden anointing as God's image-bearer also apply to them, or were the Neanderthals not included under Adam's title, since they had not evolved enough? What became of the Neanderthals either way? Did they gradually evolve to a high enough level themselves to be God's image-bearers? Were they all wiped out in the flood, leaving only Noah's descendants on earth? (Noah, one would assume, was a *physical* descendant of this hypothetical evolved Adam, rather than of the Neanderthals—which, of course, is precisely what Genesis tells us, minus the "evolved Adam" fiction.)

We are forced to assume, even if we believe by faith that Adam evolved from a lower order, that his title as God's image bearer was passed along only to his own physical offspring.[3] Any co-existing Neanderthals, one must assume by this silly exposition, had not evolved enough to exhibit God's image in the way that this one post-Neanderthal named Adam had done. This, of course, raises the question of whether the descendants of those not-quite-good-enough Neanderthals might have evolved to the point that Adam had reached, but we really need to draw a line on this hypothetical absurdity someplace; so we will allow our gnostic theologians to pretend that Adam evolved from the lower orders for the moment and leave it at that.

---

[2] See Chapter 5 for more information on Kidner's sorrowful attempt at explaining how this heresy works out in Scripture.

[3] The doctrine of imputed sin which Paul elucidates in Romans is explained more simply and succinctly in Genesis: like begets like. Adam and Eve were sinners, and as such were capable only of giving birth to sinners. They could not give birth to a holy child any more than to a fish.

So we must assume that the image of God was passed down from our evolved Adam to his physical offspring, and once we assume that then we must also recognize that we gain nothing whatsoever in assuming that Adam evolved, because we are forced to begin counting the generations of mankind from the time of Adam—even as we do when we believe by faith that Adam was created directly from the dust of the earth, as Genesis tells us. The only thing that we gain is the ability to explain away the claims of modern science concerning the "fossil record," whereby they date mankind back 100,000 years or more. Alas, our attempts to do so only gain us an Adam who lived roughly 10,000 years ago—which is roughly the time frame shown by the genealogies in the Bible, just coincidentally. So in mixing evolution into Genesis, we have once again been unfaithful to the theologies of Genesis *and* evolution.

And what about Eve? Was she a literal person, or is she merely an allegorical figure representing womanhood? If she was literal, where did she come from? Was she born to Neanderthal parents, having evolved enough to be selected by God as His image bearer along with Adam? Or did God literally create her from Adam's rib?

We cannot believe in both the evolution of Adam *and* the creation of Eve from Adam's rib at the same time, because we cannot say that Genesis 2 is a mixture of historical fact and allegory, arbitrarily deciding that Adam's creation from dust is metaphorical but Eve's creation from his rib is literal. (We cannot, of course, take this approach to Genesis as a whole, which is precisely what Christian Darwinists do when they say that Abraham was a historical man but creation is a metaphorical "narrative," or that "days" means "millions of years.") Therefore, if we say that Adam evolved and was not directly created from dust by God's own hand, then we must also say that Eve was not created from his rib but that she, too, evolved from some "lesser beings."

This opens another can of theological worms. Why would God give headship to the man, as He so clearly does throughout Scripture, when Eve had as much right to authority as Adam? After all, she evolved just as much as Adam did, having raised herself up from her ignoble Neanderthal heritage, so each was equally worthy of honor and authority.[4]

---

[4] Here, incidentally, is another way in which evolution is a self-glorifying religion: man evolved himself from the ooze, and he owes little to God.

Paul tells us clearly that it was Adam's sin, not Eve's, that brought sin and death into the world. But if Eve had evolved herself from lower orders, then she was just as responsible for bringing sin and death as was her husband. (We are not permitted to suggest that Eve was less evolved than Adam, since Genesis clearly states that both bear the image of God.) Paul further teaches that woman should not hold authority within the church, "For Adam was formed first, then Eve. And Adam was not deceived, but the woman being deceived, fell into transgression" (1 Tim. 2:13–15). In order to sustain our faith in evolution, we must now assume that Eve evolved later than Adam, and that she committed some sort of sin through ignorance while Adam did so deliberately. And here again we gain nothing, and are forced to read 1 Timothy 2 at face value while insisting that the Scripture upon which 1 Timothy is *based* is actually *not* meant to be read literally but metaphorically—which then gets us into a knot because it would mean that Paul misunderstood Genesis 2 and 3, taking those chapters literally when they were not meant to be taken literally, and that in turn would mean that his teachings on church authority were invalid.[5]

And what, exactly, is this "sin" of which we are speaking? The concept of "sin" requires two things: a law or commandment; and a sentient, responsible being who possesses the free will, understanding, and ability either to obey or disobey that law. The Christian Darwinists are forced to assume that Neanderthal man and his predecessors were not accountable for sin in some manner, whether because they lacked free will or sufficient intelligence, or for some other reason which precluded them from being considered God's image bearers. Adam, however, reached a point in his evolution where he was capable of being held accountable, according to this theory, so God presumably gave him some commandment—and Adam disobeyed. There is no other option, for without a commandment there was nothing to obey or disobey, and sin cannot be possible.

Once again, we are forced full-circle back to Genesis 3, forced to conclude that some individual human at some point in history violated some command of God and so introduced the concept of "sin" into the world. We have gained absolutely nothing by claiming that Adam evolved from lower

---

[5] Some feminists, of course, attempt to build this very argument. It is not my purpose, however, to debate Paul's teachings on church authority, but rather to demonstrate that our beliefs on creation and our reading of Genesis have a profound impact upon our Christian beliefs—upon our reading of the entire Bible.

orders, but we *have* lost the right to accept Genesis 3 at face value—as Moses intended us to—and have, therefore, lost the one sensible explanation for the doctrines of sin and death.

This brings us back to the person and work of Jesus Christ, the Last Adam. The title "Last Adam" which is ascribed to Christ (1 Cor. 15:45) implies that there was at least one preceding Adam, and perhaps many (Noah, for example, can be seen as a "second Adam"). It also implies that Jesus is the final Adam in the succession of Adams; that, after Him, there is no need for another Adam.

This whole concept is built upon the premise that Adam, the first man, failed to obey God, condemning himself and all of his descendants to death and separation from God. As I've already said, this means that Adam needed to: 1) exist literally; 2) know and understand the will of God; 3) deliberately disobey God's will of his own volition. Christ, also, had to: 1) exist literally on earth; 2) know and understand the will of God; 3) deliberately obey God's will flawlessly, completely, perfectly, and in opposition to strong temptation toward disobedience. Having done so, He fulfilled the role which was originally assigned to the first Adam, and no further Adams are required.

This bit of theology is at the very core of the Christian faith. Without an Adam, we have no Christ. The doctrines of evolution force Christian Darwinists either to arbitrarily inject a miraculous divine intervention into millennia of non-miraculous "natural" evolution—which, as we have seen, accomplishes nothing; or else to do away with Adam altogether—which accomplishes the complete negation of the Christian faith.

The only solution to this problem is to accept Genesis 3 at face value, believing by faith that a literal Adam ate from a literal tree in violation of a literal command of God. This, of course, forces us to back up and accept Genesis 2 at face value, believing by faith that God literally created Adam from the literal dust of the earth, literally creating Eve from Adam's literal rib, placing both in the literal garden with God's literal blessing. And if we have reached the point of accepting all this by faith at face value, then we must do the same with Genesis 1, accepting by faith that God literally created all that exists in six literal 24-hour days.

And having reached this point, we recognize that there is nothing whatever to be gained by *not* reading Genesis 1 at face value, understanding Moses' intended meaning that the world was created by God's word in six literal 24-hour days.

## A Simple Matter of Logic

Modern man has developed a dangerous habit of trying to compartmentalize truth, as though "theological truth" does not need to be consistent with "scientific truth." After all, we assume, they are different fields of study, different areas of expertise, different departments of a vast organization of knowledge. Marcus Dods puts it nicely when he argues that the Bible should be revered only in respect to having authority "in its own department of truth,"[6] and thus cannot be expected to provide modern readers with any sort of reliable account of creation—the origins of man, after all, are the bailiwick of modern science, not divinely inspired Scripture.[7]

We cannot expect a theologian to be conversant in the latest theories of quantum physics, nor do we expect a physicist to hold forth on the subjects of original sin and redemption. (Ironically, when a physicist such as Howard Van Till does put himself forward as a theologian, we acquiesce to his authority without a murmur—but not vice versa.[8])

Now, the modern theologian will pipe up at this point and squeak that he is trying to do just this very thing, to harmonize one department of truth—modern science—with another department of truth: the Bible. This, however, cannot be done without radically changing one or the other—and it is noteworthy that scientists (such as Van Till) and theologians (such as Gordon Wenham) always decide to change the Bible while leaving modern science intact. (Others attempt to change both, such as James Boice, with even worse results.) The reasoning which these writers use is to suggest that Moses could not be expected to understand modern science, so therefore we should feel free to change what he wrote to harmonize it with the "facts" of science. They try to override the concept of divine inspiration by claiming that human "editors" wrote Genesis, stealing ideas from pagan myths. This way, they can justify changing even the words of the Lord which Moses quotes directly, building the notion that Moses (excuse me, the "redactor") was not quoting God but merely lifting material from some Babylonian document.[9]

---

6 Marcus Dods, *The Expositor's Bible: The Book of Genesis*, 2.

7 "If any one is in search of accurate information regarding the age of this earth, or its relation to the sun, moon, and stars, or regarding the order in which plants and animals have appeared upon it, he is referred to recent text-books in astronomy, geology, and paleontology. No one for a moment dreams of referring a serious student of these subjects to the Bible as a source of information." [Dods, p. 1]

8 See, for example, Howard J. Van Till, et al., ed., *Portraits of Creation*.

9 Wenham does this when he tries to explain what "the narrator" *really* meant in Genesis 3, where

This is the flow of logic—or lack of logic—which modern theologians use to rewrite Genesis 1 and 2 as metaphor, while keeping Adam and his sin more or less intact as historical figures and events. As I have stated repeatedly, there is no change in the text to indicate that Moses is switching from allegory to history or vice versa at any point in Genesis, so the result of this vapid logic is that we either must take Abraham and his descendants as fictional characters, or else we must treat the entire book of Genesis as a historical document. Modern theologians defy reason and logic in their rewritings of Genesis.

A man might say, "God is love, and the word 'love' comes from an ancient Egyptian word meaning 'ox cart,' so we know, therefore, that love should bear all burdens." This man's etymology, of course, would be very wrong, yet both his basic thesis ("God is love") and his conclusion ("love bears all wrongs") might still be true. We might choose to overlook this error if the man is a theologian, since we know that theologians are not well-read; or we might choose to hold him accountable for his bad etymology if he claims to be a linguist. We are not, however, particularly troubled by the fact that his argument depends upon all three points being true. The man's conclusion, from a purely logical perspective, must be treated as false the moment that one of the links in the chain ("the word 'love' is from 'ox cart'") proves false.

Moses claims that God created the world; that He did it merely by speaking; and that He did it in a particular order over a specific period of time. Modern science claims that this is not so, and Christian Darwinists respond by saying, "Oh, well, that's okay, we can't expect an ancient author to know about evolution—but his conclusions [that God created the world] are still valid!" This is the most outrageously false and illogical premise that a man can put forward.

If God did not create the earth exactly as described in Genesis 1, then He did not create man from dust and woman from man, as described in Genesis 2. And if Genesis 2 is incorrect in any detail, then Adam and Eve did not fall from grace in Genesis 3.

---

Moses directly quotes God's words in the curses. "While a messianic interpretation may be justified in the light of subsequent revelation," Wenham pompously declares, "it would perhaps be wrong to suggest that this was the narrator's own understanding [in relation to the 'seed of the woman' in the serpent's curse]. Probably he just looked for mankind eventually to defeat the serpent's seed, the powers of evil" [*Genesis 1–15*, 81]. He assures us repeatedly that it is "difficult to grasp the author's precise intention"—whenever the evident intention of Moses or the directly quoted words of God Himself prove inconvenient to Wenham's desire to harmonize evolution and Scripture.

This problem is larger than the question of divine inspiration. It is a question of logic, of following an orderly sequence of reasoning—point A leading to point B which concludes with point C. The fall of mankind is predicated upon God's instantaneous creation of man, and that instantaneous creation requires, by force of logic, that Moses' six-day account be true—exactly as written, which includes the six 24-hour day timeframe. If any of these three points is *not* true—any, including six literal 24-hour days—then the very person and work of Jesus Christ also proves false.

# Section 3:
# Heretics in Our Midst

# 10
# WHAT IS GNOSTICISM?

Gnosticism is the official name for a heresy that flourished in the second century AD, during the period of the early Christian church. We have already seen, of course, that this heresy originated in the Garden of Eden, underneath the Tree of Knowledge. But for ease of understanding, we will examine the writings and thinking of the second-century Gnostics, specifically the Valentinian school. This body of literature and thinking is perhaps the best definition and clearest origin of the modern school of thought variously known as "Deconstructionism," "Revisionism," and "Higher Criticism."[1] In this chapter, I will discuss some of the basic tenets of classical Gnosticism, and will compare those ideas with the thinking of the modern gnostics.

## Gnostic Jargon

Classical Gnosticism was a syncretistic religious system which took ideas and terminology from Christianity, Judaism, Babylonian and Egyptian polytheisms, and other sources. It was a promiscuous blend of religious thought, mixing incompatible ideas together into a strange, mystical religion of chaos. So the early Gnostics, for example, blended Christian teachings on the resurrection together with Eastern notions of reincarnation, sprinkled in some mystical-sounding terminology about "gnosis" and "thought" and so forth, and cooked up their own heretical brew for the afterlife.

The early Gnostics stole concepts and terminology from the gospels and epistles, which we now know as our New Testament, which lent their writings an orthodox Christian flavor. By using such familiar names and terminology—and even sometimes referring directly to the writings of Paul and Peter and John—the Gnostics were able to seduce many Christians into believing that they were teaching truth, when in fact they were preaching a false gospel.

---

1 I do make a distinction between the "classic Gnosticism" of Valentinus and the "modern gnosticism" of writers such as Harold Bloom, Gordon Wenham, and others. I have followed the convention throughout this book of using lower-case "gnosticism" to refer to the modern gnostics, and upper-case "Gnosticism" to refer to the second-century Gnostics. I will continue to make this distinction within this chapter.

One early Gnostic was a man named Valentinus, whose writings and teachings had a wide-spread influence in Gnostic and Christian circles during the second century. This man was very nearly elected to be the Bishop of Rome—the man whom we now call Pope. In fact, this early voice of Gnosticism was probably never exposed as a heretic during his own lifetime, as his writings and thinking were ultimately exposed by Irenaeus in his classic work *Against Heresies*, written after the death of Valentinus. Little is known of Valentinus' life, but it seems that he was viewed during his lifetime as a legitimate leader within the Christian church. This is worth emphasizing because the same trend is evident in the church today, as modern gnostics are being accorded the respect and attention of legitimate Bible teachers and scholars—when, in fact, they are leading the church into grievous error.

An example of the Gnostics' use of Christian terminology was their appropriation of Colossians 2:9, where Paul tells us that "in Him dwells all the fullness of the Godhead bodily." The word translated "fullness" is *pleroma* in the Greek. The Gnostics adapted this word and used it freely to refer to a body of angelic beings (who turn out to be demonic beings when one reads their writings) who form some sort of council, comprising the "fullness of the deity." Paul is clearly stating that Christ embodies the fullness of God in His own person, but the Gnostics twisted his terminology to suggest that the full godhead was composed of a variety of angelic (that is, demonic) beings.

The use of Christian terminology was not restricted to such esoteric Greek terms as *pleroma*; the Gnostics stole freely from the early writings of the apostles and early church leaders to create their own unsound doctrines. For example, *The Treatise on the Resurrection*, a Gnostic text from the late second century, makes free use of Christian thought. The author refers to "the Word of Truth," speaking of "our Savior, our Lord Christ," assuring his readers that "the Savior swallowed up death," "for we have known the Son of Man, and we have believed that he rose from among the dead," and using other phrases and terminology that gave his writing a genuine Christian sound. But the gist of his message is that the resurrection which Christ promised is actually *not* the resurrection of a believer's body and immortal soul, but merely of a person's gnostic thoughts! "The thought of those who are saved shall not perish," the author writes. "The mind of those who know him shall not perish.... The world is an illusion!... already you have the resurrection."[2] "Why not look

---

2 *The Nag Hammadi Library in English*, James M. Robinson, editor. San Francisco: Harper, 1988, p. 54–55.

at yourself and see that you already have arisen and have been received in?"³ Paul addresses these writers in 2 Timothy 2:16–21:

> But shun profane and idle babblings, for they will increase to more ungodliness. And their message will spread like cancer. Hymenaeus and Philetus are of this sort, who have strayed concerning the truth, saying that the resurrection is already past; and they overthrow the faith of some. Nevertheless the solid foundation of God stands, having this seal: "The Lord knows those who are His," and, "Let everyone who names the name of Christ depart from iniquity." But in a great house there are not only vessels of gold and silver, but also of wood and clay, some for honor and some for dishonor. Therefore if anyone cleanses himself from the latter, he will be a vessel for honor, sanctified and useful for the Master, prepared for every good work.

These men—Hymenaeus and Philetus—were spreading the teachings of the early Gnostics among Christian believers. Paul equates Gnostic teaching with the vessels of dishonor, and urges believers to cleanse themselves from such teachings. This is precisely what the church must do again today, repudiating the modern gnosticism contained in the works of Wenham and Hamilton and their tribe, and returning to the orthodox embrace of the Scriptures as the straightforward, inspired Word of God. Irenaeus, writing in the second century, addressed the Gnostics' twisting of Christian terminology, "striving, as they do, to adapt the good words of revelation to their own wicked inventions."⁴

We see the same tendency within the modern "New Age" movement. This loosely organized group of gurus loves to borrow ideas and terminology from many religious systems—including Christianity—to teach their adherents that they can evolve into godhood by tapping some mystical "inner power." Like the New Age movement, Gnosticism was a religious system in which each philosopher was free to invent more or less his own system of thought, his own methods of working out the "higher knowledge" of Gnostic ideas. "And while they affirm such things as these concerning the creation,"

---

3 *The Nag Hammadi Scriptures*, Marvin Meyer, ed. NY: Harper One, 2007, p. 55.
4 Irenaeus, *Against Heresies*, I.3.6.

writes Irenaeus, "every one of them generates something new, day by day, according to his ability; for no one is deemed 'perfect,' who does not develop among them some mighty fictions."[5] I have touched briefly upon this trait in modern Bible criticism, where each theologian invents his own methods of working evolution into the Bible. I will address this in more depth in the next chapter, when we will confront this trick of our modern theologians, each man inventing whatever creation scheme is right in his own eyes.

Classical Gnosticism does, however, have several strands of thought which run throughout all their early writings, with only minor variations.

## The Gnostic View of Creation

**In the beginning, all was chaos.** Chaos is a vitally important concept to Gnostic thought—an interesting thing to discover when one notes how important it is to our modern theologians, as well. *The Hypostasis of the Archons* is another Gnostic tract which opens with quotations from Paul (Col. 1:13; Eph 6:12) to lend itself credibility, then describes the Gnostic concept of creation.

> "Their chief is blind; [because of his] power and his ignorance [and his] arrogance he said, with his power, 'It is I who am God; there is none [apart from me].'"[6]

This initially sounds like a reference to the fall of Lucifer, but as we read on we discover that this arrogant, ignorant, blind "chief" is none other than Jehovah, whom the Gnostics generally refer to as the *demiurge* (a Greek word meaning "craftsman" or "creator").

The author of *Hypostasis/Archons* refers to this god as Samael, meaning "god of the blind." The author informs us that this blind god sinned against the archons—the ruling body of spirit-beings—by declaring himself to be the only god. As a result, a goddess named Sophia, the "incorruptible one," cast down this blind god into "chaos and the abyss." So far, this all sounds perfectly orthodox, despite the odd names, as though this is the fall of Lucifer.

Next we find Sophia hovering over the waters of the newly created earth, and "her image appeared in the waters; and the authorities of the darkness

---

5 Irenaeus, *Against Heresies*, I.18.1.
6 Robinson, *The Nag Hammadi Library*, 162.

became enamored of her."[7] These "authorities of darkness" then conspire together to create mankind, doing their best to duplicate the image of Sophia which they saw upon the waters. Eventually, their "man" comes to life, at which point these blind authorities bring all the animals before him and watch him name them. They then proceed to place the man in a garden. And inside that garden there is a tree—"the tree of recognizing good and evil"—from which the man is forbidden to eat, because the "authorities of darkness" fear that he will become like them if he eats from the tree of gnosis—so they threaten to kill him if he touches it. At this point, of course, we become fairly certain whose perspective this creation account is actually presenting, as these are essentially the words of the serpent in Genesis 3.

These blind authorities of darkness next cause the man to fall asleep, and we are informed that this was actually the sleep of "Ignorance."[8] They open up his side and remove—not a rib, but his spirit! The man had been created a three-fold being—body, soul, and spirit—but now he was left with only his body and soul; he was doomed to spend his life searching for his soul if he was to ascend into godhood.

This is the core of the Gnostic teachings: that man has been cheated of his godhood by the very one who created him, and that he can only regain it by gaining some mystical higher knowledge or gnosis. It is for this reason that Gnostics preached a hatred of the body and the physical world: because these things had been created by the creator god—the one whom we know as Jehovah—and anything that he created was evil in the eyes of the early Gnostics.

The *Hypostasis/Archons* introduces a new character: "the snake, the instructor," a being of beauty and wisdom who set about to teach man and woman the truth about "higher knowledge." The account at this point actually follows Genesis 3, except for the important alteration of having the serpent tell the truth about the wicked trick played upon mankind by their creator. The snake tells them that they can regain their deity by eating from the tree of Gnosis, so our fallen heroes, Adam and Eve, take from the tree of gnosis and discover that they have, in fact, been cheated of their spirits, their essence of

---

7 Robinson, *The Nag Hammadi Library*, 163.

8 In Gnosticism, the most dreadful thing to fear is ignorance, the lack of knowledge or "gnosis." This is also the charge which the "higher critics" frequently level against "literalists," that those who insist upon reading Genesis as written are merely remaining in ignorance and wearing "blinders" against the "higher truths" which science has unearthed.

godhood. It is interesting that, in the Gnostic scheme, Adam was fallen *prior* to eating from the Tree of Knowledge, and it was only by eating that he found hope of redemption—not far removed from those theologians who claim that Adam was not immortal prior to eating the forbidden fruit.

Adam and Eve are disgraced at having been deceived by their creator, and in great shame they cover themselves with fig leaves. Then along comes that naughty creator, that tricky scoundrel who says one thing but means another, "and he said, 'Adam! Where are you?'—for he did not understand what had happened."[9] The writer follows Genesis 3 point by point, yet with an oddly skewed perspective—the perspective of the serpent—and he makes it clear that the creator god is asking questions because he is ignorant. Again, this concept of ignorance is the antithesis of Gnosticism, and the claim that Jehovah is ignorant reflects the utmost contempt.

Finally, we learn the origin of death, when the creator looked upon his superior, the highest god who threw him down, and the creator envied his superior, and his envy "engendered death."[10] But we are reassured that all these bad things happened according to the plan of this supreme being, the "thrown-down one" who is mightier than the creator, "so that the sum of chaos might be attained."

Obviously, this entire scheme is a mere inversion of the truth, where Lucifer is placed above Jehovah. The serpent is portrayed as telling the truth, while the Creator is a liar who has deceived mankind and cheated him of his deity. Another Gnostic text, *On the Origin of the World*, tells us, "Then came the wisest of all creatures, who was called Beast." It then proceeds to recount the words of the serpent.[11] This inversion is at the core of Gnosticism, placing Lucifer at the pinnacle and Jehovah in chaos. As Willis Barnstone puts it, "Clearly, the gnostics turned Judeo-Christian theology upside down. They had the audacity to make Yahweh into a vain creator of the earth and its imprisoned inhabitants and, in many scriptures, simply into the devil."[12] Barnstone adds, "To convert traditional Christians to their intelligence, the gnostic philosophers developed an allegorical exegesis of the gospels to prove that Christian gospel revealed gnostic truths."[13]

---

9 Robinson, *The Nag Hammadi Library*, 165.
10 Robinson, *The Nag Hammadi Library*, 168.
11 Robinson, *The Nag Hammadi Library*, 184. It is worth considering that the rise of modern gnosticism might well be preparing the world to embrace the coming Beast, prophesied in Revelation.
12 Willis Barnstone, *The Gnostic Bible*, Willis Barnstone and Marvin Meyer, ed., 777.
13 *Ibid*, 780.

## Section 3: Heretics in Our Midst

The gnostic Christians of the 21st Century are using this very same trick with Genesis, allegorizing and metaphorizing the entire account of the creation and fall of mankind, in hopes of seducing Christians into believing that the Bible actually reveals gnostic evolutionary doctrines. Harold Bloom, a self-proclaimed modern gnostic, points out that Valentinus embraced this heresy "because he had seen that a perfect cognition of the origins [of mankind] was itself more than enough to make us free."[14] This "perfect cognition of the origins" of man, however, entailed quite a change from the account which is given in Genesis. It is the same today, as our modern theologians are insisting that a "correct understanding" of Genesis 1 requires us to rewrite it entirely.

Bloom points out that the concept of chaos was central to classical Gnostic thought concerning the creation of the world. According to Bloom, the Rabbinical Jews in the second century rejected Gnosticism as a heresy because the Gnostics were teaching that God had created the world out of chaos rather than out of nothing, *ex nihilo*. "It was through this conception of a creation out of nothing over against the conquest of chaos by the Creator-God" that the Rabbinical Jews determined the Gnostics to be heretical. The heresy of Gnosticism, in the minds of the second-century Jews, was found centrally in their teachings that God had created the world from chaos, rather than from nothing. Bloom writes, "The substitution of nothingness for chaos seemed to provide a guarantee of the Creator-God's freedom as opposed to all mythical determination by fate. His Creation thus ceases to be a struggle and a crisis and becomes a free act of Love."[15] Bloom is not a Christian, yet he is honest enough to admit that creation from chaos is the opposite of creation from love. He also points out that God's creating the earth from nothing, a nothing that was devoid of chaos, proves that He is above and beyond all other creatures and powers. If God merely conquered chaos when beginning creation, as our modern Bible commentators claim, then He is merely the greatest among many gods, not the sole and supreme God of all creation.

The ancient Gnostics admit that God created the earth, they merely claim that He did it differently than what Genesis seems to say on the surface. This is precisely the same ploy that the modern gnostics are using, those "higher critics" who work so assiduously to seduce Christians into believing that the

---

14 Harold Bloom, *Agon: Towards a Theory of Revisionism*. NY: Oxford UP, 1982, p. 72.
15 Bloom, *Agon*, p. 81. The book's title is a Greek word for "contest, conflict, struggle," a concept that is closely related to *chaos*.

first three chapters of Genesis do not mean what they appear to mean. In the end, the second-century Gnostics were leading Christians away from Jehovah and toward the worship of Lucifer. In the same way, our modern theologians are pretending to find hidden meanings in the creation account in order to adulterate it with evolution, and in the end this heresy will lead the Church away from our Creator and toward serving the devil.

"Gnostic religions," writes Marvin Meyer, "typically present stories and myths of creation, especially from the book of Genesis, interpreted in an innovative manner, with the transcendent divine spirit commonly distinguished from the creator of the world, often to the point of dualism, in order to explain the origin, estrangement, and ultimate salvation of what is divine in the world and humanity."[16] Our modern "higher critics" stop just short of teaching an actual duality at creation, of utterly divorcing the Spirit from the Creator. Yet, as I have already demonstrated, following their other "innovative" readings of Genesis to their logical conclusion, we will find ourselves deprived of Adam and original sin, which will indeed leave us in the quandary of explaining the existence of sin and "estrangement" (separation from God) under which mankind suffers today. When Christians begin to recognize that they have lost the person of Adam by admitting the heresy of "day/age" theologies, they will also discover that our gnostic theologians have already laid the foundation for a duality at creation simply by their insistence upon the presence of chaos at the time of creation. By permitting these men to get away with their magicians' tricks today, we are opening the door to a full-blown gnostic Christianity tomorrow.

## Gnostic Evolution

Gnosticism was actually an amalgam of numerous ancient pagan heresies, drawn together in the second century under the disguise of being sound Christian and Jewish theology. As I have said many times, the notion of evolution is not new; it has been a staple of pagan mythologies since Adam left the garden—so it is no surprise when we find the seeds of modern evolutionary thinking in the writings of the early Gnostics.

Valentinus, for example, tells us that the Creator took many eons to produce the world, in an effort to imitate the eternal nature of Lucifer. "When the Demiurge further wanted to imitate also the boundless, eternal,

---

16 Barnstone, *Gnostic Bible*, p. 16.

infinite and timeless nature" of the true god who exists eternally apart from the Creator, "he embodied their eternity in times, epochs, and great numbers of years, under the delusion that by the quantity of times he could represent their infinity."[17]

A larger evolutionary element within Gnosticism, however, is the teaching that mankind is evolving toward godhood. The basic tenet of Gnosticism is that the Creator of mankind was evil, and that He created man out of spite, intending to make humanity suffer and remain eternally apart from the Fallen One who exists above the Creator. Man, however, can save himself by attaining a higher knowledge, by eating of the fruit of the tree of knowledge which the Creator tried to keep hidden from early man. If a person partakes of this hidden knowledge, he will gain insight into the higher god who exists beyond the Creator—the Fallen or Exiled One—thus enabling him to become one with the highest god. As Willis Barnstone puts it, Gnosticism is a "self-centered religion," drawn from "multiple strands of Jewish and Christian hopelessness"[18]—"hopelessness" referring to the gospel teaching that man cannot save himself, that he needs a Redeemer.

This self-centered religion is based upon the notion that man is capable of evolving into deity, that he has no need of a redeemer but only of higher knowledge. "The self," writes Barnstone, "may become divine. The self may become god."[19] This lie of self-evolution, of mankind evolving into deity, was first told in the Garden of Eden by none other than the serpent. "Eat that magical fruit," he told Eve, "and you shall evolve into godhood." This is the very interpretation which the second-century Gnostics put upon Genesis 3.

> "Then came the wisest of all creatures, who was called Beast. And . . . he said to her, 'What did God say to you? Was it "do not eat from the tree of knowledge [*gnosis*]?"' She said, 'He said, "Not only do not eat from it, but do not touch it, lest you die".' He said to her, 'Do not be afraid. In death you shall not die. For he [God] knows that when you eat from it, your intellect will become sober and you will come to be like gods.'"[20]

---

17 Irenaeus, *Against Heresies*, I.17.2.
18 Barnstone, *Gnostic Bible*, 781.
19 Barnstone, *Gnostic Bible*, 791–92.
20 "On the Origin of the World," in Robinson, *Nag Hammadi Library*, 184.

### Harold Bloom, Modern-Day Gnostic

Harold Bloom teaches literature at Yale University, and he has written numerous books defining his brand of "Deconstructionist Criticism," sometimes called Revisionism. He also defines himself as a gnostic, a modern-day disciple of the second-century Gnostic Valentinus.

His idea is that each reader and poet and writer must build upon the writings and ideas of others, but that they must first deliberately misread and misunderstand the ideas and writings of their predecessors. It is a good thing, Bloom argues, for a reader to deliberately misunderstand and misread a text, to perform a "deliberately perverse misreading, whose purpose is to clear away the precursor so as to open a space for oneself."[21] He writes enthusiastically that, "in such revisionary hermeneutic, Gnosticism was a great innovator."[22]

There are numerous other modern and recent writers who have embraced gnosticism, and one was the well-known poet William Blake. Blake's poem "The Tyger" famously asks, "Did he who made the Lamb make thee?" Christians incorrectly assume that Blake's answer was "yes," when in reality it was a resounding "no!" Blake's contention is that the being who made the Lamb could never have made the Tyger because the two are opposites—they are mutually negating. The Tyger represents wrath in Blake's symbolism, while the Lamb represents Love. Christians frequently misconstrue the poet's symbolism in these poems, thinking that he had Christ in mind when he wrote of the Lamb. But in Gnostic schemes, "wrath" is Jehovah, the Creator, while "love" is the Usurped One, the Thrown-Down One, also known as Abyss or Lucifer.

Blake was an early modern gnostic, a dualist, yet he called himself a Christian. Such poems as "The Lamb" and "The Tyger" are often cited by Christians as beautiful testimonies to the wonders of God's creation, when in fact they are Gnostic songs directed (ultimately) to Lucifer. The reason that this confusion occurs is that gnosticism frequently steals words and concepts from Christianity, being syncretistic, and the convoluted lingo of gnosticism seduces Christians into believing that it is a high-flown and mystical comprehension of Christianity. But the ultimate god of gnosticism is Satan.

Blake and Bloom and others exemplify the ancient trick of the Gnostics, creating their own terminology, inventing words, stealing phrases and

---

21 Bloom, *Agon*, 64.
22 *Ibid.*, p. 67.

concepts from Christianity and imbuing them with new heretical (but hidden) meanings—using words upon words to baffle and seduce their audience into believing that they are telling the truth. Here is a nice example of gnostic double-talk from Harold Bloom's *Agon*:

> The third term of the triad is extravagance, the restitution of power by a mode of figuration that moves from the symbolic or synecdochic through the Sublime or hyperbolic and ends in an acosmic, anti-temporal trope that reverses the Alexandrian predicament of belatedness. This final extravagance is the earliest instance I know of the rhetoric of transumption, which is the ultimate modal resource of post-Miltonic poetry, and which projects lateness and introjects earliness, but always at the expense of presence, by the emptying out of the living moment."[23]

And the emptying out of intelligible meaning, it would appear. Interestingly, Bloom himself confesses that "the Biblical doctrine of creation is deliberately free of speculations upon origins." "There are Talmudic warnings against the *Minim* or Jewish Gnostics that center upon warning away those who would speculate upon the origins" of the human race. "As a Jewish heresy, [Gnosticism] had to begin at the Beginnings, and thus had to challenge the orthodox doctrine of Creation, for that doctrine fixed man's place."[24]

Bloom continues, "If you are not to be hedged in by God's incomprehensible power, then you must dissent from the doctrine of creation. You must learn to speculate about the origins [of mankind], and the aim of your speculation will have to be a vision of catastrophe, for only a divine catastrophe will allow for your own, your human freedom."[25] Bloom uses the words "catastrophe" and "chaos" interchangeably, providing yet another demonstration of the importance of "chaos" in gnostic thinking. As an openly confessed gnostic, he also freely admits that the rewriting of Genesis frees a person from being "hedged in" by God—in other words, he openly acknowledges that rewriting the Genesis creation account accomplishes the work of Lucifer, the Fallen One, by removing mankind from under God's

---

23 *Ibid.*, 68.
24 *Ibid.*, 78.
25 *Ibid.*, 78.

authority. It would be better if our modern "higher critics" were as open in this confession.

## Pharaoh's Magicians as Modern-Day Gnostics

Bloom has high praise for the modern school of theology which seeks to deliberately misinterpret the Bible. He openly declares that modern "higher criticism" is a strong form of gnosticism which "confronts and seeks to overthrow the very strongest of all texts, the Jewish Bible."[26] He states that gnostics spend their efforts "trying to occupy ground where others have stood more significantly."[27] He tells us that the early Gnostics were "precisely those intellectuals who could tolerate least" the feeling that the Biblical creation account was already clearly defined.

These Gnostic writers presented themselves, Bloom tells us, as the ones who were the "true understanders" of the Biblical "mysteries," yet they simultaneously refused to call themselves revisionists. "But Basiledes and Valentinus, and all other Gnostics, indeed *are* revisionists, and they say that Genesis and Plato got everything that was crucial quite wrong."[28] They felt, per Bloom, that they needed to rewrite and redefine the Bible's account of creation if they were to "open a space" for themselves. In other words, the early Gnostics reinvented the creation of the world in order to make a name for themselves, in order to secure disciples, in order to build their careers.

It is unfortunate that so many modern Bible commentators are continuing this tradition. The modern "higher critics" are busy "trying to occupy ground where others have stood more significantly," trying to claim that Genesis has been misread for millennia, that the church has gotten its reading of Genesis concerning "everything that was crucial quite wrong."

The now-mocked Gap Theory actually grew out of ancient Gnostic writings, which taught that the "original creation" of earth had been "overcome" and "usurped by a Demiurge." By Demiurge, the Gnostics meant Jehovah, not Lucifer; but the gap theorists still maintained that God had created the earth once, then destroyed it when He threw Lucifer down from heaven. They invented this absurdity in order to harmonize Genesis with modern scientific theories about the "fossil record," but in their attempt to compromise Scripture they inadvertently embraced Gnosticism.

---

26 *Ibid.*, 70.
27 *Ibid.*, 81.
28 *Ibid.*, 82.

Bloom describes the subtle approach of modern gnostic revisionism in another book, *The Anxiety of Influence*. "And revisionism," he writes, "whether in political theory, psychology, theology, law, poetics, has changed its nature in our time. The ancestor of revisionism is heresy, but heresy tended to change received doctrine by an alteration of balances, rather than by what could be called creative correction, the more particular mark of modern revisionism. Heresy resulted, generally, from a change in emphasis, while revisionism follows received doctrine along to a certain point, and then deviates, insisting that a wrong direction was taken."[29]

He describes how revisionism has been used on poetry, a technique of interpretation that "always proceeds by a misreading" of older writings, "an act of creative correction that is actually and necessarily a misinterpretation." The history of poetry, he claims, is a history "of distortion, of perverse, wilful [sic] revisionism."[30]

This deliberate act of misreading is precisely what is being practiced by the "higher critics," who openly admit that they are attempting to perform "creative correction" on the text of Genesis in order to read evolution into it. This "wilful revisionism" of these theologians "is actually and necessarily a misinterpretation," to use Bloom's words. It is also important that we recognize that the early Gnostics themselves felt it important during the second century to misinterpret Genesis in order to insert evolution and rearrange the created order and chronology.

## The Unknowable Knowledge

Gnosticism ultimately preaches of a knowing which cannot be known, a gnosis without which God Himself cannot be known—the unknowable knowing of the Unknowable. Bloom tells us that "the Gnostic dualism of soul or *psyche* against self or *pneuma* or 'spark' is crucial for seeing just what Gnostic knowing, or Gnosis, takes as its quest." So one must first comprehend both concepts of *psyche* (soul) and *pneuma* (spirit) if one is to gain the "higher knowledge," the Gnosis, required to comprehend ultimate Truth.[31] Then, in the very next sentence, he tells us that "the *pneuma* of Gnosis is a figurative

---

29 Harold Bloom, *The Anxiety of Influence: A Theory of Poetry*, 29.
30 *Ibid.*, 30.
31 "Ultimate truth," of course, is a concept which modern gnostics disdain, believing ultimately that a man is his own ultimate truth. Jesus, however, claimed that He is Truth, and that the only way to know God was through Him.

expression for which we ought not to seek an empirical referent, because that would belong to human rather than divine knowledge."[32] In normal English, Bloom is saying that the concept of *pneuma* cannot be understood by men, because only God can comprehend it.

The inevitable conclusion of Gnosticism is insanity. It is a belief system which elevates human knowledge and human understanding and human learning and intelligence above all other aspects of being human. It teaches that one cannot know truth without "higher knowledge," then assures us that the higher knowledge is unknowable, but warns us that the only way to gain ascendancy is to perpetually pursue that unknowable higher knowledge. The modern gnostic will likely end his days in an asylum.

---

32  Bloom, *Agon*, 7.

# 11
# Pharaoh's Magicians

I speak in harsh terms of the major figures in Biblical criticism today, and it is important to stop a moment to point out that I am not castigating the men, I am denouncing their books. No man knows the heart of another, save God alone, and I have no doubt that Gordon Wenham and Victor Hamilton and their peers are fine men in their private lives. They are, however, teachers, and as such their teachings are subject to a higher level of accountability. The teachings of these men are in grievous error, some even preaching heresy, and as such the books at the very least should go out of print—if not openly corrected or recanted by the writers. Since this seems unlikely, I feel that a heavy hand is justified in thrashing out the heresies.

In this chapter, then, we will look more closely at a few of the favorite magical tricks perpetrated by Pharaoh's magicians, these self-acclaimed "higher critics."

## The Created Order

Pharaoh's magicians have worked wonderful magic in convincing the church that the order and timeline of creation in Genesis is not really what Genesis means. It *says* it, but it doesn't *mean* it—that's the basic argument of the magicians. But Satan himself entered the garden for the express purpose of inverting the created order. He approached Eve rather than Adam for the simple reason that he wanted Eve to take over headship of the race. God clearly tells Adam that the curse on mankind is "because you have heeded the voice of your wife, and have eaten from the tree" (3:17). Satan succeeded in turning upside down the created order, and Adam was held accountable for assisting the devil in his work.

One might ask, "does it really *matter* in what order God created the heavens and the earth?" Does it really matter whether the sun was created on Day 4 or Day 1 or Millennium 3,402? The gnostics claim that it *doesn't* matter, that the order and time stipulated in Genesis 1 is not really the order in which things were created nor the time that was actually required. But if we invoke great ages in creation rather than six literal days, we force ourselves to accept evolution. And if Adam evolved from the lower orders, then the animal kingdom is not under man's dominion. Mankind has no more authority over the animals than a man has over his distant cousin. If Adam evolved, Eve also evolved—and all of Paul's teachings concerning headship go out the window, since he bases them upon the created order.

So yes, it does matter what order things were created in, and it does matter how long that creation took. In rearranging the order of creation—"dischronologizing," as Pharaoh's magicians phrase it—the "higher critics" are telling the lie of the serpent, they are doing the work of the devil.

## J-E-P

As I said earlier, it is not my purpose to debate whether or not Moses wrote the book of Genesis. Nevertheless, we must address the assertion of the "higher critics" that Genesis was written by "authors" and "editors" and "redactors" long after the wilderness period, for it is on this lie that they base their other lies, including the lie that the creation account of Genesis 1 and 2 is stolen from pagan mythologies.

One of the many sleight-of-hand tricks used by Pharaoh's magicians is to mold their fictional J-E-P redactors into whatever role suits their purpose. Most of the time, Genesis is not written (in their "literary hypothesis") by any single author, but is rather a "redaction" or retelling of ancient pagan myths. A series of make-believe "editors" collected a series of make-believe ancient documents, each one selecting his favorite pieces of paganism to rewrite into a bit of propaganda for the Jews. These redactors didn't even live at the same time, according to this fairy tale, but worked on the "Genesis document" over the span of hundreds of years—the later redactors adding to what the earlier redactors had done.

But Pharaoh's magicians don't want us to read Genesis as it is written, so to accomplish this further deception they convert the redactors into the most marvelously skilled and unified writers—not mere "editors" any longer, mind you, but writers more skilled than Shakespeare—plying their gifts together with subtlety and delight (and the concept of "subtlety" within Genesis is not a flattering one), all of these independent individuals suddenly working together hand-in-hoof, united with one mind and purpose despite living hundreds of years apart, sharing the same vision and poetic skills despite the fact that writing styles and tastes change dramatically over centuries—to say nothing of linguistic nuances.

Thus, when Gordon Wenham wants to convince us that creation took much longer than six days, he clothes his redactors in the garb of the Bard and makes them grand masters of poetry. Suddenly, the six days are just a literary "device," intended by these Shakespearean redactors to be a poetic representation of "the coherence and purposiveness of the creative work," but unfortunately a poetic device that "has been seized on and interpreted over-literalistically, with the result that science and Scripture have been pitted against each other instead of being seen as complementary."[1]

The problem, according to Wenham, is that the ordinary man does not have the "higher knowledge" and therefore cannot hope to "properly" understand the poetic subtleties (that dangerous word again) of Genesis 1. "Properly understood," says Wenham, "Genesis justifies the scientific experience of unity and order in nature. The six-day schema is but one of several means employed in this chapter to stress the system and order that has been built into creation."[2] In other words, the high priests of gnosticism have the secret knowledge which enables them to see that the author(s) of Genesis *said* six days but actually *meant* six billion years. (We will disregard for now the absurdity of suggesting that there is a "system" or "order" within the death-driven chaos of evolution.)

The common man, of course, cannot be expected to recognize these subtleties without the assistance of the gnostic priests, so Wenham continues: "Other devices" in this masterpiece of poetical subtlety "include the use of repeating formulae, the tendency to group words and phrases into tens and sevens, literary techniques such as chiasm and inclusio, the arrangement of creative acts into matching groups, and so on."[3] And so on, indeed.

Thus our disparate "redactors" and "editors" (two pejorative terms, by the way, which imply that the "authors" of Genesis are ham-fisted pedantic hacks)—suddenly these hacks are transformed into gifted poets working together with the single vision of saying one thing while meaning something quite different, signaling that deeper meaning with "literary devices" which would be lost on the average reader—even though we are told at all other times that Genesis was intended as a bit of propaganda for the Hebrew masses, and even though these make-believe editors allegedly lived at vastly different periods of human history.

This in itself is like suggesting that the plays of Shakespeare were actually "redactions" of ancient texts (now lost) which were edited by three different

---

1 Wenham, *Genesis 1–15*, 39.
2 *Ibid.*
3 *Ibid.*

men who lived in the 1500s, 1700s, and 1900s respectively—all of whom worked independently and yet somehow maintained a unified poetic sense and writing skill, in spite of the vastly different literary tastes of those respective periods. This doctrine is so ludicrous that it could only be seriously believed by modern theologians and other madmen.

Why do these commentators play these tricks? Wenham himself may give us a clue when he laments that "science and Scripture have been pitted against each other instead of being seen as complimentary." There seems to be an overriding determination in modern commentaries to make science and the Bible walk hand-in-hand—and whenever the two disagree it's the Bible that must be changed, not science. But Christians are under no obligation to make the Bible accord to the learning of mankind. Science has indeed been very beneficial to modern man, providing cures for disease and increased comfort and health, and Christians *do* have an obligation to think and to wrestle with any challenges which modern learning may pose. The wrestling becomes a problem, however, when the teachings of man clearly contradict the teachings of Scripture, as is undeniably the case with evolution. At that point, God's people are commanded to abandon those false teachings and to cling by faith to the Word of God. Contemporary Bible scholars have not done this; instead of wrestling with the fallacies of scientific evolutionism, they have turned against the Word of God and attempted to wrestle the Bible into submission to the teachings of man.

Those critics who perpetuate the J-E-P fiction must also carry their faulty reasoning into the gospels if they are to be consistent. John, for example, was an uneducated fisherman and could not be expected to write such a rich, poetic, mystical document as the Gospel of John. So Pharaoh's magicians should be consistent and start writing books about how the Gospel of John was actually written hundreds of years after Christ by a series of redactors who were seeking to draw together the teachings of the early Christian church into one unified theological system. These redactors simply drew from ancient mythologies, you see, reworking them to fit the life of Christ. There are innumerable myths, after all, of gods who became men, sons of gods who performed great deeds, and our Johannine Redactors used those myths to create a polemical story which *refutes* the very myths that they use.

The church has recognized for millennia the truth of divine inspiration, believing that John the fisherman could write about Christ's role in creation

## Section 3: Heretics in Our Midst

because God Himself revealed it to him. The same approach must be taken to Genesis if we are to be consistent, and the "documentary hypothesis" must be recognized for the gnostic heresy that it is, and its adherents banned from orthodox theological studies.

One of Harold Bloom's books is entitled *Ruin the Sacred Truths: Poetry and Belief from the Bible to the Present*. His title is intended quite literally: His "deconstructionist" view is that each generation must deliberately destroy a text in order that they may then rebuild it in a fashion which suits their own age and agenda. Even the term "deconstruction" underscores this belief, as these modern gnostic critics strive deliberately and openly to misinterpret literature in order to make it fit into the beliefs and values of their own generation. The deconstructionists grew out of the same group of German theologians who are the founders of modern Biblical criticism—they are the two branches of the same Tree of Knowledge, a sacred and a secular, both equally committed to the goal of ruining the sacred truths in order to rewrite them with a new meaning.

Bloom snidely mocks those who believe that Moses wrote Genesis, and those who believe that Genesis means what it says. "J, according to a number of current Biblical scholars,[4] including many literalists who refuse to recognize a metaphor even when it confronts them,[5] has had no real existence, but merely was invented by the Wellhausen school and those who came after."[6] Bloom assures us that we are over-literalizing our reading of Genesis when we interpret the words of "J" (one of the mighty trinity J-E-P) to refer to some god called Jehovah. We need to deconstruct Genesis fully in order to set J's writing free from the "condition of enclosure" (by which he evidently means context) which we have imposed upon the text. He builds upon the teachings of Pharaoh's magicians, even interpreting parts of Genesis in precisely the same way as Wenham, et al. (e.g., Gen. 2:4ff)—but he carries them to their logical conclusion, telling us that Adam is "fictitious," and that the author ("J") of this portion of Genesis intends us to *recognize* that Adam is fictitious, that "J" has implanted "ironic" clues in the text which urge us not to read the text literally. Bloom takes us to the final conclusion of gnosticism,

---

[4] I only wish there were more such current Biblical scholars and fewer "higher critic" gnostics.

[5] Wenham similarly denigrates "literalists" when he writes that "rejection [of J-E-P] has usually come from orthodox Jews, conservative Christians, or others on the fringes of mainstream scholarship." [*Genesis 1–11*, xxxiv]

[6] Harold Bloom, *Ruin the Sacred Truths*, 3.

where his theologian comrades are afraid to go: "The first violator of the Second Commandment was Yahweh himself."[7]

## Source Criticism

Source criticism is the name given to one of the tricks of Pharaoh's magicians, by which they claim that the "authors" of Genesis stole their ideas from pagan "sources." It is actually little more than a tribe of dwarfs who run around trying to knock down giants. They are not restricted to Biblical studies; any giant of literature (and music and probably any other field of human endeavor) will find himself subjected to the annoyance of these little gnomes scurrying about in his shadow, squeaking up at him, "where did you get *that* idea? Whose plot did you copy? We know that *you* didn't write this—what are your sources??"

The basic premise of this trick goes back, once again, to the notorious German "higher critics" who simply refused to believe in miracles. The source critics cannot accept the miracle of human genius, the idea that a man such as Mozart or Shakespeare could really be so gifted, so inspired, so . . . genius! This is probably exacerbated by their teeth-gnashing recognition of their own pedestrian lack of genius.

This is not to say that Shakespeare did not use "sources" for his plays. He was not hesitant, for example, to draw ideas and characters and even some basic plots from classical mythology, historical events, and so forth. The problem is that speculating about his sources has become a bona fide field of study in its own right—more than this, it has become an obsession, to the point that students of literature today spend more time reading what modern day theorists say *about* Shakespeare than they do reading Shakespeare.

This is merely a tragic gyp for students of English literature; but it is a dangerous gnostic heresy when it is applied to the Bible. Students of the Bible today are distracted away from reading God's Word *as* the words of God Himself, spending excessive mental energy on wrestling with the theories of critics rather than on applying the Word of God to modern life. Thus, contemporary commentaries lure us away—persistently, relentlessly—from the deep truths of Genesis to worry about who *really* wrote the book and where they got their ideas. Source criticism applied to the Bible purports to be a useful scholarly tool, but it ends up being a dangerous presupposition,

---

[7] *Ibid.*, 11.

denying the inerrant inspiration of the Holy Spirit, denying the possibility of God's direct transmission of truth to a single human writer.[8]

## "Narrative"

Another of the pervasive sleights-of-hand played by Pharaoh's magicians is to refer incessantly to Genesis as "narrative." This, in fact, has become the unquestioned label by which modern critics refer to the book; one never refers to it as Scripture or history. The question must be asked, however, whether Genesis is in fact a narrative.

This leads, of course, to the primary question: what *is* "narrative?" The literary term itself refers to a story told by a narrator. The narrator may be a character within the story (first person), or he may be an unnamed storyteller who is merely relating some tale (third person). The story itself can be nearly any sequence of events which revolve around some central plot. It may be the story of events that actually occurred some time in the past (history), or it may focus upon one person's life (biography), or it may even be pure invention on the part of the author (fiction). The author may bring himself into the story to act as narrator, such as in autobiography; or he may use another person to tell the story—perhaps a real person, such as in historical fiction, or an invented character whose views further the plot in some way, a technique often found in satire.

Technically speaking, narrative is not a genre, it is a technique used in telling a story. History is a literary genre, a classification which we use to describe a certain category of literature. Historical literature describes actual events that really took place, generally involving actual people who really lived. Historical literature purports to tell the truth to the reader about what happened, how it happened, who was involved, and what each person said or did.

An author may choose to write a work of history using many different techniques to tell his reader about the historical subject. He may wish, for example, to put forward his own ideas on why an event occurred and why that event had certain results, and to do this he would use a very analytical approach. He might cite certain things that were said or done by important people, showing the reader how, in his opinion, those actions led to subsequent occurrences. Another author might choose merely to describe,

---

[8] See Appendix 1 for a look at the alleged "sources" of Genesis. The reader can judge for himself whether there is any similarity between Genesis and the pagan myths.

more or less chronologically, what happened over a given period of time, relating facts and dates and participants with little or no interjection of his own opinions—he is merely telling his reader what happened. This would be considered a narrative approach to history.

It is, therefore, inaccurate to refer to Genesis as "narrative," because narrative is a literary technique, not a literary genre. It is not entirely false to do so, since Moses is using the narrative technique to describe historical events; but his book is a historical account, not a narrative. Referring to Genesis simply as narrative is rather like referring to *Beowulf* as "an alliteration." *Beowulf* certainly makes use of alliteration, but alliteration itself is not a genre, it is a technique used within the genre of poetry.

Genesis purports to be describing for the reader certain historical events which took place in the past, and as such it is history. A straightforward, honest reading of Genesis makes it abundantly clear that the author is claiming to relate an accurate account of real historical events and people. The fact that he uses the narrative approach is of no importance; the only question that matters is whether or not the history is true and accurate.

Once again, we come back to the double-mindedness of modern biblical scholars, for the fact is that modern science claims that Genesis is wrong while Genesis claims that modern science is wrong—and the Bible scholar can't decide whom to believe. He therefore tries to rewrite Genesis in a way that will permit him also to place his faith in the teachings of men; and to enable him to do so, he refers persistently to the book as "narrative."

This sleight-of-hand trick is important to Pharaoh's magicians because they can dismiss Moses' historical account as merely a series of stories—"narratives"—torn out of pagan mythologies and sewn together into a patchwork "redaction"—a redaction which, according to the magicians, is actually a polemic or refutation of the very myths from which the "editors" got their ideas in the first place. And better still, since Genesis is merely a patchwork quilt—or better, a "mosaic"—one can feel free to remove one small section and re-attach it in another, more convenient spot. This is how Pharaoh's magicians work the trick of "dischronologizing" the six days of creation.

We must not permit Pharaoh's magicians to distract us with these sleight-of-hand tricks. Genesis is not a narrative, it is a history which uses narrative and other techniques to recount historical events. When we encounter a different historical account which conflicts with this historical account, we are certainly free to dismiss this account as inaccurate and unreliable—but we are *not* permitted to invent some new genre in hopes of embracing both conflicting accounts.

## "Polemic"

Pharaoh's magicians also incessantly refer to Genesis as "polemic," claiming (without ever providing any evidence) that Genesis is written merely to refute some ancient pagan writing which was causing confusion for God's people. I've already addressed this in an earlier chapter in passing, but it is worth pursuing a trifle further here in order to demonstrate that Genesis is *not* a polemic and to expose the "higher critics" in one of their tricks.

A polemic is a type of literature whose main objective is to address and refute someone else's beliefs. Here are some examples of polemical writing from the Bible:

> Do not defile yourselves with any of these things; for by all these the nations are defiled, which I am casting out before you. For the land is defiled; therefore I visit the punishment of its iniquity upon it, and the land vomits out its inhabitants. You shall therefore keep My statutes and My judgments, and shall not commit any of these abominations, either any of your own nation or any stranger who dwells among you (for all these abominations the men of the land have done, who were before you, and thus the land is defiled), lest the land vomit you out also when you defile it, as it vomited out the nations that were before you. For whoever commits any of these abominations, the persons who commit them shall be cut off from among their people. Therefore you shall keep My ordinance, so that you do not commit any of these abominable customs which were committed before you, and that you do not defile yourselves by them: I am the LORD your God. (Leviticus 18:24–30)

> When you come into the land which the LORD your God is giving you, you shall not learn to follow the abominations of those nations. There shall not be found among you anyone who makes his son or his daughter pass through the fire, or

one who practices witchcraft, or a soothsayer, or one who interprets omens, or a sorcerer, or one who conjures spells, or a medium, or a spiritist, or one who calls up the dead. For all who do these things are an abomination to the LORD, and because of these abominations the LORD your God drives them out from before you. You shall be blameless before the LORD your God. For these nations which you will dispossess listened to soothsayers and diviners; but as for you, the LORD your God has not appointed such for you. (Deuteronomy 18:9–14)

You have heard that it was said to those of old, "YOU SHALL NOT COMMIT ADULTERY." But I say to you that whoever looks at a woman to lust for her has already committed adultery with her in his heart.... You have heard that it was said, "AN EYE FOR AN EYE AND A TOOTH FOR A TOOTH." But I tell you not to resist an evil person. But whoever slaps you on your right cheek, turn the other to him also.... You have heard that it was said, "YOU SHALL LOVE YOUR NEIGHBOR and hate your enemy." But I say to you, love your enemies, bless those who curse you, do good to those who hate you, and pray for those who spitefully use you and persecute you. (Matthew 5:27–28, 38–39, 43–44)

Likewise also these dreamers defile the flesh, reject authority, and speak evil of dignitaries. Yet Michael the archangel, in contending with the devil, when he disputed about the body of Moses, dared not bring against him a reviling accusation, but said, "The Lord rebuke you!" But these speak evil of whatever they do not know; and whatever they know naturally, like brute beasts, in these things they corrupt themselves. Woe to them! For they have gone in the way of Cain, have run greedily in the error of Balaam for profit, and perished in the rebellion of Korah. These are spots in your love feasts, while they feast with you without fear, serving only themselves. They are clouds without water, carried about by the winds; late autumn trees without fruit, twice dead, pulled up by the roots; raging waves of the sea, foaming up their own shame; wandering stars for whom is reserved the blackness of darkness forever. Now Enoch, the seventh from Adam, prophesied about these men also, saying, "Behold, the Lord comes with ten thousands of His saints, to execute judgment on all, to convict all who are ungodly among them of all their ungodly deeds which they have committed in an ungodly way, and of all the harsh things which ungodly sinners have spoken against Him." These are grumblers, complainers, walking according to their own lusts; and they mouth great swelling words, flattering people to gain advantage. (Jude 1:8–16)

But these, like natural brute beasts made to be caught and destroyed, speak evil of the things they do not understand, and will utterly perish in their own corruption, and will receive the wages of unrighteousness, as those who count it pleasure to carouse in the daytime. They are spots and blemishes, carousing in their own deceptions while they feast with you, having eyes full of adultery and that cannot cease from sin, enticing unstable souls. They have a heart trained in covetous practices, and are accursed children. They have forsaken the right way and gone astray, following the way of Balaam the son of Beor, who loved the wages of unrighteousness; but he was rebuked for his iniquity: a dumb donkey speaking with a man's voice restrained the madness of the prophet. These are wells without water, clouds carried by a tempest, for whom is reserved the blackness of darkness forever. For when they speak great swelling words of emptiness, they allure through the lusts of the flesh, through lewdness, the ones who have actually escaped from those who live in error. (2 Peter 2:12–18)

If Moses had been writing polemic, as Pharaoh's magicians constantly claim, then Genesis 1 would have sounded like this:

"You have heard it said that in the beginning, the gods wrestled and the seas roared, but I tell you that God alone created all things."

"One of their own writers has said that the sun could not bring forth the moon; as indeed, how could it? For the sun and moon were not created until the fourth day."

"And you shall hear of lies and rumors of lies; do not follow after them. For in the last days, false prophets shall arise among you, even in the midst of the body of believers, and they shall tell you that Adam grew up out of the apes. Do not believe them, for they are clouds of hot vapor, billowing bags of gas, which preach false doctrines by which they shall seek to lure away, if possible, even the elect. Their doom shall come swiftly, and their end shall be destruction."

As I have reiterated throughout this book, Genesis is a history book. It is not a collection of short stories, it is not an allegory, and it is not a polemic. Each of these literary forms is a specific genre which follows specific rules, and the book of Genesis does not follow any of the rules or forms associated with the genre of polemical literature.

But even Pharaoh's magicians themselves abandon the "polemic" lie when it suits their purposes to do so. The *Enuma Elish*, for example, teaches that "long were the days" of creation, that "ages increased" during which various gods appeared. Pharaoh's magicians claim that this is the primary "source" from which nameless "redactors" stole the plot for Genesis—and, they claim, Genesis is actually a polemic which openly strives to *refute* the *Enuma Elish*.[9] Then—and this is where our gnostic theologians really make your head spin—then they turn around and tell us that Genesis actually *doesn't* refute the "ages" claim of pagan myths, that Genesis actually is teaching the same great ages whenever it says "day," that Genesis really *isn't* refuting *Enuma Elish* even though it is allegedly a polemic—a document whose sole purpose is to *refute*. At the one point where they might actually find support for their "polemic" claim—six literal days of creation refuting the "great ages"

---

9 I will address this fairy tale in more depth in Appendix 1, for those interested in seeing what the *Enuma Elish* and other supposed "sources" *really* say.

espoused in pagan myths—they reverse their stand and claim that Genesis *isn't* polemic, and that it actually endorses pagan myth!

Frankly, this is not mere incompetence on the part of Wenham and Hamilton and their gang of criminals, it is deliberate deception and falsehood. It is one of the sleight-of-hand tricks played by Pharaoh's magicians, making unsubstantiated claims (Genesis is polemic) in order to lend credence to some false assertion (Genesis is not divinely inspired), then turning around and contradicting those claims (Genesis is *not* polemic) in order to support a different false assertion (Genesis endorses evolution).

Pharaoh's magicians use this same magical trick to force the concept of "chaos" upon Genesis 1, as I have already addressed. There is no element of chaos present in Moses' account of creation—quite the opposite, as he underscores God's gentleness—but our magicians need to make chaos magically appear in order to prove that Genesis is stolen from *Enuma Elish*, so they once again decide that Genesis really *isn't* polemic by pointing out that *Enuma Elish* preaches chaos. These head-spinning arguments truly are chaotic, and chaos is the realm of the devil. It gives a reader pause when considering the source of the magicians' teachings.

A bitter irony exists in the writings of Pharaoh's magicians. The modern commentators are so wrapped up with long-forgotten pagan myths, so hell-bent on proving that Moses stole his ideas from the *Enuma Elish*, that they fail utterly to offer any insights for the modern reader who is faced with the modern paganism of scientific evolutionism. They are so busy claiming that Genesis is a polemic that they forget to gain any polemical value from it for today!

## Taking Away the Bible

This brings me to one of the most damning charges against the works of Wenham and his ilk: that their commentaries are of little or no practical value to the modern Christian. They are little more than treatises on the history of modern gnostic thought, focused overwhelmingly on "sources" and linguistic debates and playing pimp to Darwin, while offering no helpful insight on why modern Christians should care a whit about the serpent in the Garden of Eden.

I once wrote a treatise on Chaucer's "Squire's Tale" from *Canterbury Tales*, addressing the question of whether Chaucer ever finished it. This is a topic of interest to Chaucerian scholars, and much lively debate has been carried on for many years. But even the most ardent Chaucerian will recognize that the answer to the question, should we ever know it, will really have no significant impact on one's life—apart, perhaps, from gaining some recognition for one's own scholarship within the academic world. It's merely an ancient text, and it's entertaining to speculate on Chaucer's sources and whether our "received manuscript" represents his authorial intentions and what his contemporary audience thought about it—but it's only a story, and in the end it makes little difference one way or another.

The Bible, however, is not *Canterbury Tales*. Men read it in the 21st Century because they want to learn about the God who created them, because they want wisdom and guidance as to how to live their lives in a God-pleasing way, because they desperately yearn for eternal life. They do *not* read the Bible because they are curious about what Wellhausen said in 1852 concerning the Elohist redactor. Yet this is precisely the sort of drivel that fills the books of Pharaoh's magicians.

This failure of the commentators is far more serious than mere bad writing. By treating Genesis as though it were merely a "narrative text," they have seduced others into *not* turning to it for practical guidance. This can be seen by the fact that this "higher criticism" perpetuates itself generation after generation, until now it is very difficult to find a commentary on Genesis which offers insight on how to apply its principles to daily life.[10] It's little wonder that this generation is seeking answers elsewhere, for the church has been led astray by her leading theologians.

Victor Hamilton will provide us with one example out of the volumes of possible examples. He comes to the Trees of Life and Knowledge of Good and Evil, and spends four full pages summarizing the various ways in which other gnostics have interpreted the "symbolism" of the Tree of Knowledge—complete with copious footnotes and quotations from every modern gnostic back to the original German founding fathers of the 1800s. Some think that the Tree of Knowledge, Hamilton lectures, is symbolic for sexual knowledge; others that it stands for omniscience; and so forth. He pompously puffs out that "we mention the view" which best fits "our position"—the plural, of course, referring to himself—droning tediously on and on ad infinitum

---

10 One notable exception is Henry Morris, whose works on Genesis offer both scholarly refutation to the higher critics and, more importantly, practical insight into the character of God and man. Morris is generally treated patronizingly—if not with outright contempt—by the "higher critics," which is a significant endorsement in its own right.

about various academic, dry-as-bones symbolisms that might be read into the "Genesis story."

But none of Hamilton's theories even comes close to suggesting that the account in Genesis 2 and 3 refers to a literal tree bearing literal fruit. Here is a chance for a theologian to address free will and obedience and original sin and the Adamic nature and Jesus Christ who is the Last Adam, but Hamilton does not touch upon any of these topics. He is infatuated with the seductive lies of his gnostic forebears and peers, and that is the only topic which he discusses in this passage.

These "higher critics" have castrated Christianity; they themselves are spiritual eunuchs, incapable of producing any spiritual seed with which to grow the church in the coming generations. They hope to bring some reconciliation between the teachings of modern science and the traditional teachings of Scripture, but instead they only serve to instill doubt in the ordinary Christian—doubt that an ordinary believer can ever again trust his own uneducated reading of the Bible. It is sad to think that William Tyndale was martyred for bringing the Bible to the common man, while modern theologians are being praised for taking it away again.

## Higher Criticism and the Deconstructionists

The fact is, the modern biblical "higher critics" are merely a Christianized version of the secular school of Deconstructionist thought, of which Harold Bloom is a leading light. Bloom, however, openly confesses his Gnosticism, while the biblical "higher critics" pose as orthodox Christians. In doing so, the "higher critics" are merely emulating their great ancestor, Valentinus, that second century heretic who was almost made Pope.

"Every deep reader is an Idiot Questioner," Bloom happily tells us. "Criticism is the art of knowing the hidden roads that go from poem to poem."[11] By these things, he means exactly what the modern Idiot Questioners—the self-proclaimed "higher critics"—boast themselves of: their supposed ability to detect Scripture's hidden sources, the hidden roads and webs which interconnect and intertwine Genesis with its pagan antecedents.

Gnosticism itself is a descent into chaos. Modern gnostics practice the art of "deconstruction" upon literature, effectively scrambling the great works of Shakespeare and Milton and so forth into an incoherent and meaningless

---

11 Bloom, *Anxiety of Influence*, 96.

string of empty words. Their basic approach to literature is to claim that a story can mean absolutely anything that any individual reader wants it to mean—anything, that is, except what it *seems* to mean. For "seeming" is the great bugaboo of gnosticism, the obvious superficial meanings of all things in our world. The world—the whole of creation—is detestable to the gnostic, because the foundation of Gnosticism is the teaching that the Creator is evil while the "thrown-down one," the "displaced one," is the highest of all beings, above the gods, supreme over the Creator Himself, usurped by a jealous Jehovah but calmly waiting for mankind to gain the "higher knowledge" which will free him from the bondage of the Creator God into the eternal nothingness of Abyss.

The "higher critics" also practice their chaos upon Scripture, assuring the modern reader that the words do not mean what they seem to mean, that true understanding and "right reading" can only come through a higher knowledge of ancient pagan myths (many of which do not even exist but are merely asserted as hypothetical "sources") and hidden meanings of words, rearranging meaning and scrambling truth and assassinating common sense until the reader is left with nothing but another chaotic gnostic text—a "creation narrative" that can mean absolutely anything you want it to mean except that which makes the most sense. It is no wonder that these critics insist upon putting "chaos" into Genesis 1, because Chaos is the god whom they serve.

Gnostics strive to move knowledge backward on the premise that man can gain true gnosis only by reaching back to the time before creation. This is also a subtle but powerful force within modern biblical "higher criticism," which teaches that we cannot properly understand Genesis unless we look backward at earlier texts and beliefs—we must discover Moses' "sources" before we can comprehend Genesis. This, of course, becomes a self-defeating wild goose chase because, even if we did have documents in our possession which were obviously used by Moses (which we don't), we would still be forced by this approach to search for *their* sources before we could properly understand them or Genesis—and so on, back to infinity.

The Christian, however, seeks to understand Moses by looking forward, looking to later writers for clarification and support, ultimately looking to Jesus and the New Testament authors to help us know what to do with Genesis. And Jesus, we discover, accepted Genesis at face value—as do Paul and Peter and John and others. This backward insistence is the reason that

Gnostics of all ages have been fascinated with questions of their origins. This is the reason that evolution has gained ascendancy in the west. This is the reason that modern gnostic theologians insist upon rewriting the Bible's accounts of creation by looking backward at more ancient texts, just as their forefathers did in the second century.

It is not a new phenomenon to have gnosticism corrupting the Christian church. As I have already mentioned, the early Gnostics of the second century pretended to be orthodox Christians and managed to seduce some Christians and create confusion for others. Willis Barnstone, editor of *The Gnostic Bible*, builds the case that the early Christian church was severely threatened by the Gnostics of the second century simply because the church did not have an established canon yet—a Bible as we know it today. The Gnostics, however, were churning out a vast body of literature. Without a recognized canon of Scripture, the Gnostics were free to appropriate the gospels and epistles as their own. Today's gnostics are attempting to return us to that condition.

"For its part," writes Barnstone, "gnosticism with immense vitality challenged and widely subverted Christian theology—which had its own divisions—and remained Christianity's most serious rival, even when muted [rejected as heresy], until the birth of Islam."[12] This time around, the threat of gnosticism is even more serious to the church, because the gnostic teachers are being placed into the very pulpits and seminaries of Christianity. This time, the gnostics might just make it to Popehood.

## Conclusion

It is important that we understand the rules of logic. If a man builds an argument upon a false premise, then all subsequent points of his argument must be treated as false. Even if he should make a point by coincidence that is not false, he still cannot be cited as proof of the truth of that point, because his entire argument is false. Gordon Wenham and others have built an argument upon the premise that Genesis is not the inspired Word of God, claiming that it is the work of mere men who have taken their ideas from other mere men. This premise is false, so therefore all the subsequent claims made by Wenham must be assumed false. Even if Wenham and company should accidentally hit upon truth now and again, they still cannot be cited as authoritative evidence on those points because their overall writings are false. Serious students of

---

12 Barnstone, *The Gnostic Bible*, 783.

the Bible must recognize that these gnostic theologians are not credible sources of accurate Biblical interpretation.

The poison of their gnosticism has spread throughout the teachings of the church today. Even teachers whose works are usually conservative and profitable, such as James M. Boice, have been perverted with the false teachings of the "day/age" theory, purporting that the six days of creation were actually six millennia. As I have demonstrated repeatedly, this lie will lead the church away from the person and work of Jesus Christ when followed to its logical conclusion. The gnostic "higher critics" have succeeded in their seduction of the church by telling little lies every step of the way, and the church has fallen prey because the "higher critics" have not been held to account for each and every one of those little lies.

It is time for the church of Jesus Christ to repudiate these lies and to reject outright the false religions of evolution and gnosticism. "Choose you this day whom you will serve."

# Appendix 1

# The So-Called "Sources" of Genesis

The modern "higher critics" claim that the "authors" of Genesis stole their ideas from a number of ancient pagan myths—some of which we have today, some of which the critics have invented out of thin air. This claim of "sources" is very important to the arguments of Pharaoh's magicians, because they base many of their subsequent claims, particularly their insistence upon evolution and the "great age" of creation, upon the notion that Genesis is nothing but a cleaned-up version of ancient pagan myths. Therefore, it is worthwhile to take a look at these alleged "sources" to see for ourselves whether they bear any resemblance to Genesis.

Gordon Wenham pompously puffs that only "modern scholars familiar with Mesopotamian accounts. . . can appreciate"[1] the correlations and differences between pagan myths and Genesis. He is, as usual, wrong. Read the following excerpts for yourself; judge for yourself. Do not be misled into thinking that you need some "higher knowledge" to "properly understand" these dreadful texts; they are well translated by the very scholars who claim to hold that "higher knowledge," and a simple reading will suffice to demonstrate that there is no correlation whatsoever between these pagan myths and the inspired Word of God.

## Enuma Elish

The *Enuma Elish* is a pagan myth inscribed on seven stone tablets, written roughly around 650 BC—easily 800 years after Moses probably wrote Genesis. But facts never get in the way of the "higher critics," and many volumes have been written which strive to demonstrate that the story itself dates way way back in history—before the time of Moses, of course, which is the sole objective in these dating games, but just for good measure they claim that the story was told as far back as the Sumerians who predated the Egyptians. They base these speculations on very little evidence, such as the fact that some of the characters in the story have Sumerian-sounding names. Absolutely no concrete evidence has ever been found to support this claim, but for the sake of argument we will pretend that the *Enuma Elish* really *does*

---

1 Wenham, *Genesis 1-11*, 244.

date back to hundreds of years before Moses. Even if it did exist when Moses wrote Genesis, an honest reader will quickly recognize that the story contains no similarity to Genesis whatsoever.

*Enuma Elish* is not actually an account of creation at all—it is a long, dull story about a war amongst pagan gods which includes, in passing, a number of lines that refer to the earth's creation. These lines are spread out through the seven tablets, but counted together they amount to a small percentage of the entire dreary tale. For the sake of brevity, I will include all the passages in the dreadful story which have anything even approaching a similarity to Genesis. The rest of the story is largely concerned with pagan gods talking.

Here are the opening lines of *Enuma Elish* from Tablet 1 (the ellipses (. . . ) at the end of some lines indicates that material is missing from those lines):[2]

> When in the height heaven was not named,
> And the earth beneath did not yet bear a name,
> And the primeval Apsu, who begat them,
> And chaos, Tiamut, the mother of them both
> Their waters were mingled together,
> And no field was formed, no marsh was to be seen;
> When of the gods none had been called into being,
> And none bore a name, and no destinies were ordained;
> Then were created the gods in the midst of heaven,
> Lahmu and Lahamu were called into being...
> Ages increased...
> Then Ansar and Kisar were created, and over them. . . .
> Long were the days, then there came forth. . . . .
> Anu, their son,...
> Ansar and Anu...
> And the god Anu...
> Nudimmud, whom his fathers, his begetters. . . . .
> Abounding in all wisdom...
> He was exceeding strong...
> He had no rival...
> Thus were established and were... the great gods.

---

2 From L. W. King, tr., *The Seven Tablets of Wisdom*. This text can also be read in its entirety on the Internet at www.sacred-texts.com.

# Appendix 1: Alleged "Sources"

> But Tiamat and Apsu were still in confusion...
> They were troubled and...
> In disorder...
> Apsu was not diminished in might...
> And Tiamat roared...
> She smote, and their deeds...
> Their way was evil...
> Then Apsu, the begetter of the great gods,
> Cried unto Mummu, his minister, and said unto him:
> "O Mummu, thou minister that rejoicest my spirit,
> Come, unto Tiamut let us go!"
> So they went and before Tiamat they lay down,
> They consulted on a plan with regard to the gods, their sons.
> Apsu opened his mouth and spake....

And so on and so forth. The gods in this tale spend most of their time opening their mouths and speaking. The following extract is from Tablets 4 and 5:

> And the lord stood upon Tiamat's hinder parts,
> And with his merciless club he smashed her skull.
> He cut through the channels of her blood,
> And he made the North wind bear it away into secret places.
> His fathers beheld, and they rejoiced and were glad;
> Presents and gifts they brought unto him.
> Then the lord rested, gazing upon her dead body,
> While he divided the flesh of the ... and devised a cunning plan.
> He split her up like a flat fish into two halves;
> One half of her he established as a covering for heaven.
> He fixed a bolt, he stationed a watchman,
> And bade them not to let her waters come forth.
> He passed through the heavens, he surveyed the regions thereof,
> And over against the Deep he set the dwelling of Nudimmud.
> And the lord measured the structure of the Deep,
> And he founded E-sara, a mansion like unto it.
> The mansion E-sara which he created as heaven,
> He caused Anu, Bel, and Ea in their districts to inhabit.

***TABLET 5***
He (Marduk) made the stations for the great gods;
The stars, their images, as the stars of the Zodiac, he fixed.
He ordained the year and into sections he divided it;
For the twelve months he fixed three stars.
After he had... the days of the year... images,
He founded the station of Nibir [the planet Jupiter] to determine their bounds;
That none might err or go astray,
He set the station of Bel and Ea along with him.
He opened great gates on both sides,
He made strong the bolt on the left and on the right.
In the midst thereof he fixed the zenith;
The Moon-god he caused to shine forth, the night he entrusted to him.
He appointed him, a being of the night, to determine the days;
Every month without ceasing with the crown he covered him, saying:
"At the beginning of the month, when thou shinest upon the land,
Thou commandest the horns to determine six days,
And on the seventh day to divide the crown.
On the fourteenth day thou shalt stand opposite, the half....
When the Sun-god on the foundation of heaven... thee,
The... thou shalt cause to..., and thou shalt make his...
... unto the path of the Sun-god shalt thou cause to draw nigh,
And on the... day thou shalt stand opposite, and the Sun-god shall...
... to traverse her way.
... thou shalt cause to draw nigh, and thou shalt judge the right.
... to destroy..."

What similarities to Genesis do we find in these passages? Well, there is a vaguely similar opening formula—very vaguely similar to Genesis 1:1. "In the beginning God created the heavens and the earth." Actually, there is no similarity at all, other than the fact that Genesis and *Enuma* both begin at the creation of the world. *Enuma* also mentions "heaven" and "earth," but that is hardly surprising when one discusses creation, now is it? The "waters" are also mentioned in *Enuma*—again, one would expect that in a discussion of earth's creation, but we will not cavil. We shall pretend that it is deeply significant that both Genesis and *Enuma* mention "waters." So what about

## Appendix 1: Alleged "Sources"

those waters? Well, nothing as it turns out. There is not Spirit or wind or breath or anything else "hovering over" those waters, and rather than being separated we find them "mingled together" in *Enuma*.[3]

But let us not be discouraged. Scholars assure us that the similarities are profound—nay, earth-shattering—between *Enuma* and Genesis, so let us press onward. Ah, here's something important: *Enuma* informs us that in the beginning "no field was formed, no marsh was to be seen." Undoubtedly, this is where the "authors" of Genesis (who wrote Genesis, of course, sometime shortly after World War 2) stole their ideas for Genesis 2:4–6: "This is the history of the heavens and the earth when they were created, in the day that the LORD God made the earth and the heavens, before any plant of the field was in the earth and before any herb of the field had grown. For the LORD God had not caused it to rain on the earth, and there was no man to till the ground; but a mist went up from the earth and watered the whole face of the ground."

Striking, isn't it? Or maybe not. Perhaps it is just coincidence that two stories about the creation of the world use a similar formula to establish the fact that they are talking about the very beginning of everything; perhaps it isn't even a coincidence—perhaps it is actually just that: a *formula*. Modern literature uses formulas for certain genres of writing, as well. Fairy tales, for example, frequently begin with "Once upon a time." Epic poems, such as Milton's *Paradise Lost*, begin with an invocation to the muses. And let us not forget one very important possibility: it is entirely possible that the Genesis account is *true*, that it is actually historical fact, and that at the beginning there were no "marshes" or "fields" or herbs or anything else. If Genesis is actually *true*, then it stands to reason that other accounts, even pagan myths, might bear some of the same facts.

---

3 Scholars speculate that the Babylonian gods Apsu, Tiamat, and Mummu represented three types of water. According to Alexander Heidel [*The Babylonian Genesis*, 3], "Apsu was the primeval sweet-water ocean, and Tiamat the salt-water ocean, while Mummu probably represented the mist rising from the two bodies of water and hovering over them." If one treats the *Enuma Elish* as a sort of allegory, it is conceivable that one might read in a "spirit hovering over the waters" in this account. But even then, it requires a severe stretch to suggest that the "redactors" of Genesis translated the allegory into the literal description in Genesis 1. It is also interesting to note, however, that Gordon Wenham provides the following mistranslation of Genesis 2:6: "But the fresh water ocean used to rise from the earth and water the whole surface of the land" [Wenham, *Genesis 1-15*, 44]. If anyone got his ideas from the *Enuma Elish*, it was Gordon Wenham, not Moses.

Now, I said above that "wind" is not mentioned at the time of creation, but that is not strictly accurate: we do find it blowing about aimlessly, three tablets and hundreds of mind-numbing lines later. I point this out merely to fully exhaust every possible point of similarity with Genesis—even though the "wind" mentioned in *Enuma* is not hovering over the waters or doing anything else in the work of creation. It is just in the story, but that evidently is enough for our "higher critics" to claim that Genesis is based upon this myth.

Tablet 4 tells us that the gods created "heaven," meaning the sky. Wow! Now *there's* a striking similarity to Genesis! Who would have expected a "creation narrative" to include something about how the sky got created? And the account of the sky's creation is so very close to that of Genesis: the god Marduk kills the goddess Tiamat, then slices her in half like a filleted fish and stretches her body out to become the sky—after he "made the North Wind" carry her blood away "into secret places" and plugged her up so as "not to let her waters come forth." Yes, that sounds like Genesis.

And then, after all this exertion, the god Marduk takes a rest. Any self-respecting pagan god would do the same after all the talking and fighting he's been doing. Assuredly, this is where the "authors" of Genesis got the idea to make Jehovah rest on the seventh day. After all, according to Pharaoh's magicians, the "authors" wrote Genesis long after the time of King David, and they needed some way of justifying the Sabbath laws to the Jews—so clearly this is where they got it!

If you think this is exciting, wait until we move on to Tablet 5, which opens with Markuk creating "stations for the great gods"—which is as close to a Garden of Eden as the *Enuma* gets. Oh, but that won't stop us. Next Marduk "fixed" the stars in their places. Clearly, this is where the "authors" of Genesis got the idea for "fixing" the stars in *their* "narrative/story," since the idea of addressing the stars in a creation account would not normally occur to a writer. The same goes for measuring time, as we're told that Marduk "ordained the year and into sections he divided it."

I will even go beyond the self-evident and point out that the *Enuma* mentions "bounds" and "gates" and "bolts," items used in fixing things in their places and setting up boundaries. Genesis mentions boundaries. No doubt this is where the "Genesis authors" got the idea. And finally, the gods in *Enuma* make the seventh day special, in some incomprehensible way, which underscores the fact that the "authors" of Genesis stole the Sabbath idea from it.

# Appendix 1: Alleged "Sources"

These points which I have addressed are actually *more* than what most of the "higher critics" claim as proof that the *Enuma Elish* is the primary source of Genesis 1 and 2. I don't think it's necessary to point out how very *dis*similar these two creation accounts are; a simple, honest reading of the *Enuma* will suffice to make that evident. This is the reason that you will never catch the "higher critics" actually quoting from *Enuma*: they don't want you to read it, they just want you to take their word for it that it's the source of the "Genesis narrative." By now, we have discovered just what their word is worth.

Scholars are now beginning to confess that *Enuma Elish* could not possibly be the "source" for Genesis. They grudgingly admit that the differences far outweigh any similarities. No kidding. As Alexander Heidel argues, "the divergences [between Genesis and *Enuma Elish*] are much more far-reaching and significant than are the resemblances, most of which are not any closer than what we should expect to find in any two more or less complete creation versions (since both would have to account for the same phenomena and since human minds think along much the same lines) which might come from entirely different parts of the world and which might be utterly unrelated to each other."[4]

So what do these scholars do next? Do they go back and question their fundamental presuppositions to see whether they are true? Do they stop and question whether there really *are* pagan "sources" from which Genesis was written? Do they wonder whether the whole J-E-P fairytale might be merely a fairytale? Do they consider the possibility that Genesis really *is* divinely inspired?? No. They admit that *Enuma Elish* is not the "source" for Genesis, and then turn around happily and tell us that the real "source" is Atrahasis! So let's take a look at that.

## Atrahasis

*Atrahasis* is a Babylonian myth dating from around 1600 BC and written on three tablets. Like the *Enuma Elish*, it is a tedious recounting of the gods opening their mouths and speaking. Also like *Enuma*, it is not a creation story, in spite of being billed as such by the "higher critics;" it is, rather, a poem of praise to the gods of Babylon which mentions, in passing, a few lines concerning the creation of mankind and the great flood.

---

4 Heidel, *The Babylonian Genesis*, 130.

Here are the only relevant excerpts. Words within brackets, apart from my own interjections, are supplied by the translator, indicating that text is missing from the original.[5]

> When the gods like men
> Bore the work and suffered the toil—
> The toil of the gods was great,
> The work was heavy, the distress was much—
> The Seven great Anunnaki
> Were making the Igigi suffer the work.
> Anu, their father, was the king;
> Their counsellor was the warrior Enlil;
> Their chamberlain was Ninurta;
> And their sheriff Ennugi.
> The gods had clasped hands together,
> Had cast lots and had divided.

[Here follow nearly 200 lines of the gods opening their mouths and attacking one another. Eventually, they get down to creating mankind.]

> "While [Bēlet-ilī, the birth-goddess], is present,
> Let the birth-goddess create offspring,
> And let man bear the toil of the gods."
> They summoned and asked the goddess,
> The midwife of the gods, wise Mami,
> "You are the birth-goddess, creatress of mankind,
> Create *Lullû* that he may bear the yoke,[6]
> Let him bear the yoke assigned by Enlil,
> Let man carry the toil of the gods."
> Nintu opened her mouth
> And addressed the great gods,
> "It is not possible for me to make things,
> Skill lies with Enki.
> Since he can cleanse everything
> Let him give me the clay so that I can make it."

---

5 From W. G. Lambert and A. R. Millard, *Atra-Hasis: The Babylonian Story of the Flood*.
6 *Lullû* refers to mankind.

# Appendix 1: Alleged "Sources"

Enki opened his mouth and addressed the great gods,
"On the first, seventh, and fifteenth day of the month
I will make a purifying bath.
Let one god be slaughtered
So that all the gods may be cleansed in a dipping.
From his flesh and blood
Let Nintu mix clay,
That god and man
May be thoroughly mixed in the clay,
So that we may hear the drum for the rest of time
Let there be a spirit from the god's flesh.
Let it proclaim living (man) as its sign,
So that this be not forgotten let there be a spirit."
In the assembly answered "Yes"
The great Anunnaki, who administer destinies.
On the first, seventh, and fifteenth day of the month
He made a purifying bath.
Wê-ila, who had personality,[7]
They slaughtered in their assembly.
From his flesh and blood
Nintu mixed clay.
For the rest [of time they heard the drum],
From the flesh of the god [there was] a spirit.
It proclaimed living (man) as its sign,
And so that this was not forgotten [there was] a spirit.
After she had mixed that clay
She summoned the Anunnaki, the great gods.
The Igigi, the great gods,
Spat upon the clay.
Mami opened her mouth
And addressed the great gods,
"You have commanded me a task, I have completed it;
You have slaughtered a god together with his personality.
I have removed your heavy work,

---

[7] There is a delicious though unintentional irony here, that these gods—so busy opening their mouths and saying nothing—should murder the only one among them who had a personality.

I have imposed your toil on man.
You raised a cry for mankind,
I have loosed the yoke, I have established freedom."
They heard this speech of hers,
They ran together and kissed her feet, (saying,)
"Formerly we used to call you Mami,
Now let your name be Mistress-of-All-the-Gods."

[Here follow another hundred lines describing pagan rituals involved in human birth.]

Twelve hundred yeas [had not yet passed]
[When the land extended] and the peoples multiplied.
The [land] was bellowing [like a bull],
The god got disturbed with [their uproar]
[Enlil heard] their noise
[And addressed] the great gods,
"The noise of mankind [has become too intense for me],
[With their uproar] I am deprived of sleep.

[The remainder of tablet 1 and all of tablet 2 are concerned with the gods trying to make man quiet down so that they can get some sleep. They send a plague, followed by a famine and a drought, then finally try a flood.]

Atra-hasis opened his mouth
And addressed his lord,
"Teach me the meaning [of the dream],
[....] that I may seek its outcome."
[Enki] opened his mouth
And addressed his slave,
"You say, 'What am I to seek?'
Observe the message that I will speak to you:
Wall, listen to me!
Reed wall, observe all my words![8]
Destroy your house, build a boat,

---

8 The god at this point is evidently talking to Atrahasis' house.

# Appendix 1: Alleged "Sources"

Spurn property and save life.
The boat which you build
[…..] be equal [.....]
[missing lines]
Roof it over like the Apsû.
So that the sun shall not see inside it
Let it be roofed over above and below.
The tackle should be very strong,
Let the pitch be tough, and so give (the boat) strength.
I will rain down upon you here
An abundance of birds, a profusion of fishes."
He opened the water-clock and filled it;
He announced to him the coming of the flood for the seventh night.
Atra-hasis received the command,
He assembled the elders to his gate.
Atra-hasis opened his mouth
And addressed the elders,
"My god [does not agree] with your god,
Enki and [Enlil] are angry with one another.
They have expelled me from [my house (?)],
Since I reverence [Enki],
[He told me] of this matter.
I can[not] live in [your …..],
I cannot [set my feet on] the earth of Enlil.
With the gods …..
[This] is what he told me …...
[Four or five lines missing to end of column]
The elders …...
The carpenter [carried his axe],
The reed-worker [carried his stone].
[The child carried] the pitch,
The poor man [brought what was needed].
…...
He/They …...
…...
Atra-hasis …...
[11 lines missing]

Bringing.....
Whatever he [had].....
Whatever he had.....
Clean (animals).....
Fat (animals).....
He caught [and put on board]
The winged [birds of] the heavens.
The cattle (?).....
The wild [creatures (?)].....
..... he put on board
..... the moon disappeared.
..... he invited his people
..... to a banquet.
..... he sent his family on board,
They ate and they drank.
But he was in and out: he could not sit, could not crouch,
For his heart was broken and he was vomiting gall.
The appearance of the weather changed,
Adad roared in the clouds.
As soon as he heard Adad's voice
Pitch was brought for him to close his door.
After he had bolted his door
Adad was roaring in the clouds,
The winds became savage as he arose,
He severed the hawser and set the boat adrift.
[Three lines missing]
.....
..... the storm
..... were yoked
[Zu] with his talons [rent] the heavens.
[He .....] the land
And shattered its noise [like a pot].
..... the flood [set out],
Its might came upon the peoples [like a battle array].
One person did [not] see another,
They were [not] recognizable in the destruction.
[The flood] bellowed like a bull,

# Appendix 1: Alleged "Sources"

[Like] a whinnying wild ass the winds [howled].
The darkness [was dense], there was no sun
..... like .....
..... of the flood
.....
.....
..... the noise of the [flood]
It was trying ..... of the gods.
[Enki] was beside himself,
[Seeing that] his sons were thrown down before him.

[Some 75 lines follow, in which the gods feel sorry that they destroyed the human race out of spite for one another.]

To the [four] winds .....
He put .....
Providing food .....
.....
[The gods sniffed] the smell,
They gathered [like flies] over the offering.
[After] they had eaten the offering
Nintu arose to complain against all of them,

[And the gods open their mouths and talk for another 75 dreary lines.]

The only portion of this mess that has anything to do with creation is the opening stuff about the gods wanting man to be created so that they didn't have to grow their own food. No comment is needed for this; it is abundantly self-evident that there is no parallel of any kind between this and Genesis.

I have included the extraneous nonsense about the flood in order to demonstrate what a text *does* look like when it gets its ideas from another text. For this, I must burden my reader with another lengthy selection from another pagan myth.

## Epic of Gilgamesh

Another ancient pagan text is the *Epic of Gilgamesh*, written sometime in the seventh century BC. It is another long story about the adventures of the gods (although it is a good deal more interesting to read than *Enuma* or *Atrahasis*) which bears no similarity whatsoever to anything found anywhere within the Bible. The sole point of comparison is found in one passage, in which the hero builds a boat, gathers together all living creatures, and survives a great flood. Once again, missing information is suggested within brackets.[9]

> Gilgamish unto him spake, to Uta-Napishtim the Distant:
> "Uta-Napishtim, upon thee I gaze, (yet) in no wise thy presence
> Strange is, (for) thou art like me, and in no wise different art thou;
> Thou art like me; (yea) a stomach for fighting doth make thee consummate,
> [Aye, and to rest (?)] on thy back thou dost lie. [O tell me (?)], how couldst thou
> Stand in th' Assemblage of Gods to petition for life (everlasting)?"
> Uta-Napishtim (addressing him thus) unto Gilgamish answer'd:
> "Gilgamish, I unto thee will discover the (whole) hidden story,
> Aye, and the rede of the Gods will I tell thee.
>       The City Shurippak—
> (O 'tis) a city thou knowest!—is set [on the marge] of Euphrates,
> Old is this city, with gods in its midst. (Now), the great gods a deluge
> Purposed to bring: . . . . . . there was Anu, their sire; their adviser
> Warrior Enlil; Ninurta, their herald; their leader(?) Ennugi;
> Nin-igi-azag—'tis Ea—, (albeit) conspirator with them,
> Unto a reed-hut their counsel betray'd he: "O Reed-hut, O Reed-hut!
> Wall, wall! Hearken, O Reed-hut, consider, O Wall! O thou Mortal,
> Thou of Shurippak, thou scion of Ubara-Tutu, a dwelling
> Pull down, (and) fashion a vessel (therewith); abandon possessions,
> Life do thou seek, (and) thy hoard disregard, and save life; every creature
> Make to embark in the vessel. The vessel, which thou art to fashion,
> Apt be its measure; its beam and its length be in due correspondence,
> (Then) [on] the deep do thou launch it." And I—sooth, I apprehending,

---

9 R. Campbell Thompson, tr., *The Epic of Gilgamesh*. *Gilgamesh* is the only existing ancient pagan myth with anything close to literary merit—yet another sharp difference between these gross texts and Genesis. However, *Gilgamesh* is actually moderately entertaining to read, and there are many paraphrases on the market, such as that of N. K. Sandars (Penguin, 1960).

# Appendix 1: Alleged "Sources"

(This wise) to Ea, my lord, did I speak: '[See], Lord, what thou sayest
Thus, do I honour, I'll do—(but) to city, to people, and elders
Am I, forsooth, to explain?' (Then) Ea made answer in speaking,
Saying to me—me, his henchman!—'Thou mortal, shalt speak to them this wise:
"'Tis me alone (?) whom Enlil so hateth that I in your city
No (more) may dwell, nor turn my face unto the land which is Enlil's.
[I will go] down to the Deep, (there) dwelling with Ea, my [liege] lord,
(Wherefore) [on] you will he shower down plenty, yea, fowl [in great number(?)],
Booty of fish .... [and big] the harvest.
 ........ causing a plentiful rainfall (?) to come down upon you."'

[(Then) when something] of morning had dawn'd ....
(*Five lines mutilated*).
Pitch did the children provide, (while) the strong brought [all] that was needful.
(Then) on the fifth day (after) I laid out the shape (of my vessel),
Ten *gar* each was the height of her sides, in accord with her planning(?),
Ten *gar* to match was the size of her deck (?), and the shape of the forepart (?)
Did I lay down, (and) the same did I fashion; (aye), six times cross-pinn'd her,
Sevenfold did I divide her ...., divided her inwards
Ninefold: hammer'd the caulking within her, (and) found me a quantpole,
(All) that was needful I added; the hull with six *shar* of bitumen
Smear'd I, (and) three *shar* of pitch [did I smear] on the inside; some people,
Bearing a vessel of grease, three *shar* of it brought (me); (and) one *shar*
(Out of this) grease did I leave, which the tackling (?) consumed; (and) the boatman
Two *shar* of grease stow'd away; (yea), beeves for the ... I slaughter'd,
Each day lambs did I slay: mead, beer, oil, wine, too, the workmen
[Drank] as though they were water, and made a great feast like the New Year,

(*Five mutilated lines* "I added salve for the hand(s)," "the vessel was finish'd ... Shamash the great." "was difficult," "..? I caused to bring above and below," "two-thirds of it"):

[All I possess'd I] laded aboard her; the silver I laded
All I possess'd; gold, all I possess'd I laded aboard her,
All I possess'd of the seed of all living [I laded aboard] her.
Into the ship I embark'd all my kindred and family (with me),
Cattle (and) beasts of the field (and) all handicraftsmen embarking.
(Then) decreed Shamash the hour: " .... (?)
Shall in the night let a plentiful rainfall(?) pour down ....
(Then) do thou enter the vessel, and (straightway) shut down thy hatchway."
Came (then) that hour (appointed), ...... (?)
Did in the night let a plentiful rainfall(?) pour down .... (?)
View'd I the aspect of day: to look on the day bore a horror,
(Wherefore) I enter'd the vessel, and (straightway) shut down my hatchway,
(So, too) to shut down the vessel to Puzur-Amurri (?), the boatman,
Did I deliver the poop (of the ship), besides its equipment.

(Then), when something of dawn had appear'd, from out the horizon
Rose a cloud darkling; (lo), Adad (the storm-god) was rumbling within it,
Nabu and Sharru were leading the vanguard, and coming as heralds
Over the hills and the levels: (then) Irragal wrench'd out the bollards;
Havoc Ninurta let loose as he came, th' Anunnaki their torches
Brandish'd, and shrivell'd the land with their flames; desolation from Adad
Stretch'd to (high) Heaven, (and) all that was bright was turn'd into darkness.
(*Four lines mutilated* "the land like...," "for one day the st[orm]...," " "fiercely blew...." " "like a battle..." ").
Nor could a brother distinguish his brother; from heaven were mortals
Not to be spied. O, were stricken with terror the gods at the Deluge,
Fleeing, they rose to the Heaven of Anu, and crouch'd in the outskirts,

# Appendix 1: Alleged "Sources"

Cow'ring like curs were the gods (while) like to a woman in travail
Ishtar did cry, she shrieking aloud, (e'en) the sweet-spoken Lady
(She of the gods): 'May that day turn to dust, because I spake evil
(There) in th' Assemblage of Gods! O, how could I utter (such) evil
(There) in the Assemblage of Gods, (so) to blot out my people, ordaining
Havoc! Sooth, then, am I to give birth, unto (these) mine own people
Only to glut (with their bodies) the Sea as though they were fish-spawn?'
Gods—Anunnaki—wept with her, the gods were sitting (all) humbled,
(Aye), in (their) weeping, (and) closed were their lips amid(?)]the Assemblage.
Six days, a se'nnight the hurricane, deluge, (and) tempest continued
Sweeping the land: when the seventh day came, were quelléd the warfare,
Tempest (and) deluge which like to an army embattail'd were fighting.
Lull'd was the sea, (all) spent was the gale, assuaged was the deluge,
(So) did I look on the day; (lo), sound was (all) still'd; and all human
Back to (its) clay was return'd, and fen was level with roof-tree.
(Then) I open'd a hatchway, and down on my cheek stream'd the sunlight,
Bowing myself, I sat weeping, my tears o'er my cheek(s) overflowing,
Into the distance I gazed, to the furthest bounds of the Ocean,
Land was uprear'd at twelve (points), and the Ark on the Mountain of Nisir
Grounded; the Mountain of Nisir held fast, nor gave lease to her shifting.
One day, (nay,) two, did Nisir hold fast, nor give lease to her shifting.
Three days, (nay), four, did Nisir hold fast, nor give lease to her shifting,
Five days, (nay,) six, did Nisir hold fast, nor give lease to her shifting.
(Then), when the seventh day dawn'd, I put forth a dove, and released (her),
(But) to and fro went the dove, and return'd (for) a resting-place was not.
(Then) I a swallow put forth and released; to and fro went the swallow,
She (too) return'd, (for) a resting-place was not; I put forth a raven,
Her, (too,) releasing; the raven went, too, and th' abating of waters

Saw; and she ate as she waded (and) splash'd, (unto me) not returning.
Unto the four winds (of heaven) I freed (all the beasts), and an off'ring
Sacrificed, and a libation I pour'd on the peak of the mountain,
Twice seven flagons devoting, (and) sweet cane, (and) cedar, and myrtle,
Heap'd up beneath them; the gods smelt the savour, the gods the sweet savour
Smelt; (aye,) the gods did assemble like flies o'er him making the off'ring.
Then, on arriving, the Queen (of the gods) the magnificent jewels
Lifted on high, which Anu had made in accord with her wishes;
'O ye Gods! I will (rather) forget (this) my necklet of sapphires,
Than not maintain these days in remembrance, nor ever forget them.
(So), though (the rest of) the gods may present themselves at the off'ring,
Enlil (alone of the gods) may (himself) not come to the off'ring,
Because he, unreasoning, brought on a deluge, and therefore my people
Unto destruction consign'd.'
Then Enlil, on his arrival,
Spied out the vessel, and (straightway) did Enlil burst into anger,
Swollen with wrath 'gainst the gods, the Igigi: 'Hath any of mortals
'Scaped? Sooth, never a man could have lived through (the welter of) ruin.'
(Then) did Ninurta make answer and speak unto warrior Enlil,
Saying: 'O, who can there be to devise such a plan, except Ea?
Surely, 'tis Ea is privy to ev'ry design.' Whereat Ea
Answer'd and spake unto Enlil, the warrior, saying: 'O chieftain
Thou of the gods, thou warrior! How, forsooth, how (all) uncounsell'd
Couldst thou a deluge bring on? (Aye,) visit his sin on the sinner
Visit his guilt on the guilty, (but) O, have mercy, that (thereby)
He shall not be cut off; be clement, that he may not [perish].
O, instead of thy making a flood, let a lion come, man to diminish;
O, instead of thy making a flood, let a jackal come, man to diminish;
O, instead of thy making a flood, let a famine occur, that the country
May be [devour'd(?)]; instead of thy making a flood, let the Plague-god
Come and the people [o'erwhelm];
   Sooth, indeed 'twas not I of the Great Gods the secret reveraléd,

# Appendix 1: Alleged "Sources"

(But) to th' Abounding in Wisdom vouchsafed I a dream, and (in this wise)
He of the gods heard the secret. Deliberate, now, on his counsel'.
(Then) to the Ark came up Enlil; my hand did he grasp, and uplifted
Me, even me, and my wife, too, he raised, and, bent-kneed beside me,
Made her to kneel; our foreheads he touch'd as he stood there between us,
Blessing us; 'Uta-Napishtim hath hitherto only been mortal,
Now, indeed, Uta-Napishtim and (also) his wife shall be equal
Like to us gods; in the distance afar at the mouth of the rivers
Uta-Napishtim shall dwell'. (So) they took me and (there) in the distance
Caused me to dwell at the mouth of the rivers.

I have included this selection for two purposes: to allow an honest reader to confront another pagan myth which the "higher critics" claim to be a source of Genesis, and to allow an honest reader to see for himself what a text really *does* look like when it is drawn from another source. If you have labored through this section of *Gilgamesh* as well as *Atrahasis* above—well, you deserve a reward for your diligence—and you'll also be quick to notice that the two accounts are very similar.

The author of *Gilgamesh* has definitely drawn his material from an older source, quite possibly from *Atrahasis* itself. This can be seen from the many details—both important and insignificant—which the two accounts have in common: mankind bellowing like a bull, keeping the gods awake; the description of birds and fish raining down from above; an "ark" made of reeds and roofed like the vault of heaven; the elders being called together; a great feast prior to setting sail; the flood lasting seven days; the gods repenting of their naughty behavior; the gods gathering together "like flies" when they smell the aroma of the hero's burnt offering; etc.

Needless to say, not one of these details is to be found in Genesis, nor are the writing styles similar in any way, nor is there any similarity beyond coincidence and common sense between Genesis and either of these myths.

Yet men like Gordon Wenham and his disciples assure us that these pagan myths are very similar to Genesis, which proves that the "authors" of Genesis stole their ideas from the pagans. I'm not sure who is more culpable in this crime: the "higher critics" for telling such an audacious lie, or the church itself for allowing them to get away with it for 150 years.

## Egyptian Creation Myths

The "higher critics" also are fond of alluding to the Egyptian myths of creation as being "secondary sources" of the "Genesis narrative." So let's take a look at what the Egyptians had to say.

Ah, but this is not quite so easy, you see, because there actually isn't a unified Egyptian "creation narrative" to look at. The creation theology of the ancient Egyptians is known only from reading inscriptions inside coffins and burial chambers. These inscriptions have been somewhat codified in *The Egyptian Book of the Dead*, which is as close as we can come to any unified Egyptian theology of creation. The *Book of the Dead* is actually nothing more than a series of "spells," rituals that were read on various occasions—mostly associated with someone dying. Contained within these spells are clues as to what the Egyptians believed concerning the creation of the world—but none of these elements bears the slightest resemblance to Genesis whatsoever.

The only elements that have any bearing upon Genesis are the theme that the earth was originally surrounded by "dark water," and that creation came about as a result of chaotic conflict. This latter, of course, is the opposite of what Genesis teaches—although the "higher critics" do their best to insert "chaos" into chapter 1—but even the absence of chaos in Genesis is a point that the "higher critics" claim as proof that these Egyptian theologies are a "source" of Genesis. This is why they love to call Genesis a "polemic," because they can point to texts which say something entirely different from Genesis and claim that the "authors" of Genesis were deliberately changing their "sources" in order to write a polemic against the pagans. This particular scheme of Pharaoh's magicians enables them to make virtually any claim that they like!

The closest we can come to any Genesis-similarities is found in *The History of Creation*, which was written on a scroll sometime around 400 BC or thereabouts. Once again, the "higher critics" find ways of antedating this creation account to be older than the time of Moses, and we will not waste our time debating the complete lack of evidence of such a claim. The text is enough to see that it is no source of Genesis. Here it is in its entirety:[10]

> The book of knowing the evolutions of Ra, and of overthrowing Apep. [These are] the words which the god Neb-er-tcher spake after he had come into being: "I am he

---

10 From E. A. Wallis Budge, *Legends of the Gods*.

## Appendix 1: Alleged "Sources"

who came into being in the form of the god Khepera, and I am the creator of that which came into being, that is to say, I am the creator of everything which came into being: now the things which I created, and which came forth out of my mouth after that I had come into being myself were exceedingly many. The sky (or heaven) had not come into being, the earth did not exist, and the children of the earth, and the creeping things had not been made at that time. I myself raised them up from out of Nu, from a state of helpless inertness. I found no place whereon I could stand. I worked a charm upon my own heart (or will), I laid the foundation [of things] by Maat, and I made everything which had form. I was [then] one by myself, for I had not emitted from myself the god Shu, and I had not spit out from myself the goddess Tefnut; and there existed no other who could work with me. I laid the foundations [of things] in my own heart, and there came into being multitudes of created things, which came into being from the created things which were born from the created things which arose from what they brought forth. I had union with my closed hand, and I embraced my shadow as a wife, and I poured seed into my own mouth, and I sent forth from myself issue in the form of the gods Shu and Tefnut.

Saith my father Nu: "My Eye was covered up behind them (i.e., Shu. and Tefnut), but after two *hen* periods had passed from the time when they departed from me, from being one god I became three gods, and I came into being in the earth. Then Shu and Tefnut rejoiced from out of the inert watery mass wherein they were, and they brought to me my Eye (i.e., the Sun). Now after these things I gathered together my members, and I wept over them, and men and women sprang into being from the tears which came forth from my Eye. And when my Eye came to me, and found that I had made another [Eye] in place where it was (i.e., the Moon), it was wroth with (or, raged at) me, whereupon I endowed it (i.e., the second Eye) with [some of] the splendor which I had made for the first [Eye], and I made it to occupy its place in my Face, and henceforth it ruled throughout all this earth.

When there fell on them their moment through plant-like clouds, I restored what had been taken away from them, and I appeared from out of the plant-like clouds. I created creeping things of every kind, and everything which came into being from them. Shu and Tefnut brought forth [Seb and] Nut; and Seb and Nut brought forth Osiris, and Heru-khent-an-maati, and Set, and Isis, and Nephthys at one birth, one after the other, and they produced their multitudinous offspring in this earth."

And what similarities do we have here? Well, the god who is speaking claims to have created everything that exists—all by himself, without any help. More startling still, he claims to have begun as one god but made himself into three gods—an Egyptian trinity! Of course, he accomplished both "creative acts" by masturbating into his own mouth and spitting out new life, but that small detail shouldn't stop us from seeing this as a source for the Genesis account of creation. I apologize for this crass description, but it is difficult to avoid crassness when one is forced to discuss crass subject matter.

It seems to me far more blasphemous, however, to suggest that such pagan mythologies as this are a "source" of the Word of God. Indeed, in this vein, it is worth noting that the religion of Egypt truly was a religion of death. Their gospels are written mostly inside coffins and on the walls of tombs. Man has been faced with only two choices since creation: worship death or worship Life. There are no other options, and all world religions fall into one category or the other. It is no coincidence that those who try to read evolution into the Bible turn to these pagan death religions as their inspiration.

And once again we find Pharaoh's magicians not following their own rules. They tell us that these Egyptian myths are a source of the "Genesis narrative," then tell us that God cannot be speaking to the Holy Spirit when He says "let us create man in our own image." But if this Egyptian myth *were* a source, then surely Moses would have gotten the idea of God speaking to Himself from this "trinitarian dogma" which we find here. The hypocrisy and self-contradictions of Pharaoh's magicians make one dizzy.

# Appendix 1: Alleged "Sources"

## Code of Hammurabi

Hammurabi was king of Babylon somewhere around 1800 BC—a few hundred years or so before Moses wrote Genesis. He is remembered today because he wrote the laws of Babylon on a big stone and set it up in the public square so that his people would know the laws of the land. Critics assure us that nobody could read at that time, of course—in fact, writing itself was barely even invented yet, according to the "higher critics"—but these people never let logic cloud their thinking. Presumably, Hammurabi wrote the laws before writing was invented and then put them up for his people who couldn't read. Here are the opening lines:[11]

> 1. If any one ensnare another, putting a ban upon him, but he can not prove it, then he that ensnared him shall be put to death.

> 2. If any one bring an accusation against a man, and the accused go to the river and leap into the river, if he sink in the river his accuser shall take possession of his house. But if the river prove that the accused is not guilty, and he escape unhurt, then he who had brought the accusation shall be put to death, while he who leaped into the river shall take possession of the house that had belonged to his accuser.

> 3. If any one bring an accusation of any crime before the elders, and does not prove what he has charged, he shall, if it be a capital offense charged, be put to death.

I include this merely because our "higher critics" tell us that the fictitious "redactors" (J-E-P) stole the idea for the ten commandments from the *Code of Hammurabi*. The code contains 282 laws, none of which are contained within the Ten Commandments, but once again facts are irrelevant—it's the *idea* that counts. What the "authors" of the Pentateuch stole from Hammurabi, you see, was the idea of codifying the Hebrew law in a series of commandments. After all, who would ever think of writing down the laws of

---

[11] Translated by Leonard William King, 1910.

a society so that the people could know them? Certainly not the dumb-as-mud "authors" of the Pentateuch—they needed to steal this brilliance from the pagans.

These ham-fisted "authors," by the way, are the same brilliant poets who "crafted" the intricate subtleties of hidden meanings in Genesis 1 and 2. Their status of stupidity or genius depends entirely at any given moment upon the private agenda of our gnostic "higher critics."

## Conclusion

When one reads through these ancient pagan texts, looking for similarities to Genesis, one realizes that the only thing which the "higher critics" have proven is that the Genesis creation account is unique—there is none other like it. This makes the crime all the greater when the gnostics attempt to rewrite our sacred text to make it like the pagan myths.

It is also interesting to notice that there is no similarity among the Egyptian myths, the *Enuma Elish,* and the *Epic of Gilgamesh.* The "higher critics" claim that the "authors" of Genesis stole their creation ideas from these sources, but if that were the case then there would also be evidence that the Egyptians were familiar with and influenced by *Enuma Elish* and *Gilgamesh* and other myths from other cultures. After all, if the Israelites drew *their* ideas from other cultures, so also would the other cultures have done. I find no evidence of any "cross-pollination" of theologies and ideas, apart from the flood story in *Gilgamesh* which I've already pointed out.

The gnostics will answer this with their most basic lie, saying that Moses did not write Genesis, that it was written during or after the Kings period when the "redactors" had been exposed to Babylonian myths and other pagan ideas. Thus, once again, we see how the lies of the "higher critics" are intertwined and interdependent. They have created an entire system of false thought, and they have gotten away with it because their little lies have gone unchallenged for over 100 years.

When one investigates the claims and allegations of the "higher critics," in fact, one discovers that they have lied and cheated every step of the way. Each of their little lies is like the little foxes of Song of Solomon: not particularly threatening individually, but when gathered en masse they destroy the roots of the vineyard. This is why the church cannot afford to permit the "higher critics" to get away with any of their little lies; they must be called to account every time they open their mouths or put pen to paper.

# BIBLIOGRAPHY

Barnstone, Willis and Marvin Meyer, ed. *The Gnostic Bible*. Boston: Shambala, 2003.

Bloom, Harold. *Agon: Towards a Theory of Revisionism*. NY: Oxford UP, 1982.

Bloom, Harold. *The Anxiety of Influence: A Theory of Poetry*. NY: Oxford UP, 1997.

Bloom, Harold. *Ruin the Sacred Truths*. Cambridge, MA: Harvard UP, 1989.

Boice, James M. *Genesis, vol. 1*. Grand Rapids, MI: Baker Books, 1998.

Brown, Francis, ed. *The New Brown-Driver-Briggs-Gesenius Hebrew and English Lexicon*. Peabody, MA: Hendrickson Publishers, 1979.

Brown, Lesley, ed. *The New Shorter Oxford English Dictionary*. Oxford: Clarendon Press, 1993.

Budge, E. A. Wallis, tr. *Legends of the Gods*. London: Kegan Paul, etc., 1912.

Dods, Marcus. *The Expositor's Bible: The Book of Genesis*. NY: Hodder and Stoughton, n.d.

Eddy, Mary Baker. *Science and Health with Key to the Scriptures*. Boston: Trustees Under the Will of Mary Baker G. Eddy, 1934.

Ferguson, J. Wesley. *What the Bible Teaches: Genesis*. Kilmarnock, Scotland: John Ritchie Ltd., 2000.

Garrett, Duane A. *Rethinking Genesis: The Sources and Authorship of the First Book of the Bible*. Ross-Shire, GB: Christian Focus Publications, 2000.

Green, Jay P. Sr., ed. *The Interlinear Hebrew-Aramaic Old Testament*. Peabody, MA: Hendrickson, 1985.

Green, Jay P., ed. *The New Thayer's Greek-English Lexicon of the New Testament*. Peabody, MA: Hendrickson Publishers, 1981,

Hamilton, Victor P. *The Book of Genesis: Chapters 1–17*. Grand Rapids, MI: William B. Eerdman's, 1990.

Heidel, Alexander. *The Gilgamesh Epic and Old Testament Parallels*. Chicago, IL: Univ. Chicago Press, 1963.

Heidel, Alexander. *The Babylonian Genesis*. Chicago: U. Chicago Press, 1951.

Henry, Matthew. *Matthew Henry's Commentary on the Whole Bible, vol. 1*. Peabody, MA: Hendrickson Publishers, 1994.

Hughes, R. Kent. *Genesis: Beginning and Blessing*. Wheaton, IL: Crossway, 2004.

Irenaeus, *Against Heresies*. Volume I.

Jordan, James B. *Creation in Six Days: A Defense of the Traditional Reading of Genesis One*. Moscow, ID: Canon Press, 1999.

Keil, C. F. *Commentary on the Old Testament*. Peabody, MA: Hendrickson, 1989, Vol. I.

Kidner, Derek. *Genesis: An Introduction and Commentary*. Downers Grove, IL: Inter-Varsity Press, 1967.

Lambert, W. G. and A. R. Millard, ed. *Atra-Hasis: The Babylonian Story of the Flood*. Oxford: Clarendon Press, 1970.

King, L. W., tr. *The Seven Tablets of Wisdom*. London: Luzac and Co., 1902.

Lewis, C. S. *The Abolition of Man*. NY: Macmillan Publishing Co., 1977.

Lewis, C. S. *The Magician's Nephew*. NY: Macmillan Publishing Company, 1988.

Liddell, H. G. and R. Scott. *A Greek-English Lexicon*. Oxford: Clarendon Press, 1977.

Mathews, Kenneth A. *The New American Commentary: Genesis 1–11:26*. Nashville, TN: Broadman and Holman, 1996.

Meyer, Marvin, ed. *The Nag Hammadi Scriptures*. NY: Harper One, 2007.

Morris, Henry M. *The Genesis Record: A Scientific and Devotional Commentary on the Book of Beginnings*. Grand Rapids, MI: Baker Books, 2006.

Morris, Henry M. *The New Defender's Study Bible*. Nashville, TN: World Publishing, 2006.

*New World Translation of the Holy Scriptures*. Brooklyn, NY: Watchtower Bible and Tract Society of New York, Inc., 1961.

*The NIV Study Bible*. Grand Rapids, MI: Zondervan, 1985.

Pipa, Joseph and David Hall, ed. *Did God Create in 6 Days?* White Hall, WV: Covenant Foundation, 2005.

Robinson, James M., ed. *The Nag Hammadi Library in English*. San Francisco: Harper, 1988.

Sandars, N. K., ed. *The Epic of Gilgamesh: An English Version with an Introduction*. Baltimore, MD: Penguin Books, 1966.

Stanton, Elizabeth Cady. *The Woman's Bible: A Classic Feminist Perspective*. NY: Dover, 2002.

Strong, James. *Exhaustive Concordance / Dictionaries of the Hebrew and Greek Words*. MacLean, VA: MacDonald Publishing, n.d.

Thompson, R. Campbell, ed. *The Epic of Gilgamesh*. London: Luzac and Co., 1928.

Van Till, Howard J., et al., ed. *Portraits of Creation: Biblical and Scientific Perspectives on the World's Formation.* Grand Rapids, MI: William B. Eerdmans, 1990.

Waltke, Bruce K. *Genesis: A Commentary.* Grand Rapids, MI: Zondervan, 2001.

Wenham, Gordon J. *Word Biblical Commentary: Genesis 1–15.* Nashville, TN: Nelson Reference, 1987.

Youngblood, Ronald. *The Book of Genesis: An Introductory Commentary.* Eugene, OR: Wipf and Stock, 1999.

www.ingramcontent.com/pod-product-compliance
Lightning Source LLC
Chambersburg PA
CBHW070305230426
43664CB00014B/2640